DIE

THEIR CONSTRUCTION A
MODERN WORKING OF SHEET METALS

A TREATISE
ON THE DESIGN, CONSTRUCTION AND USE OF DIES,
PUNCHES, TOOLS, FIXTURES AND DEVICES, TOGETHER
WITH THE MANNER IN WHICH THEY SHOULD BE USED
IN THE POWER PRESS, FOR THE CHEAP AND RAPID
PRODUCTION OF SHEET METAL PARTS AND ARTICLES.

COMPRISING
FUNDAMENTAL DESIGNS AND PRACTICAL POINTS BY
WHICH SHEET METAL PARTS MAY BE PRODUCED AT
THE MINIMUM OF COST TO THE MAXIMUM OF OUT-
PUT : WITH SPECIAL REFERENCE TO THE HARDENING
AND TEMPERING OF PRESS TOOLS, THE USE OF FILES,
AND TO THE CLASSES OF WORK WHICH MAY BE PRO-
DUCED TO THE BEST ADVANTAGE BY THE USE OF
DIES IN THE POWER PRESS.   :   :   :   :   :   :   ·

BY

JOSEPH V. WOODWORTH

AUTHOR OF

" Punches, Dies and Tools for Manufacturing in Presses,"
" Hardening, Tempering, Annealing and Forging of Steel," and
"American Tool Making and Interchangeable Manufacturing."

SIXTH EDITION

DIES
Their Construction and Use for the Modern Working of Sheet Metals

by Joseph V. Woodworth

ISBN 0-917914-30-9

6 7 8 9 0

WARNING

Remember that the materials and methods described here are from another era. Workers were less safety conscious then, and some methods may be downright dangerous. Be careful! Use good solid judgement in your work, and think ahead. Lindsay Publications, Inc. has not tested these methods and materials and does not endorse them. Our job is merely to pass along to you information from another era. Safety is your responsibility.

Write for a catalog or other unusual books available from:

Lindsay Publications, Inc.
PO Box 12
Bradley, IL 60915-0012

TO

FREDERICK J. BRYON,

THE AUTHOR'S FRIEND AND ASSOCIATE,

WHOSE KINDLY INTEREST AND ENCOURAGEMENT WILL EVER BE REMEMBERED,

THIS BOOK IS AFFECTIONATELY DEDICATED.

PREFACE.

The use of the power press for the cheap production of sheet metal parts (both large and small) has progressed in a truly wonderful manner during the last few years, and, by the adoption and use of suitable dies and fixtures, this modern machine tool has demonstrated its efficiency for turning out work formerly (and even now in a large number of shops) produced by the milling machine, the shaper, the drill press and the forge. Especially is this so where the parts required are of flat soft steel or iron; and in not only one line of machine manufacturing has the power press been used in this manner, but in every line.

The management of the manufacturing establishments in which the power press has been adopted for the production of parts as referred to above, understand and appreciate the full value of dies : and in such shops they and the machines in which they are used have become as great factors in production as any of the other tools in general use.

The rapidity with which the use and adaptation of dies and press fixtures are becoming understood, the endless variety of articles which they turn out, and the great numbers of mechanics who are in various ways engaged in devising and constructing such tools, have suggested to the author that a practical, comprehensive treatise on this subject would be of value and interest to all persons who might be in any way interested in modern sheet-metal working.

In writing this book the author has done so with the purpose of giving to practical men a book which would treat these preeminent factors in modern manufacturing—Dies—as they should be treated; and that is, from the viewpoint of a practical man. In the pages following are shown engravings of dies, press fixtures and sheet-metal working devices, from the simplest to the most intricate in modern use, and the author has endeavored to describe their construction and use in a clear, practical manner, so that all grades of metal-working mechanics will be able to understand thoroughly how to design, construct and use them, for the production of the marvelous variety of sheet-metal articles and parts which are now in general use, and form an integral part of our twentieth century civilization. Many of the dies and press fixtures shown and described herein were constructed by the author, others under his supervision; while others were constructed by some of our most skillful mechanics and used in some of the largest sheet-metal goods establishments and machine shops in the United States. A number of the tools shown have been selected from over 150 published articles which have been written for the columns of "The American Machinist," "Machinery" and "The Age of Steel," under the author's own name and various pen names. For a number of practical "points" and "kinks" which have been written into the text of the volume the author acknowledges his indebtedness, with thanks, to the following individuals and establishments: Mr. J. E. Fillman, Brooklyn, N. Y.; Mr. W. B. Bailey, Brooklyn, N. Y.; Mr. Robert Leith, Hoosick Falls, N. Y.; Mr. Walter J. Woodworth, Brooklyn, N. Y.; Mr. Charles Colligan, Hartford, Conn.; E. W. Bliss Company, Brooklyn, N. Y.; The Cleveland Punch and Shear Company, Cleveland, O.; Perkins Machine Company, Boston, Mass.; Nicholson File Company, Providence, R. I.

We have endeavored to keep all obsolete matter out of this volume, and to make every die and device and press shown represent the highest that has been attained in the development of each type described. The description of the construction and application of the tools, it is to be hoped, will enable the practical man to adopt them for the production of sheet-metal parts and articles to the maximum of output at the minimum of cost and labor. It is the earnest wish of the author that a perusal of the contents of this volume will enable all who may be in any way interested in sheet-metal working to contribute to the manufacture of sheet-metal parts in a manner which is up-to-date, both as to efficiency and working qualities of the output and to cheapness in production.

Of the origin or antiquity of the art of sheet-metal working the author knows very little; and although he realizes that the marvelous numbers of ingenious tools and devices which are used to-day to produce articles ranging from the modest trouser button to the massive boiler head are but the results of a long course of evolution, he is convinced that a treatise describing the tools and devices of the present day is what the practical man wants.

Although the origin and history of obsolete methods and tools may be of interest to the antiquary, the present-day machinist prefers to spend his hours of leisure in acquainting himself with the design, construction and use of tools with which he may increase the output and lower the cost of production, and thereby increase his earning capacity. With this object in view, and trusting that all metal-working mechanics may be helped by it, this book is modestly submitted to the public.

JOSEPH V. WOODWORTH.

Brooklyn, N. Y.

CONTENTS.

CHAPTER IV.

THE ADAPTATION AND USE OF SIMPLE DIES AND PRESS FIXTURES FOR THE ECONOMIC PRODUCTION OF SHEET-METAL PARTS.

CHAPTER V.

BENDING AND FORMING DIES AND FIXTURES.

CHAPTER VI.

PERFORATING DIES AND PROCESSES FOR THIN AND HEAVY STOCK.

CHAPTER VII.

CURLING, WIRING AND SEAMING PROCESSES.

CHAPTER VIII.

DRAWING PROCESSES FOR SHEET METAL SHELLS.

CHAPTER IX.

COINING PROCESSES—PUNCHES AND PRESSES FOR OPERATIONS ON HEAVY STOCK.

CHAPTER X.

THE FEEDING OF SHEET METAL TO DIES—LUBRICATION OF PRESS WORK.

CHAPTER XI.

ANNEALING TOOL STEEL, AND HARDENING AND TEMPERING PROCESSES FOR PRESS TOOLS—INCLUDING HINTS AND SUGGESTIONS ON THE PROPER USE OF FILES.

CHAPTER XII.

MISCELLANEOUS DIES, PRESSES, FIXTURES, DEVICES AND SPECIAL ARRANGEMENTS FOR SHEET METAL WORKING.

CHAPTER XIII.

CHAPTER I.

INTRODUCTORY.

In this, the opening chapter, we will illustrate and describe dies which, if adopted, will supersede processes for the production of metal parts which are now obsolete in a large number of machine manufacturing establishments. The only reason for their non-adoption in other establishments is that their application and use are not understood. In such shops, where these strictly up-to-date methods are not being used, special tools and fixtures are being constantly designed and constructed for the machining and finishing of metal parts by milling, drilling or other means, which could be accomplished in half the time by means of dies of simple and most inexpensive construction, in the power press. Aside from the reduced cost of production, the lightness, interchangeability, and fine finished appearance of sheet-metal blanks add greatly to the appearance of the machines to which they are attached, and in many cases improve the working qualities as well.

Let any manager of an establishment which does not number a power press or two among its machine tools stroll through his shop with a power press catalogue in his hand and he will not go far before realizing that he is paying for a lot of unnecessary work. After finishing his inspection he will lose no time in placing an order for a power press, and his toolmakers will be kept busy for some time constructing sets of blanking, piercing, bending, shearing and finishing dies to take the place of expensive milling, drilling and polishing fixtures.

Steel.

In no branch of the machinist's art should more attention be given to the importance of the proper selection of steel than in die making, as the working qualities of the tools when finished and their efficiency depend upon this more than anything else.

When ordering steel which is to be used for dies be sure to specify that annealed steel is wanted, as the saving of time and labor in the working of it and the results in the hardening and tempering of the finished tools will be a source of gratification to the die-maker. When these results are considered the slight extra cost of annealed steel is insignificant.

As to the grade of steel to use; be sure to get a good grade, and as there are several brands of steel on the market which are used principally for dies and punches no difficulty should be experienced in procuring a grade or brand which will prove suitable for any special class of work.

When steel forgings are required the job should be given to a smith who understands this branch of his art, as in order for the forgings to machine well and allow of being hardened and tempered as desired, so that the finished tools will accomplish the required results, the smith must understand such work.

The Construction of a Simple Punch and Die.

During a long experience in the making of dies the author has come to know of a number of different methods for constructing single blanking dies, and double or piercing and blanking dies. Every one of these methods has possessed some little kink or way by which the desired results might be accomplished in a manner superior to other methods. So after getting together the best and most practical kinks and ways of all methods, the method of construction here described and illustrated has been evolved.

The Bolster.

Before taking up the description of the die, we will devote a short space to the die-block or bolster. Although these bolsters are made in a variety of shapes and sizes, the one shown in Fig. 1 is of a type most generally used for fastening and locating the kind of die indicated. A number of different styles of bolsters for blanking and piercing dies are shown in Figs. 2 to 5. A large number of shops, which make dies for their own use, make a bolster with each die, so as to leave the die permanently within it. But for economy, where dies of an average shape and size are used, two or three are all that are required. When a number of dies are kept in action all the time, or at the same time, then, of course, each die must have a separate bolster.

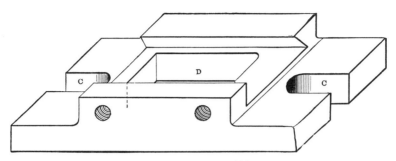

FIG. 1.—THE BOLSTER.

In the preparation and machining of the bolster, first a cut should be taken off the top and bottom, and then a finishing cut

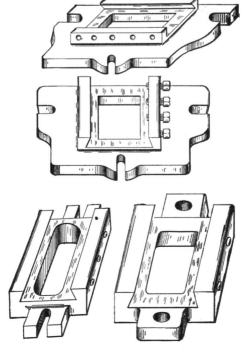

FIGS. 2 TO 5.—TYPES OF BOLSTERS.

off the bottom, after which the face or die seat may be planed
to an angle of 10 degrees, as shown, this being a standard taper
for die blanks among die-makers. The slots C C are cast in the
position shown, in width sufficient to allow of clearance sideways
for the fastening bolts with which it is afterward secured to the
press. The hole D, in the center of the bolster, should be large
enough for the largest blank, from the set of dies which are to
be used in the bolster, to drop through after being punched.

The Die Blank.

In Figs. 6, 7 and 8 are shown a double punch and die used
for the production of blanks like
Fig. 9; this die is of a type in
general use. The punch and die
consist of the following parts:
The punch holder or stem A, of
cast iron, the punch plate or pad
B, of mild steel, the blanking

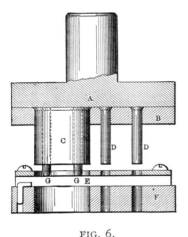

FIG. 6.

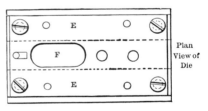

Plan
View of
Die

FIG. 7.

punch C, of tool steel, the piercing punches D, of the same, the
stripper and gage plates E, the die F, of tool steel, and the pilot
pin G. The shape of the piece to be produced in a die of this type
may be any circular or irregular shape desired, as the method of
construction here shown is applicable to all, excepting when the
blank to be produced is of a very large size or when the metal to
be punched is very thick.

As most presses in which punches and dies of this type are
used require a punch holder with a round stem, we show one
of this sort. When machining the holder great care must be
taken to get the working surfaces square with the stem; the
faces of the punch plate and stripper plate must be perfectly

parallel. When planing the die no great care is required, as it has to be ground after hardening. It should be finished with beveled sides, to fit the bolster, with the edges of the face smooth so as to have a square edge from which to lay out the die.

We will now lay the punch plate, punch holder and stripper plate aside, as they will not be touched until the die proper has been finished.

The Templets.

Now in order to lay out the die a templet or master blank is required; this should be made from sheet steel about 3-32 inch thick, and should be filed and finished all over to the exact shape

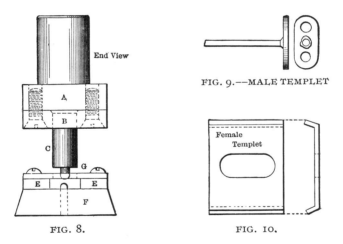

End View

A

B

C

G

E   E

F

FIG. 8.

FIG. 9.—MALE TEMPLET

Female
Templet

FIG. 10.

and size required. The two holes should then be laid out in the exact location desired and drilled and reamed to size. Care and accuracy in the preparation of the templet are necessary, as the quality of the work to be produced depends on it. Now take a piece of, say, ⅛-inch brass rod about 2½ inches long, and solder one end of it to the back of the templet as shown in Fig. 9. The templet is now complete and there is no possibility of getting the wrong side up.

We now take a piece of soft sheet brass, of the same thickness as the templet, and bend it to the shape shown in Fig. 10, that is to fit across and over the face of the die with the bent ends projecting down the inclined sides of the die about 5-16 inch.

This is the female templet, and it should be long enough to allow of its being worked out in the center to fit the male templet, Fig. 9. After having done this the face of the die (which should be polished with a rough piece of emery cloth) should be "blue-stoned" and the female templet placed upon it in the proper position, and an outline of the blank marked through it on the face of the die with a sharp scriber. We now remove the templet and proceed to finish the blanking die, which must be accomplished by working the blank through it.

Working the Templet Through the Die.

To work a templet through a die proceed as follows: After the surplus stock has been removed by drilling holes about 1-64 inch apart around the inside of the outline and drifting it out, file through from the back to within a shade of the line. Now take the male templet and, holding it by the end of the brass rod, enter it into the die from the back, holding it as parallel as possible with the face of the die. By holding a piece of white paper in front of the die it will be noticed that the die touches the templet at only a few narrow spots; take a lead pencil and mark these spots, making a line at each spot as long as the surface touched. Now remove the templet and file where the marks appear. Keep inserting the templet, marking the spots and filing them away, and in a surprisingly short time the templet will be even with the face of the die, which will be the exact shape and size desired, fitting the templet perfectly.

There are a great many dies of this type in use (which are used for cutting out blanks which are not required to have smooth sides) that it is not necessary to finish the insides smoothly. But there are a greater number in which the finish of the blanks with smooth sides is one of the objects sought. In dies for producing smooth and well-finished blanks the insides should be finished highly, either with a dead smooth file or a scraper.

Giving Clearance to the Die.

In giving clearance to a die a few things must be considered in order to decide upon the proper amount to give. For a die which will only be used to produce a few thousand blanks excessive clearance should be given, say, five degrees, as this will allow of the die being finished quickly. In dies which are to produce large quantities of blanks, and in which the blanks produced are required to be of approximately the same size, one degree is plenty. In giving this one degree of clearance to the die so that it will have one degree of clearance all the way through, the holes that are drilled to allow of removing the surplus stock should be reamed from the back with a reamer of about the taper of 1-32 inch to 1 inch of length. The reaming of the holes when constructing a blanking die will save a vast amount of filing and the giving of the one degree of clearance will not be difficult.

Locating the Piercing Dies.

The next step in the construction of the die is the locating of the two piercing dies. To accomplish this, place the master blank within the female templet and clamp it to the face of the die in the correct position, allowing for a thickness of metal between blanks. We now take a center drill, which fits the holes in the master blank, and transfer the two holes through it to the face of the die; we drill these holes and then ream them from the back with a reamer of the same taper as the one used for the blanking die. After the holes for the dowel pins and screws by which the stripper and gage plates are to be fastened to the die have been drilled and tapped, and the hole for the stop pin located and drilled, we are ready to harden and temper the die.

Hardening a Blanking Die.

In order to harden a die properly great care should be taken; first in the heating of the steel, and second in the quenching. In all shops where dies, or other tools which require hardening, are constructed, a gas furnace or "muffler" should be used for heating them. But when a "muffler" is not handy charcoal should be used. After a good clean fire has been built, all screw and dowel holes in the die should be plugged with fire clay or asbestos. By taking these precautions the tendency of the steel to crack around the holes is, as far as possible, eliminated. We now heat the die to an even cherry red, so that the entire plate will be the same temperature; then remove it from the fire and dip it endwise into the water (which should be warmed slightly to take the chill out), being careful to dip down straight, and not to move it or shake it around, as that would increase the possibility of the die warping or shrinking excessively. After removing the die from the water it should be immediately warmed. Now grind the face of the die; heat a thick piece of cast iron red hot, and place the die upon it; it can then be drawn evenly to any temper desired. By taking a piece of oily waste and wiping the face of the die as it is heating the different colors will show up clear. When the color denoting the temper required appears remove the die and allow it to cool off slowly.

Making the Blanking Punch.

Now for the blanking punch: Take the master blank or male templet; remove the wire rod and mark the spot where it was attached, so as to know the back from the front of the blank. Then solder the blank, front up, to one end of the piece of tool steel which is to be used for the blanking punch. The punch can now be machined, either in the shaper or the milling machine, so that its entire length will be the shape of the blank, finishing it as close to the edge of the blank as possible. Now heat the steel slightly and the blank will drop off. Clean the blank, lay it aside and proceed to fit the punch. If it is to punch very thin stock make it a tight fit within the die; if for heavy stock, a trifle loose. In order to make a punch a perfect fit for thin stock the edges of the cutting face should be beveled with a file. The punch should then be sheared through the die in the press in much the same manner as a broach is used, being careful to have it in perfect alignment with the die.

Before hardening the punch it is necessary to locate the holes for the pilot pins G. These pins are necessary in order to produce pierced blanks that will be interchangeable. Take the master blank, enter it into the die from the back with the front up. It will fit the die tightly because of the shrinkage in hardening. Now enter the blanking punch from the top and locate the holes for the pilot pins through the holes in the blank with a centering drill. Drill the holes to size and harden and draw the punch to the temper desired, which should be in most cases a dark blue. In tempering the punch draw it from the back, allowing the temper to run out to the front; thus the back will be almost soft while the remainder will be as hard as required.

The drawing of the punch so that the back will be soft is done to strengthen it and also to allow of upsetting it when locating it within the punch plate.

Locating the Blanking Punch in the Punch Plate.

To locate the punch in the punch plate, take the plate and clamp it true on the face of the die and transfer the outline of the blanking die to the face of the plate. Then work a hole of the shape of this outline through the plate, so that the punch can be entered face first through from the back. Then place both punch and plate under the ram of the press and set the punch dead square with the face of the pad and proceed to force it through, using the punch as a broach. It will be necessary to repeat this operation several times in order to get the punch through the plate, as the surplus stock curled up by the punch has to be removed. After having forced the punch into the pad until the face is through, force it back and out again. Now chamfer the edges of the hole at the back of the pad and force the punch in again, until the back is a shade above the plate, and upset or rivet as shown and finish it flat with the plate; when this is done there will be no danger of the punch pulling out when in use.

Locating the Piercing Punches in the Punch Plate.

To locate the holes for the piercing punches, enter the blanking punch into the die until the faces of the punch plate and the die are within 3-16 inch of each other, with a pair of parallels between them. Then use the die as a jig and locate the holes for the piercing punches; spot them deeply. With a drill about two sizes smaller than the piercing dies drill entirely through the punch plate and then ream the holes to size. Use the die as a jig for all three operations.

For the two piercing punches use drill rod and upset the heads before hardening, as all small punches should be hardened for their entire length, as otherwise they would bend or break. If after hardening the punches are found to have sprung they must be carefully straightened before forcing them into the punch plate. Fasten the punch plate to the cast iron holder A, with four flat-head screws as shown.

Finishing the Die.

All holes for screws and dowels in the stripper and gage plate should be transferred through the die. The holes for the two piercing punches in the stripper should be the same size as the dies, as by fitting tightly the punches are strengthened and supported while piercing the metal.

After the gage plates and stripper have been located and fastened upon the die as shown, with the stop pin located so that its locating face is the same distance from the edge of the blanking die as the width of surplus stock allowed between the blanks, the die is complete.

If the method of construction described and illustrated in the foregoing is properly carried out there will never be any possibility of failure in the accomplishment of the desired results.

Fundamental Points to be Remembered.

The practical points to be remembered when constructing a die of this type are as follows: Be sure to make an accurate pair of templets. Machine the punch holder and stripper plate accurately. Work the blank through the die, and use it for locating all the holes for the pilot pins and piercing punches. Finish the die before starting on any of the other parts. Transfer all holes in the punch plate through the die; and, lastly, be sure to have the front of the master blank up during all operations in which it is used. By keeping in mind these practical points a punch and die of this type can be constructed in which the alignment between all parts will be perfect.

Setting the Die and Using It.

To operate the die, drive the die proper into the die block or bolster, Fig. 1, and then set it up in the press. The proper way to set a die of this kind is to first place the punch within the ram of the press and fasten it there. The punch should then be brought down until the faces are within ⅛ inch of the die face. Then, using the left hand through the press bolster, the die should be raised up until all punches have entered it. The punch should then be brought down about 5-16 inch and the die will rest squarely on the press bolster in perfect alignment with

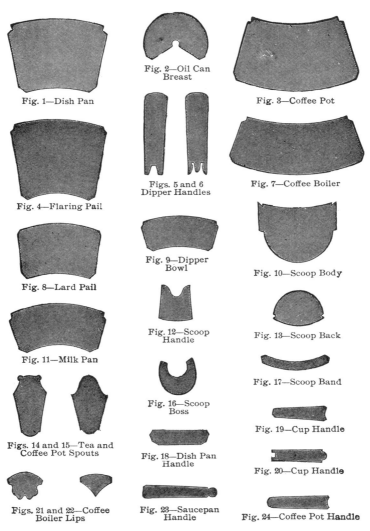

Fig. 1—Dish Pan

Fig. 2—Oil Can Breast

Fig. 3—Coffee Pot

Fig. 4—Flaring Pail

Figs. 5 and 6 Dipper Handles

Fig. 7—Coffee Boiler

Fig. 8—Lard Pail

Fig. 9—Dipper Bowl

Fig. 10—Scoop Body

Fig. 11—Milk Pan

Fig. 12—Scoop Handle

Fig. 13—Scoop Back

Figs. 14 and 15—Tea and Coffee Pot Spouts

Fig. 16—Scoop Boss

Fig. 17—Scoop Band

Fig. 19—Cup Handle

Figs. 21 and 22—Coffee Boiler Lips

Fig. 18—Dish Pan Handle

Fig. 20—Cup Handle

Fig. 23—Saucepan Handle

Fig. 24—Coffee Pot Handle

FIG. II.—DIAGRAMS OF BLANKS FROM CUTTING DIES.

the punch. Now fasten the die to the press bolster and give it
a rap with a hammer at either end to set it; then go ahead.

The stock to be punched should be entered beneath the
stripper and pushed up against the stop pin. At the first stroke
of the press the two holes are pierced and a scrap blank punched
out. Now feed the stock forward until the back edge of the
blanked hole rests against the stop pin, and at the next stroke
as the punch descends the pilot pins in the blanking punch will
enter the holes pierced at the first stroke and a blank will be
produced which will be an exact duplicate of the master blank.
The stock may then be fed along until the entire strip has been
worked up.

A Plain Blanking Die.

When a plain blanking die is desired, to produce blanks of
any circular or irregular shape such as the smaller ones shown
in Fig. 11, the description given herein for the construction of

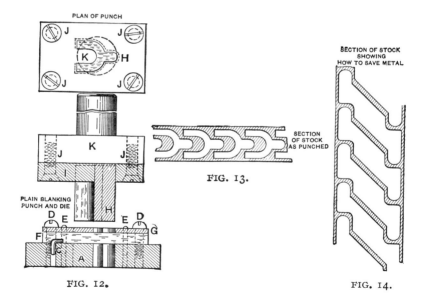

FIG. 12.   FIG. 13.   FIG. 14.

the blanking die and punch portions of Figs. 6 to 8 should be
followed, and instead of making two templets make only one—
the male.

As shown, plain blanking dies of the class shown in Figs.

12 and 15 are very simple in construction.   They are used to produce blanks of any flat shape from tin, iron, steel, aluminum, brass, copper, zinc, silver, paper, leather, cloth, etc.   In Figs. 12 and 15, K is the punch holder or stem, I the punch plate, H the punch which is let into the punch plate and upset at the back, as shown.   The punch plate is fastened to the holder face by four flat-head screws J J J J.   The die A is worked out at B and finished to templet, C is the stop pin, F F the two gage plates, and G the stripper plate fastened and located by the four screws D and the two dowels E E.   All plain blanking dies for punching stock up to 3-16 inch thick should be constructed, like this one.

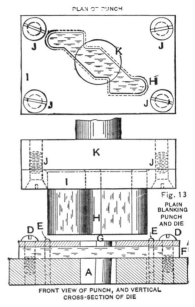

Fig. 13

PLAIN
BLANKING
PUNCH
AND DIE

FRONT VIEW OF PUNCH, AND VERTICAL
CROSS-SECTION OF DIE

FIG. 15.

Dies for Large Blanks.

Blanking or cutting dies for punching out large blanks from comparatively thin stock are made in almost every shape and size for cutting all kinds of metal.   A number of different shapes and sizes are shown in Figs. 16 and 17, and a set of blanks produced in dies of this construction are shown in Fig. 18.   This class of dies consists of an upper or "male" die, commonly called the punch, and a lower or "female" die, rightly called the die. As a rule the female die is hardened and tempered to the degree best suited for the stock to be punched, while the male die, or punch, is left soft, so that it can be upset at the cutting edges when worn, so that blanks may be produced which will be free from burrs and fins.   The cutting edges of dies of this class are always sheared, the size of the blank and circumstances determining the amount of shear to be given.   For punching blanks from thin stock such as tin, brass, iron, etc., a moderate amount of shear will give the best results, while for heavy stock a greater amount must be given. These dies are usually made

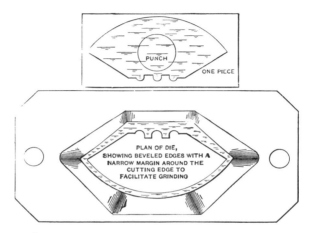

FIG. 16.—BLANKING DIE CONSTRUCTED FROM FORGINGS.

from forgings and the finest work in this line that we know of is done in the shops of E. W. Bliss Co., Brooklyn, N. Y., where probably more dies are constructed than in any other shop in the

FIG. 17.—" BLANKING " OR " CUTTING " DIES.

world. They make their large cutting dies by first welding steel cutting rings, which have been first forged to somewhere near the desired shape, to wrought-iron bases or plates. These bases are

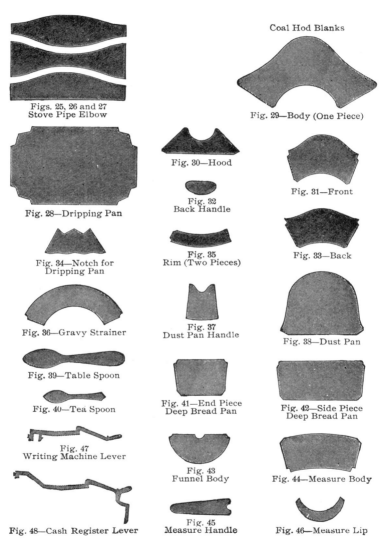

Figs. 25, 26 and 27
Stove Pipe Elbow

Coal Hod Blanks

Fig. 29—Body (One Piece)

Fig. 28—Dripping Pan

Fig. 30—Hood

Fig. 32
Back Handle

Fig. 31—Front

Fig. 34—Notch for
Dripping Pan

Fig. 35
Rim (Two Pieces)

Fig. 33—Back

Fig. 36—Gravy Strainer

Fig. 37
Dust Pan Handle

Fig. 38—Dust Pan

Fig. 39—Table Spoon

Fig. 40—Tea Spoon

Fig. 41—End Piece
Deep Bread Pan

Fig. 42—Side Piece
Deep Bread Pan

Fig. 47
Writing Machine Lever

Fig. 43
Funnel Body

Fig. 44—Measure Body

Fig. 48—Cash Register Lever

Fig. 45
Measure Handle

Fig. 46—Measure Lip

FIG. 18.—DIAGRAMS OF BLANKS FROM CUTTING DIES.

then planed and the die machined to almost the finish size and the cutting edges beveled, as shown, on upright milling machines. The templets are then fitted to the dies by filing, after which the faces are sheared and the dies hardened. The cutting faces are then ground on special machinery and a number of bent pins located around the die to act as strippers when the die is in use. For punching heavy or thick sheet iron, steel, brass and other heavy stock they harden both male and female dies, drawing the male somewhat lower than the female, and provide them with stripping plates and construct the dies somewhat dif-

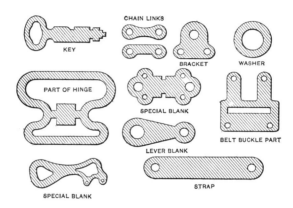

FIG. 19.—BLANKS FROM PIERCING AND BLANKING DIES.

ferently from those used for thin stock. A set of these dies are shown in Figs. 20 to 22.

The Use of a Power Press.

In shops in which a power press has not as yet found a place, and where it is thought that one or a few could be used to advantage, the management should write press manufacturers fully, describing the work to be done. If a new article is to be manufactured, which can be produced to the best advantage by means of suitable dies in the power press, a sample of the work or an exact drawing of the same should be submitted to the manufacturers of such tools. As very often the shape, size or general construction of such parts are modified, before the articles are manufactured in large quantities, it is absolutely necessary that such points should be settled before placing an order for a set of tools for their production, as otherwise, if a slight alteration is made in the parts afterward, it will involve considerable alteration in the tools.

In sheet-metal goods establishments the chief desire is the increasing of the daily production of the presses and tools, and this object can only be attained by keeping the presses constantly producing parts of the same shape and size and using the presses which are best adapted to the work. In small establish-

FIG. 20.—PUNCH AND DIE WITH STRIPPER.

ments, or in machine shops where only a given number of parts of sheet-metal of the same shape and size are required at intervals, a press should be used which will take in a wide range of work of widely varying dimensions, thus allowing the production of a large variety of sheet-metal articles and parts with one press and different sets of tools, which in the larger establishments require a number of presses of different sizes.

When a press is to be used exclusively for punching, before ordering particular attention should be given to the thickness of the material to be punched, the size and number of holes and their relative position to each other. If parts are to be produced in which more than one hole is to be pierced, their position in the sheet must be determined. By giving the maximum dimensions of the above a press of the required strength and depth of throat will be obtained.

Open Back Presses.

The best style of press to use for general work, wherever possible, is the "open back" style, as the advantages of a press of such construction over those with a solid back are numerous. First, instead of having the crank on one end of the shaft, it is

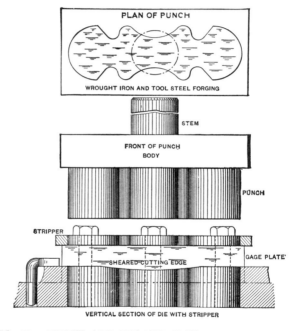

FIG. 21.—PUNCH AND DIE FOR CUTTING HEAVY STOCK.

supported by journals on each side which prevents the shaft from springing and wearing unevenly; second, the opening at the back, admitting plenty of light, makes an accurate adjustment of the dies possible without trouble on the part of the operator when setting them; lastly, where, in a "solid back" press the balance wheel is at the back, and thereby out of reach of the operator when setting the dies, in the "open back" press it is on the right side and within easy reach, thus enabling the operator to revolve it with his right hand while he is setting the tools with his left.

Lining Up and Leveling a Power Press.

Line up and level a power press as you would any other machine tool from which satisfactory results are desired, and fasten it securely to the floor. The position of the press in relation to

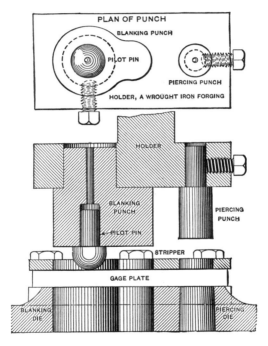

FIG. 22.—PUNCH AND DIE FOR PIERCING AND CUTTING
HEAVY STOCK.

the driving shaft should be such as to allow of using a straight belt and having the balance wheel run toward the operator, and thus the belt can be thrown off and slipped on again without trouble. The gib screws for adjusting the fit of the ram should not be very tight, for if they are there will be undue friction on the strap—a clicking sound of the clutch will warn the operator of this.

The diameter of the pulley on the driving shaft should be large enough to allow the press to be speeded according to the directions given by the manufacturer. When setting the dies throw the belt off the driving pulley and set the die according to the directions given herein under "Setting and Using the Die."

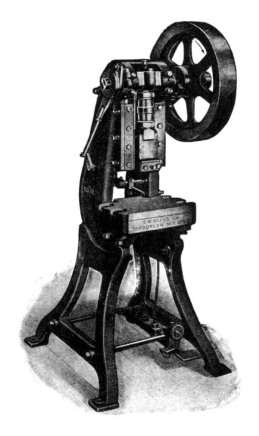

FIG. 23.—A POWER PRESS FOR PRODUCING SMALL OR MEDIUM SIZED BLANKS, EQUIPPED WITH AN AUTOMATIC ADJUSTABLE STOP OR FINGER GAGE.

Allow the punch to enter the die just far enough to do the work required and no further. Have the operator locate all oil holes and see that he oils all parts regularly. Lastly do not allow *everybody* to take a turn at running the press; have a man or a bright boy to run it and *keep* him at it, and there will then be very little probability of finger clipping.

Using the Proper Tools.

When in doubt as to the best press or classes of tools to use for a special job, write to manufacturers or experts who make a specialty of such tools. It is often possible to have dies made in their establishments at a lower cost to the buyer than if they were constructed in his own tool room; because, where the foreman or toolmakers might understand the construction of one type of dies which would do the work required, the specialist will understand a number of different types, and he will choose the one which will be at once the cheapest and the best. What is more, there will be no guess work about it.

For the production of small and medium sized parts, a press of the design and construction shown in Fig. 23 will be found to meet all requirements. In connection with a press of this type a "finger gage attachment" or automatic stop-pin may be used wherever the nature of the work will allow it. As shown in the engraving, the attachment consists of an adjustable stop, resting with its pointed end on the face of the die, from which it is automatically raised after each stroke, allowing the metal to be fed forward for the next stroke. By dropping back at the proper time into the hole last punched, it acts as an accurate gage without impeding the progress of the stock.

Dies of the types shown and described in this chapter should prove adaptable for the rapid and cheap production of a large variety of sheet metal parts. The methods of construction given cover all plain or single blanking dies, and double or piercing and blanking dies used in the general run of sheet-metal work.

CHAPTER II.

In this chapter are shown a number of dies that are invaluable for use in the average machine shop—especially in the jobbing shop. The dies shown are the most simple and inexpensive of their class for producing work of the kind indicated.

An Emergency Die.

The first die, shown in Fig. 24, is known among die-makers as an "Emergency Die," that is—a punch and die for producing

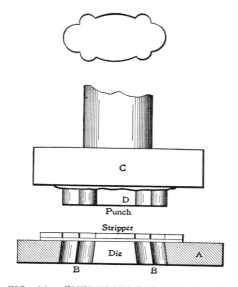

FIG. 24.—EMERGENCY DIE AND BLANK.

a small number of blanks of a given shape and size, of which the blank shown in Fig. 25 is a type. The die A is made from a piece of 5-16 inch flat tool steel, planed and fitted to bolster, with the shape of the blank worked out at B B. In dies of this type, when only a small number of blanks are to be punched, the clearance or taper of the die, from the cutting edge, should be considerable, as the more clearance given, the less labor and skill required to finish. Allow the master blank to just fit the die at the cutting edge, and then draw and harden the die.

The punch consists of the cast iron holder C, and the punch D; a piece of ¼-inch flat tool steel, which is worked out to shape and sheared through the die and left soft. It is then hard soldered to the face of the holder C as shown, and the punch and die are complete.

For punching blanks from thin stock to the number of 100 to 2,000, a die of this type will prove all right, and although some may say "a botch job," the results will be found to be all that can be desired. This style of die is used universally in almost all of the fancy sheet metal goods houses, as the number of differ-

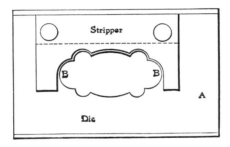

FIG. 25.—PLAN OF EMERGENCY DIE.

ent shapes and the small quantities required necessitate the elimination of all unnecessary expense in the production of the same.

A Shearing Die for Finishing Heavy Blanks.

The punch and die shown in Fig. 26 is known as a shearing or finishing die for heavy blanks, and it may be used for finishing work that is often finished in the milling machine, or by grinding. The blank finished in this die is shown in Fig. 27. It is a small wrench punched from 7-32-inch mild steel. In the punching of heavy stock the punch is always fitted very loosely to the die, with the result that the blanks produced are generally concave at the edges, and have a ragged appearance where they have cut away from the rest of the stock. To remove these defects and marks, the blanks should be sheared through a finishing die like the one shown in Fig. 11, when by trimming or cutting off a shaving of stock all around the blanks, they are left smooth and have the appearance of having been milled.

In making a die of the finishing type, one of the blanks that

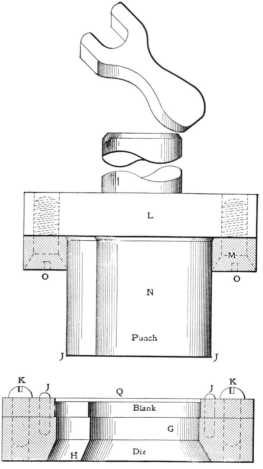

FIGS. 26 AND 27.—BLANK, AND SHEARING PUNCH AND DIE.

has been punched is taken and filed and finished all around the edges, removing about .003 of stock all around. The blank is then used as a templet in finishing the die F, letting it through from the back and filing the die straight, giving it just the least clearance possible and having the templet a tight fit at the cutting edge. The inside of the die is then polished as smooth as possible at G, and then filed taper, downward from H. As shown, I is the gage plate which is worked out to allow of the rough blank fitting nicely within it. This plate is fastened and located upon the face of the die accurately, by the screws J J, and the dowels K K, so that the blank will rest on the face of the die I, with an equal margin for trimming all around. Great care should be taken to locate this gage plate in its proper position, as the small amount of stock to be trimmed from the blanks will not allow of much leeway. The die should be carefully hardened and drawn to a very light straw temper, and the face ground and oilstoned, so that the cutting edge will be as sharp as possible.

The punch is constructed in the same manner as the blanking punch shown in Chapter I, L being the holder, M the pad and N the punch. The punch N is sheared through the die to a snug fit within it, after which it is highly polished and left soft. When using the die, the blank Fig. 27 is placed within the gage plate L; the punch descends and it is sheared into the die F at G, trimming and finishing it all around. If the die has been highly polished the results produced will be as good as if the blanks were finished in a milling machine or by more expensive means.

Burnishing Dies.

There is a large number of different small pieces which are in great demand in the average machine shop, which, when the quantity permits, could be finished at a greatly reduced cost by a die of this type. When a high finish or polish is desired, the blanks should be forced through another die, in construction the same as the first, except that it should taper slightly from the cutting edge, and be about .002 smaller at the back than at the cutting edge. This die should also be highly polished and left very hard. In forcing the blank through this die the metal around the edge is compressed and then polished by the friction as the smaller part is passed through. Blanks treated in this manner have the appearance of having been polished or buffed. A die of this type is called a burnishing die, and it is a "hummer" for rapid and cheap production.

Die for Finishing Holes in Heavy Stock.

The punch and die shown in Fig. 29, although of the simplest construction, is a great tool for accomplishing by inexpensive means results that usually require considerable time and cost to produce. It is used for finishing square holes that have been punched in the strip of flat 5-16-inch machine steel shown in Fig. 30. The upper view shows the holes after the first operation, and the lower view, the appearance after being finished. Of course they could be finished by broaching, but the means shown here are best by a long shot. After the holes have been

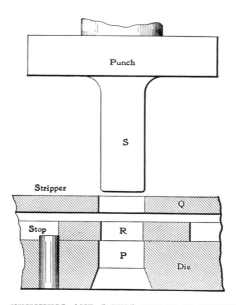

FIG. 29.—FINISHING AND SIZING HOLES IN HEAVY STOCK.

punched, their edges are uneven and ragged and, as they are left about .003 smaller than the required size, this punch and die are used to square, polish and size them.

The punch S is machined in the miller to a perfect square of the size to which the holes are to be finished, that is .003 larger than the punched holes. After being polished, the face is finished dead square and the edges left sharp; it is then hardened and drawn slightly and the face oilstoned. The die P is then made and worked out until the face of the punch can be entered. It is then used as a broach and forced into and through the die, finishing it to an exact duplicate of its shape. The die is then filed taper from the back, and left straight for about 5-16 inch from the cutting edge. The edges of the punch are then rounded so that it will enter the holes easily. The stripper Q is of ½-inch flat machine steel, with a channel milled down through the center, in depth and width sufficient to allow of the strip of stock in which the holes are punched to pass through it freely without side play. A small pin projecting above the die P, at the left acts as a gage for locating the stock in position.

When in use the strip of stock is entered beneath the stripper with the first hole under the punch. The punch descends and enters the hole, gradually compresses the sides and finishes it,

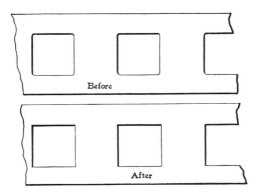

FIG. 30.—THE WORK.

leaving a dead square hole with a smooth finish on all sides. The punch shown should enter the work for a full inch of its length. This type of die can be used for finishing a large variety of different shaped holes in heavy iron or mild steel, where they are all required to be the same shape and size. By using the means shown, the holes have a finish that it would be impractical to accomplish by other means.

A Curling Die for a Hinge.

In Figs. 31 and 33, respectively, are shown two dies called curling dies, accomplishing, as they do, the curling of sheet metal. The one shown in Fig. 31 is for curling the hinge, Fig. 32, while the one in Fig. 33 is for curling a flat piece of metal into the form of a tube as shown in Fig. 34, in which is shown the metal before and after curling.

These dies, although simple in design and construction, are required to be accurately made in order to work well; there are several points in each where close work is necessary for rapid and first-class production. In the hinge die, Fig. 31, the punch holder V, is turned and faced and a dovetailed channel let into

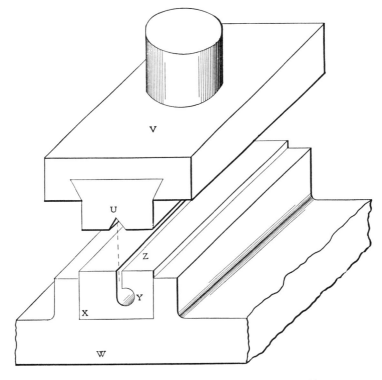

FIG. 31.—A HINGE-CURLING PUNCH AND DIE.

the face to admit the tool steel punch U, which is worked out and fitted to the holder, as shown, and a slot milled down the face to an angle of 45 degrees. It is hardened and drawn to a light temper and driven into the holder V. The die consists of the bolster W, and the die X, which is located as shown. After the radius to which the hinge is to be curled has been found, the piece of steel which is to be the die, is centered at each end for the hole Y. A drill 1-32 inch under size is then used, drilling from each end, in the lathe, keeping one end of the die on the tail center, and then reversing it, until the hole is completely through the die. A "gun" reamer is then used to ream and finish the hole to the exact size required. The hole should then be lapped to a smooth finish. A mandrel is now forced into the hole Y, the die is set on the centers of the miller, and a cut is taken off the bottom, thereby squaring it with the hole Y. The two sides and top are then finished as shown, after which a cutter or metal saw (in width equal to the thickness of the stock to be curled) is used to cut the slot Z, being careful to get the outer edge of it in line with the side of the hole Y. After removing all burrs and polishing the edges, the die should be hardened, and drawn just a little, leaving it as hard as possible without

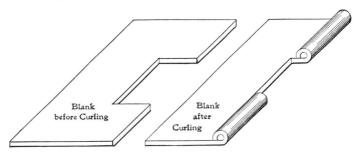

Blank
before Curling

Blank
after
Curling

FIG. 32.—THE WORK.

danger of cracking. In order to harden a die of this type properly, and eliminate as far as possible all chances of its warping, it should be heated slowly and evenly, and quenched down straight into a tub of water with about two inches of oil on the top. Passing through the oil toughens and prepares the steel, so to speak, for the sudden chill of the water. The manner in which this die is used can be understood from Fig. 31. One of the blanks shown in Fig. 32, is entered into the slot Z, in the die, and the punch is set in line with it as shown by the dotted line. The punch descends and forces the metal into the die Y, and it takes and follows the radius all around; the punch descending far enough to curl and finish the blank to the shape of the finished piece shown in Fig. 32. Care must be taken to have all working parts of this die smooth and well polished, as the finish of the work depends on it. Also, in the adjustment of the

stroke of the punch allow it to descend just far enough to accomplish the curl—as if it descends too far, the work will be
jammed into the die, from which it will be very difficult to remove without marking the die itself.   When set properly, the

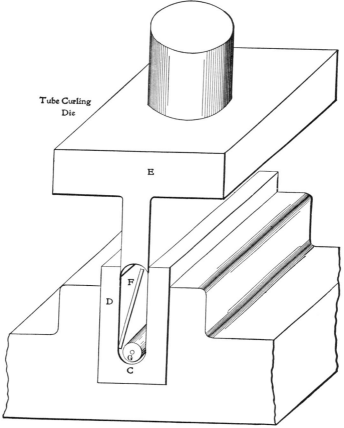

Tube Curling
Die

FIG. 33.—TUBE CURLING DIE WITH BLANK IN POSITION.

finished work, after the punch ascends, can be easily removed
from the die by hand.

Die for Making Metal Tubes.

The die shown in Fig. 33, for curling a tube, although an old
principle and well known in die shops, is a stranger in a large
number of others where it could be used to advantage. The design and construction of both punch and die is clearly shown in

the engravings, as is also the method of operation, and it requires very little description to be understood.

In the die, B is the bolster with a slot let in to admit the die A. A hole C, in diameter the same as the outer size of the finished tube, is let through and reamed to size, and then polished and finished in the same manner as Y, Fig. 31. A slot S, exactly the same width as the hole C, is milled down through the face as shown, being sure to get both sides in line with the sides of the hole. The die is then carefully hardened in the same manner as that described for the other.

The punch is made from a mild steel forging with a tool steel face for the punch F. After being turned to size and machined as shown, it is chucked in the miller and a half round groove is let into the face, using a concave cutter of the same radius as the die C. The sides of the punch are then milled to just fit the slot D,

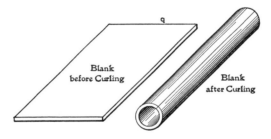

FIG. 34.—THE WORK.

in the die, running out at each side to a feather edge. The face of the punch is then polished, after which it is hardened and drawn from the back, leaving the face very hard.

The mandrel G, of tool steel is now made to the proper diameter, which should be two thicknesses of metal smaller than the die, and then polished lengthwise with emery cloth so as to allow of the easy removal of the tubes. A stud, not shown, is then let through one end to act as a handle. This mandrel is left soft, except for very accurate work, when all working parts of the die should be hardened and ground to size.

To operate, the punch and die are set up in the press as shown, and the horn or mandrel G, inserted in the die C. The blank Fig. 34, is then slipped into the die as shown at H, and the punch F, descending, forces the metal around and between the horn G, and the die C, until, at the bottom of the stroke, the punch at F, strikes the metal, forms and finishes it around the horn G, to the shape shown in Fig. 34, leaving a tube sufficiently perfect for all ordinary purposes with a close joint where the two edges of the metal meet. The horn is then pulled from the die and the tube, relaxing a bit through the spring in the metal, is stripped of the horn by hand.

The two curling dies shown here are the simplest and best to use for the class of work shown, and with proper care, will last a long while. The few points necessary to successfully construct them, are: Close work, a smooth finish on all working parts, care in hardening, and to have them as hard as possible as there is considerable wear on the parts from the friction of curling the blanks.

A Washer Die.

The die shown in Fig. 35 is a washer die, and its type may

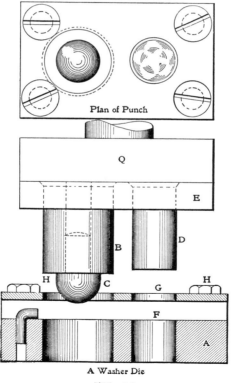

A Washer Die

FIG. 35.

be used for the production of washers of any description. Its construction is that of the piercing and blanking type described

FIG. 36.

and shown in Chapter I. A is the die, F the gage plate, and G the stripper, located and fastened to the die by the two cap screws H H. In the punch E is the pad, Q the holder, D the piercing punch for piercing the hole in the washer, and B the blanking punch, while C C is the pilot pin which enters the hole pierced by punch D, and trues the stock on the blanking die.

In operating this die, the stock is fed in and held against the gage plate and the stop-pin. At the first stroke the hole is pierced and a waste washer punched out, and at the next stroke a finished washer is produced and the hole pierced in the one following. For punching thin stock, fit the punches tight; for heavy stock, loose.

A Burnishing Die for Finishing Heavy Blanks.

Fig. 37 shows a burnishing die for finishing heavy blanks. As shown, I is the die finished at J and tapering inward a trifle

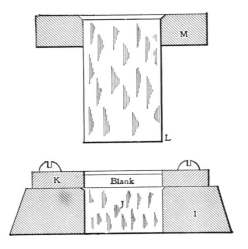

FIG. 37.—A BURNISHING DIE.

from the face. K is the gage plate for locating the work, and M the pad into which the punch is located. All working parts of this punch and die are finished very smooth and when the blank shown on the die is forced through J, a nice smooth finish on all sides results. This die is substantially the same as the one shown in Fig. 29, for finishing square holes, except that it is for external use instead of internal. For both uses the principle of construction shown will produce equally good results. The degree of finish on the product depends entirely on the smoothness of the working parts.

A Bending Die for Right Angle Bends.

The die shown in Fig. 38, is used for bending sheet metal blanks at right angles. N is the die, finished to admit the pad O,

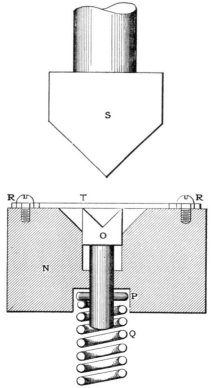

FIG. 38.—A RIGHT-ANGLE BENDING DIE.

and the spring Q. The pad is first let into the die tightly and then a 45 degree angle is milled as shown, finishing die and pad at the same time, thereby insuring an even surface when the pad bottoms at the end of the stroke. R R are the two gage plates for locating the work T, and S the punch. The spring Q is located in the bolster, after the die N has been fastened within it, by means of an adjustable screw in the bottom. The pin P prevents the pad from rising beyond the proper height, as shown. In angular bending where exact duplicates in size and shape are required, a pad as shown should be used, while for ordinary purposes a plain die without a pad will be sufficient.

Planing the Angle on Die Blanks.

The illustrations in Figs. 39 and 40 are self-explanatory, they show the wrong and the right way respectively of holding steel die blanks in the vise for planing or milling the angles. In Fig.

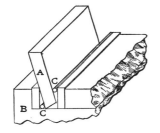
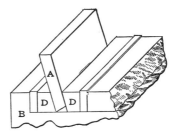
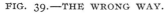

FIG. 39.—THE WRONG WAY.   FIG. 40.—THE RIGHT WAY.

39 A is the blank and C C two pieces of drill rod for throwing the blank off to the angle required. As will be seen, this way is very unreliable, and not consistent with good work. The method shown in Fig. 40 is the proper way; that is by using two angular parallels D D, which are simple to construct and cheap. A pair of such parallels should find a place in all shops where dies are made or used.

Blanking and Bending in One Operation.

The punch and die shown in Fig. 41 will serve to illustrate how a number of different bends can be accomplished in one operation in a plain blanking die, by shearing or cutting away the face of the punch to the shape desired in the blank. The pieces of work shown in Fig. 42 will convey an idea of the variety of bends which it is possible to accomplish by doing this; the top one is the product of the die shown. As will be seen, the face of the die is left perfectly flat, while the punch is finished to the shape desired in the piece.

When in use, the metal is placed on the face of the die and as

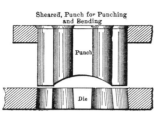

Sheared, Punch for Punching and Bending

Punch

Die

FIG. 41.

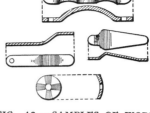

FIG. 42.—SAMPLES OF WORK.

the punch descends, the two ends commence to cut first, and enter the die before the center begins to cut; thus, the stock clings and forms itself to the shape of the face of the punch, while the part still attached to the stock is held by the die, so that when at length the blank is punched out completely it has assumed the shape of the face of the punch. A large number of different bends can be produced in this manner, which otherwise would require a second operation to accomplish.

Punching Heavy Stock.

In Fig. 43 are shown the same principles transferred to the die, in order to punch heavy stock in a press that is not strong enough to stand a straight cut, and when the blanks are re-

Sheared Die for Heavy Punching

FIG. 43.

quired to be flat. The shearing of the die, as shown, is the remedy, the punch entering and cutting at both ends first and cutting the center last, the blank resulting clings to the face of the punch and comes out flat.

In shearing either a punch or die as described here, it is always advisable to do it so that both ends of the punch will enter the die first and at the same time, as by doing this the die will be steadied and sustained while the blank is being punched. This also adds to the rigidity; as otherwise, where only one end of the punch, or the center, enters first, the tendency is to draw away and shear or mark the cutting edges of the die.

A Set of Dies Showing How Sheet Metal May Be Drawn and Formed Into Various Shapes.

In order to illustrate how sheet metal parts may be drawn and formed into various shapes, we show here a complete set of dies, which will be the means of suggesting to the reader how desired results may be accomplished with very simple and inexpensive tools. We will describe the dies as adopted and constructed for the production of a special article and leave it to the reader to decide upon the best manner of adapting them for special purposes.

The piece or article to be made was a shoe clasp, or hook, for laced shoes, with a ball 17-64 inch in diameter at one end and a cup shaped eyelet at the other, 17-32 inch deep by .185 in diameter of the small part and 19-64 inch diameter of the large part. A $\frac{1}{8}$-inch hole was to be pierced in the bottom and the article was to be made from soft sheet brass .022 thick, finished and formed as shown, slightly exaggerated, to bring out its points better, up at the right of Fig. 49. The object of the ball instead of the flat, projecting hook now in use, was to prevent the lace from catching or tearing.

After much discussion we concluded that the quickest way to get out a few sample lots for trial was by the following set of dies, which we have endeavored to show as clearly as possible in the drawings, showing the work in two views after each successive operation. Fig. 44 being the first, forming so on to Fig. 50, which shows the last.

It required eight operations to produce the result shown in Fig. 49, all of which were done in the foot press, with the exception of the first which was done in the power press by blanking two at a time, as shown in Fig. 51. Of course the blanking die was made last, as it took some time, work and patience to find the exact shape and size of the blank, for this reason the drawing and forming dies were made first.

The first punch and die is shown in Fig. 44, the blank being shown up at the left. B is the die of round tool steel, $1\frac{1}{8}$ inch in diameter, turned and finished as shown. We then finished out a die block so that all the dies for the various operations, except the first, would fit within it, thereby saving a separate die block for each operation. The drawing shows a gage plate C fastened with two screws, shown, and two dowel pins not shown; also the

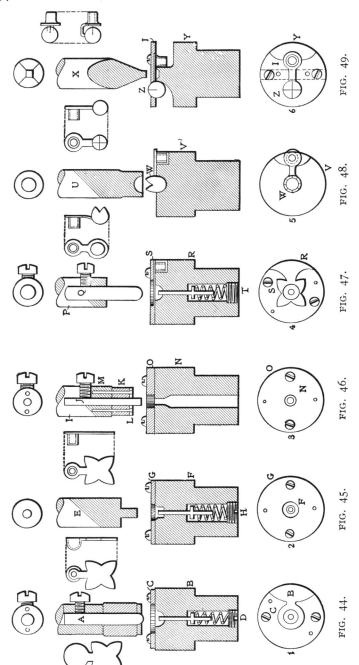

FORMING SHEET METAL IN SUCCESSIVE STAGES.

FIG. 49.

FIG. 48.

FIG. 47.

FIG. 46.

FIG. 45.

FIG. 44.

pushout spring and headless screw D for adjusting at the bottom. The die was finished with a butt mill to templet. A was the punch worked down and finished with a hand tool to templet; that is two thicknesses of metal less in diameter than the die. The rubber spring and blank-holder are shown on the punch and

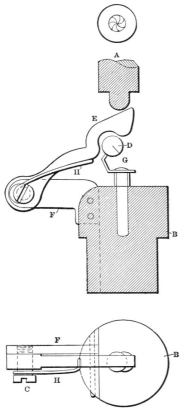

require no description. Both punch and die were hardened. The result of this operation appears up in between Figs. 44 and 45.

Fig. 45 shows the tools for the second operation. They are on the same plan as Fig. 44 except that the eyelet is drawn to the finish size. E is the punch, G the gage plate, F the die and H the adjusting screw. The result of the operation is shown between Figs. 45 and 46.

Operation No. 3 is for piercing the hole in the eyelet. N is the die, O the gage plate, I the punch holder, J the punch of Stubs wire, K a piece of $\frac{1}{2}$-inch round spring rubber, and M two pins for holding the stripper plate L, the plate moving up and down freely when the rubber was compressed. The rubber acted as a stripper to strip the finished work from the punch.

FIG. 50.—LAST BENDING OPERATION.

Fig. 47 shows the fourth operation of drawing the other ends, that is, half forming the ball. P is the punch holder, Q the punch held by screw, as shown, S the gage plate, R the die and T the adjusting screw for the push out. The finishing of the ball is shown in Fig. 48; the punch and die are respectively finished out to one-half of a sphere 17-64 inch in diameter, U the punch, V the die and W the work in position, the punch descending, causing the four wings to curl and close in, thereby filling out and forming the ball round enough to satisfy the eye, if not quite perfect.

The drawing of the work being finished, the next operation was to bend and form it to the shape shown up at the right of Fig. 49, which was done in the following manner. Fig. 49 shows the first bending with the work in position. X is the punch, Y the die, I the gage plate and Z the work. The result of this operation is shown in Fig. 50 in position for the next and last operation,

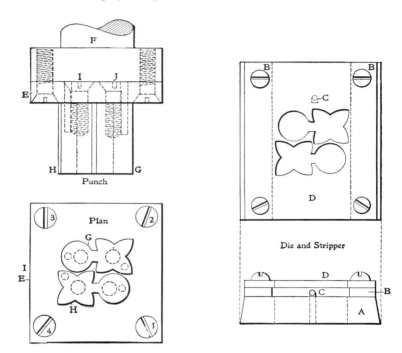

FIG. 51.—PUNCH AND DIE FOR THE BLANK .

which was accomplished in the way there shown. B is the holder, G the horn to hold the work, E the bending rig, which was of tool steel swinging on arm F and held by shoulder screw C, H being a flat spring to bring it back to place. It was worked out in the way shown, and this completed the job.

The blanking punch and die was made as shown in Fig. 51 and requires no description to be understood. By blanking two at a time the work was produced quicker and with less waste than otherwise. The die was carefully hardened so as to retain its shape as far as possible, as much variation would have caused a "heap" of trouble.

Forming Dies for Square Grooved Tubes.

The following description, with illustrations, of a method of forming sheet metal should prove suggestive for a variety of work. The job was the forming of a tube to be made of sheet iron .012 inch thick to the shape shown in Fig. 54. The finished tube was ⅜ inch in diameter outside, and 8 inches long, with a groove 3-32 inch deep and 5-32 wide, running the entire length. It was required to be within .001 inch of all these dimensions.

We figured to do the job in two operations. In the first place,

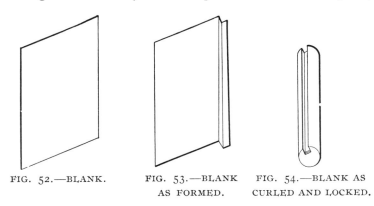

FIG. 52.—BLANK.   FIG. 53.—BLANK   FIG. 54.—BLANK AS
                   AS FORMED.   CURLED AND LOCKED.

strips of sheet iron of the right thickness were cut to the proper width and length as shown in Fig. 52; they were then ready for the first operation. The tools for this consisted of a punch and die, shown in Fig. 55. A being the punch-holder or stem, of cast iron, and B the punch, which was of tool steel and was worked down and finished very smooth, 5-32 inch in width plus one thickness of metal, which left room in the die for the opposite side to be forced in, and 3-32 inch from the face to shoulder plus one thickness of metal. C was the die of tool steel, a little over 8 inches long by 2 inches wide, dovetailed and driven into the die-block E. D was the gage plate. The die C was planned and finished so that when there was a thickness of metal in it, the punch would come down and produce a piece like Fig. 53, with two sharp corners, as shown.

For the second operation the punch, die, and mandrel, as

shown in Figs. 56 and 57, were used. The die of tool steel was
8 inches long by two inches wide, dovetailed and fitted to the
bolster J, with a ⅜ inch reamed hole through its entire length.
This hole was lapped and polished very smooth.   A slot· was
milled down its length, running into the hole, as shown in Fig.
56. It was then hardened. The mandrel was a piece of Stubs
steel, round, .350 inch in diameter, with a groove milled down its
entire length, 3-32 inch deep, by 5-32 inch plus two thicknesses
of metal wide. This was drawfiled very smooth, and hardened,

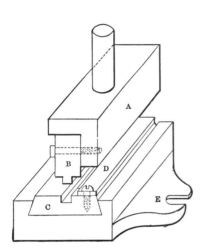

FIG. 55.—DIE FOR BENDING.

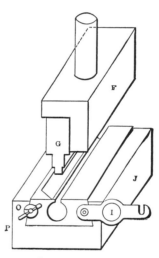

FIG. 56.—DIE FOR CURLING
AND LOCKING.

leaving the edges of the groove sharp. I was the stripper, ⅜ inch
thick. When in use the stripper I was thrown over on pin O,
and the thumb-screw P tightened, thus holding it in place. The
hole in the stripper was a nice fit on the mandrel, which was
necessary, as otherwise the metal would curl up or bruise at
the ends. It was of tool steel, and was hardened so as to wear
well.

When the die was in use the mandrel, Fig. 57, was inserted
within the die through the stripper, and the handle L turned until
a mark placed on the handle corresponded with one on the die,
thus showing that the groove in the mandrel was in line with the
punch G. The strip of metal, Fig. 53, is then inserted into the die

from the side, and with the side which has been formed resting in the groove in the mandrel. The handle L is turned one complete turn, which curls the metal and brings the groove again in line with the punch, which now descends and enters the groove in the mandrel, and bends and forces the other edge of the metal into the groove, thereby completing a tight and perfect grooved tube with sharp edges and corners. The mandrel is then pulled out, by hand, through the stripper, leaving the tube in the die, from which it is easily removed by throwing back the stripper and pushing it out. Some may think this slow work, but, as they say, results tell. There was not the slightest variation in size over the entire length of the tube, each and every one being the same with a good tight joint. Also, as the metal was drawn around the mandrel, it came out smooth and clean. To attain these results a good finish on all working parts, sharp edges on the punch dies and mandrel were necessary, as well as hardening and drawing them carefully.

FIG. 57.
HORN.

Adoption of Simple Dies in the Machine Shop.

In stating at the beginning of this chapter that the tools shown in it were applicable and can be used to advantage in the machine shop, the inference to be taken is this: There are throughout the country a number of small shops where duplicate small parts of standard shape and size are being constantly made for various special machines and attachments, and what is important about them, they are being produced by the same old means in the same old way. The adaptation of tools and devices of the kind shown in this chapter for producing or finishing this class of work—whenever possible, that is, using sheet metal blanks instead of castings where practical—would cause some of the people that run such shops to open their eyes and double their production. It is a common sight when strolling through a small machine shop in any of the up-to-date localities to see a couple of power presses punching away and producing work that a few years ago was produced by drilling or cut out with a chisel, or filed or milled down to size. Another thing, in this age of close competition, in order to keep up with the "band" it is absolutely necessary to adopt any labor-saving tool or device that will be the means of increasing the output and the income.

An Inclinable Press.

For general press work in a machine shop an inclinable power press should be used. It should be of sufficient strength to cover a wide range of work. An inclinable power press can be used for a large variety of work for which presses that are not inclinable cannot, as it is possible to adjust them from an upright to an incline position by a few turns of the wrench, thus facilitating the discharge of work from dies in which the finished work is delivered at the top, when the work will slide off by gravity.

FIG. 58.—INCLINABLE POWER PRESS FOR GENERAL WORK.

CHAPTER III.

"GANG" AND "FOLLOW" DIES, HOW TO ADAPT AND USE THEM.

The Use of "Gang" and "Follow" Dies.

For the production of small sheet metal articles which are
required to be pierced, bent, formed or stamped at one or more
points, the dies used should be, whenever possible, of the "gang"
or "follow" type, i. e., dies in which gangs of punches and dies
are assembled and located so that the results desired in the
finished blanks will be accomplished in one operation progressively. It is only by the use of such dies that small sheet metal
articles can be produced in large quantities at a profit. All too
frequently dies of the plain or single type are used, and three or
more sets of dies are required where the same results could be accomplished in one operation. Where sheet metal articles or parts
are required in large quantities an operation saved means a great
deal, and if two operations can be saved, even at the outlay
of considerable money and time, the results attained will more
than pay for all.

A Simple Gang Die and Its Work.

The piece, Fig. 59, is made of 1-16 inch hard sheet brass, and
is used, after being formed and bent to the shape shown in Fig.
60, as a buckle clasp for leather belts. The blank has two holes

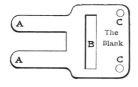 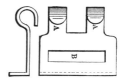

FIG. 59.—BLANK AS CUT.　　　FIG. 60.—BLANK AS FORMED.

C C and a long square-ended slot at B. The two holes C C were
required to be of different sizes in different lots of blanks, and
for this reason the gang die for producing them was made so

as to allow of this. The punch and die are shown in Fig. 61.
The die Q is laid out in the regular way from templet, and the
blanking die is worked out at R to lines and so that the templet
will fit at the top, giving it only slight clearance so as to
allow of frequent grinding without changing the size and

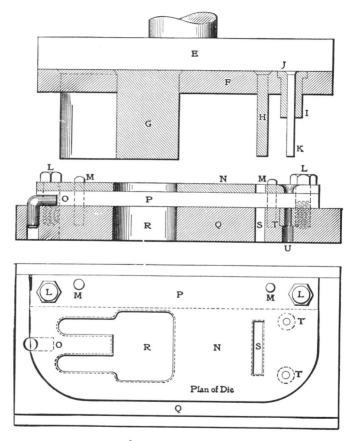

FIG. 61.—SIMPLE GANG DIE.

shape of the blanks to any extent. The oblong piercing die S
is finished as shown. The round piercing dies were not made
in the usual way. They were two hardened and ground and
lapped bushings T T forced into counterbored holes in the die
plate. After drilling and tapping the holes for the stripper
plate screws L L, and letting in those for the two gage plate

dowels M M and the stop pin O, the die was hardened and tempered in the usual way, drawing it to a light straw.

The construction of the punch is slightly different from the general practice. The holder E is of cast iron with the stem to fit the press plunger and the face finished square and true with it, for the machine steel pad F, within which the oblong piercing punch H and the blanking punch G are located. These punches were roughed out in the shaper and then sheared through the dies and finished with the file. They were both hardened and drawn to a dark-blue temper and then let into the pad and upset at the back, as shown. The construction of the small piercing dies and punches as shown allows a change, to pierce holes of different sizes, with very little trouble. The use of hardened and tempered Stubs wire lengths for the piercing punches was satisfactory and economical, as when one broke another could be substituted for the old one in short order. The same thing can be said of the use of hardened, lapped and ground bushings for the piercing dies, as when one becomes chipped or sheared another can be located with very little trouble.

A Gang Die for a Sheet Metal Bracket.

The piece shown in Fig. 62, to be made in this die, was of

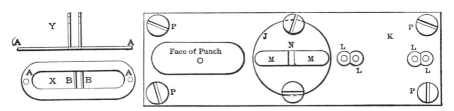

FIG. 62.—BLANK.   FIG. 63.—PLAN OF PUNCH.

1-16-inch sheet brass, and was pierced, the wings B B thrown up, and the piece blanked in one operation. There were to be four small holes in the piece, one at each end and one in the end of each wing.

At first a templet of sheet steel was made to the exact shape of the outside of Fig. 62, and the four holes drilled. The inside of the templet (except for the holes) was left intact. The die A was then bluestoned on the face and three outlines of the templet transferred to it with a sharp scriber, getting them all in line with 1-16 inch space between them. The small holes were also marked off in each outline made. These holes were then drilled and those on the right-hand end were enlarged

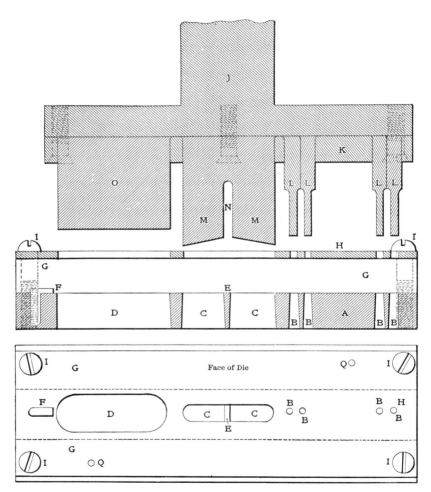

FIG. 64.—VERTICAL SECTION OF PUNCH AND DIE AND PLAN OF DIE.

and reamed to 3-32 inch, and tapered as shown. In the center outline the inner holes were enlarged and reamed to ¼ inch, thus forming the ends of the dies for blanking and throwing up the wings. These wing shapes were then worked out as shown at C C, with a rib between them at E. Using the center of the two inner holes in the last outline and enlarging them to the width of the templet, the stock between them was machined away, tapering about one degree, until the templet was let through from the back. The edges of the rib E were slightly rounded to allow the metal to bend over easily. The hole for the stop pin F, and those for the screws I, were drilled and tapped, after which the die was hardened and drawn to a light straw temper and the face ground.

The construction of the punch is plainly shown, and no description is necessary, except a few words relative to the punch M M for blanking and bending the two wings B B. This punch was made in one piece, as shown, with the slot N in the center enlarged, so as to leave space for a thickness of metal to lie in freely between it and the rib of the die. The face was sheared inwardly from each end; this was done so as to cut and start to bend at the same time. The punch was hardened and drawn to a light straw at the cutting face and a blue above it. The locating of the punches in the pad was accomplished in the manner described in Chapter I.

When in use, this punch and die were set up in the press, and the strip of metal to be worked was inserted in the channel between the gage plates G G and against the stop pin. The first two blanks were waste. The holes being pierced, the strip was moved along one space, and the wings M M cut and bent into the die C C, the space in the slot N allowing them to lie within it. The strip was then moved another space and the punch O blanked out the finished piece, as shown at X and Y.

Dies of this construction are used quite extensively where several operations are necessary to produce the finished piece. The manner shown of holding and riveting the punches within the pad is more reliable and conducive of good results than another way of fastening by set screws, though taking more time and skill in locating.

A Gang Die for Metal Tags.

Figs. 65 and 66 show another of the type of die shown in Fig. 64. It is used to produce the pronged metal tag shown in Fig. 67. As shown in the blank, the operations consist of, first, piercing the three holes T T T, then cutting and bending

the three prongs V V V, and, lastly, punching out the finished
blank to the shape and size shown. The cast iron holder and

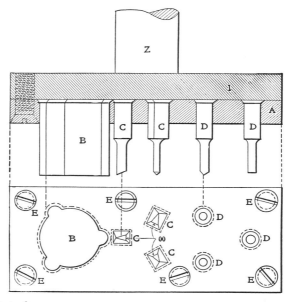

FIG. 65.—CROSS-SECTION AND PLAN VIEWS OF PUNCH.

method of fastening the punches are the same as described
in the other, and the method of construction carried out in both

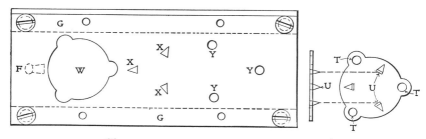

FIG. 66.—PLAN OF PUNCH.   FIG. 67.—METAL TAG.

punch and die is clearly shown in the engravings and can be
intelligently understood without a detailed description.

As will be seen this kind of a die will commend itself and

prove adaptable for the production of a large variety of different shapes of blanks, which are required to be pierced and bent at certain points, or wherever it may be necessary to throw up or bend one or more portions of the blanks. These two types of dies cover a wide range of dies used in the general run of small sheet metal working, the design and principle of construction being pretty much the same in all of them. In the die shown in Figs. 65 and 66 it will be seen that the punches C C C are left taper at the cutting face so as to cut and commence to bend at the same time. The reason for leaving the smaller or more delicate punches shorter than the blanking punch is to allow of the blanking punch having entered the die before the others commence to cut. This steadies and strengthens them and eliminates, as far as possible, the tendency to break or snap off, which is a frequent occurrence when all are left the same length. All small punches should be tight fits in the stripper for the same reason.

A Gang Die and Two Forming Dies for Umbrella Rib Tips.

The dies herein described and illustrated were used for producing umbrella rib tips of black tin .010 inch thick, and they illustrate in their design and construction many practical

points which can be adopted to advantage in the rapid production of various small sheet metal parts. The three operations necessary to produce the rib tip are shown in Fig. 68. The first operation comprises piercing the two holes a a, forming the two sides b b and punching out the blank to the shape shown. The punch and die for the first operation are shown in Fig. 69, which gives a vertical longitudinal section of both, and in Fig. 70, which shows a plan of the punch. The punch and die are

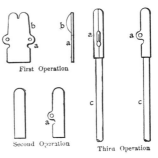

FIG. 68.—UMBRELLA RIB TIP.

of the gang type and are constructed to produce two finished blanks with each stroke of the press, and as the stock to be punched is very thin, it was far cheaper and more expedient to produce the blanks this way than by two separate dies.

The die was made first, and, after being planed and fitted to the bolster, the face was ground and polished and six outlines of the templet transferred to it, getting them in the relative position and all exactly the same distance apart, as shown in Fig. 69. The two blanking dies M M were then worked out by letting the templet through them, and the four piercing dies O, Fig. 69, were finished. The two forming dies N N were then finished to the shape of the face of the blank, Fig. 68, by first using a round face end mill to rough out and then a graver; they were then lapped and polished on the drill press. After

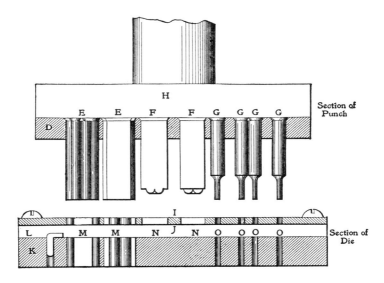

FIG. 69.—CROSS SECTIONS OF PUNCH AND DIE FOR BLANKS.

the hole for the stop pin L and those for the stripper screws and gage plate, dowels were let in and tapped as required, the die was hardened and drawn slightly, leaving it as hard as possible without danger of cracking or chipping. The piercing dies were then lapped to size, and the face of the die ground and oilstoned.

The punch consists of the cast iron holder H, and the pad D, of machine steel, in which the punches are located. The two blanking punches were made first and finished to size by shearing them through the dies M M, leaving them a tight fit, as the metal to be punched necessitated. Both punches were left soft and let into the pad D, as shown. The four piercing punches were got out and located within the pad, as shown, transferring the holes for them through the dies O, and then enlarging them to the size required. The two forming punches F F were of pieces of square tool steel, first let into the pad and the face of each then worked away to fit within the dies N N. These two punches were the only ones hardened, as, by leaving the blanking and piercing punches soft, and having the die as hard as possible, it could be worked steadily for a long time without being ground. After the stripper plate I and the two gage plates J J were located and fastened on the face of the die and the gage pin L let in, the punch and die were set up in the press.

The metal to be punched came in rolls of the proper width,

Plan of Punch

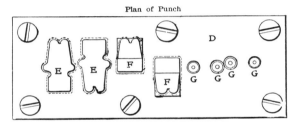

FIG. 70.—SHOWING ARRANGEMENT OF PIERCING, FORMING AND BLANKING PUNCHES.

and was set on a reel at the side of the press. The end was fed against the stop pin L. For the first two strokes the four blanks produced were waste, but after that two complete blanks were produced at each stroke. As will be seen, the two blanking punches E E and the four piercing punches G are left longer than the two forming punches; this is so that the metal will be held securely while the forming punches are drawing it, thereby allowing the metal to be drawn sideways without disturbing the relation of the operations to any extent and also allowing of upsetting the piercing and blanking punches when they become dull.

For the second operation, that of bending and forming the blank to the shape shown in the center drawing of Fig. 68, the punch and die shown in Fig. 71 were used. It is what might be called a common push-through die, and is about the simplest and cheapest that could be adopted. The punch holder P is of cast iron and is fitted to the ram of the foot press. The face is dovetailed to admit the punch Q. The face R of the punch is rounded to the proper radius to which the tips are to be finished —that is, one-half of a circle as shown. The die T is fitted to the bolster X and is worked out at U in width two thicknesses of metal wider than the punch. The gage plate S is fastened to the face of the die and worked out at V to allow the blanks to fit nicely. The edges of the die are slightly rounded and the inside polished smooth. Both punch and die are hardened and drawn slightly.

For the last operation the punch and die shown in Fig. 72

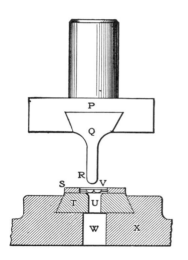

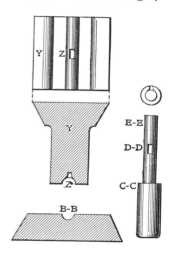

FIG. 71.—SECOND OPERATION
DIE.

FIG. 72.—TOOLS FOR THIRD
OPERATION.

are used. This operation consists of finishing the tip and closing it around the rib c, Fig. 68, so that the two eyelets a a of the blank will match. The punch Y and the die, after being finished all over and fitted to holder and bolster, have the faces ground, and are then clamped together, and a hole drilled and reamed through them, so that a perfect half-circle will remain in each face. A half-round groove is then let into the center of the punch face and the edges are rounded; this acts as an inlet and sizer for the eyelets. Both punch and die are hardened. To set this punch and die in line with each other the gage shown at the right of Fig. 72 is used, the portion E E fitting the half-circle of each and the tit D D fitting within the groove in the punch. One of the second operation pieces is placed on the die, resting within the portion B B and against a stop at the back. The rod on which it is to be fastened is then laid within it, thereby serving as a horn. The punch descending forms the tip to a perfect circle, rivets it on the rod, or rib, and sizes the eyelets a a.

A Gang Die for an Odd-shaped Piece.

As an illustration of what can be accomplished by the use of a gang die of comparatively simple design and inexpensive construction we show here a punch and die adaptable for the production of a large variety of pierced and formed articles. The product of this die is shown in two views in Fig. 73. It is punched from hard sheet brass with a central hole pierced at a, four pear-shaped holes b, and the ends c split and bent downward as shown. Three operations are required, but as they are all combined in the one die there is practically only one operation, producing one complete piece at each stroke of the press.

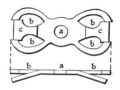

FIG. 73.—THE BLANK.

The two lower illustrations in Fig. 74 are a plan and vertical section of the die, and the upper two the same of the punch. The stock used for the die was of the composite iron and steel kind, which has been found to give the best results, especially in dies where two or more portions are worked out, and which are irregular in shape, as when hardening the tendency to shrink or warp excessively is eliminated. E E E E are the four pear-shaped dies, F F the splitting and bending dies, and G the round piercing die, while H is the blanking die. All of the dies are worked out straight for about 5-16 inch in depth and then tapered away for clearance.

While explaining the construction of the die, a few remarks as to the best method of laying out a die of this type so as to insure accurate location may not be amiss. In the first place, finish the templet, Fig. 75, to the exact size and shape required, with all pierced holes to size and shape and in the exact position, only leaving two points on the outer edges of the blank unfinished. These points are for locating the outlines of the

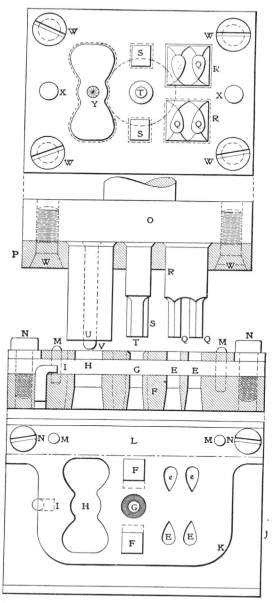

FIG. 74.—GANG DIE FOR AN ODD-SHAPED PIECE.

different operations square with the side of the die and in line with each other, and also to get the same amount of space between the different operations or the same amount of scrap between the blanks, as if this is not done accurately the locating of the stop pin is impossible. The unfinished points on the templet are at A and B respectively, the part A being bent and finished to allow of resting it against the inclined side of the die, and the edge of B finished to project from the side of the templet the same distance as the amount of metal to be left between the blanks.

We grind the face of the die, bluestone it and locate the templet on it for the first outline H, which is the blanking die, holding the part A against the side of the die and clamping the templet to the face with a die-maker's clamp and then with

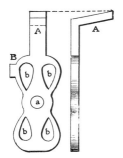

FIG. 75.—THE TEMPLET.

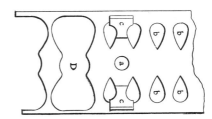

FIG. 76.—SECTION OF STOCK.

a sharp scriber transferring the outline to the face of the die. This done we move the templet along until the edge of B is in line with outline of the opposite side, clamp it in position and with a sharp center drill, which should fit nicely in the hole a, drill the center for the piercing die G and transfer the outline of the blank as before. We move the templet once more, relocate the edge B and scribe the outlines of the four pear-shaped dies E E E E. The templet is now removed. Now drill and ream the hole for the piercing die G, lay out the two splitting and bending dies F F from the center of G and from the sides of the blank outline. We then remove the projecting parts A and B, so as to have the templet perfect. The die can now be finished in the usual manner, first the blanking die, working to lines, and letting the templet through it, then the splitting dies F F and lastly the pear-shaped dies E. After drilling the holes for the screws N N and the gage and stripper plate dowels M M and also that for the stop pin I, the die should be hardened.

The upper two views of Fig. 74 show a plan and section of the punch, with all punches let into a machine steel pad and upset or riveted on the back, as shown. O is the stem or punch holder, P the punch pad which is fastened to the holder face by the four screws W and located by the dowel pins X. U is the blanking punch with the pilot pin in the center at V, S S the splitting and bending punches, T the round piercing punch, and Q Q Q Q the four pear-shaped piercing punches. The only punches hardened were the two S S, and they were drawn to a dark blue.

In Fig. 76 is shown a section of the stock used. The stock is fed in so as to project slightly over the edge of the blanking

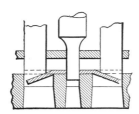

FIG. 77.—HOW THE BEND-
ING IS DONE.

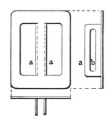

FIG. 78.—BLANK AS
PRODUCED.

die H, and as the punch descends the end is trimmed and the other holes are pierced. At the next stroke the blank produced is useless, as it is incomplete, but after that a perfect blank of the shape shown in Fig. 73, and with the ends c c split and bent to the angle shown, is produced at each stroke. The manner of splitting and bending the ends is shown in Fig. 77. As shown in the sectional view of the punch, Fig. 74, the blanking punch is considerably longer than the others. This is done so that the blank will have been located and punched out before the other punches start to cut, thus insuring the accurate locating of the stock. This leaving the blanking punch longer than the others, has been found practical for all dies of this class, as it makes the punching of the stock progressive, and also holds and locates it positively. When the piercing and blanking punches require grinding, which shortens them, to accommodate the two splitting and bending punches S S to them, the pad P is removed, the punches S S are driven partly out and filed off at the back the required amount, then driven back and re-riveted as before, this being possible as the backs are soft.

A Gang Die for Producing the Blank of a Compass Sliding Bracket.

The punch and die for producing the blank shown in Fig. 78 are shown in Figs. 79 and 80, Fig. 79 showing a longitudinal cross-section of both, and Fig. 80 a plan view of the die, in

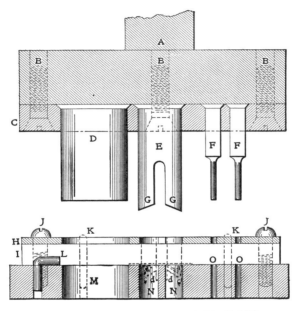

FIG. 79.—CROSS-SECTION OF GANG DIE.

which can be clearly seen the tension buttons P P which are used to keep the stock firmly against the back gage plate as it is fed along.

As the stock to be punched was quite thin, and had to be produced with nice clean edges at all points, perfectly free from burrs and fins, the punch and die had to be constructed accurately; and as the article was to be produced in large numbers, it was necessary to finish both in a manner favorable to their longevity. The method of construction followed out in the die

can be clearly understood from the cross-section view Fig. 79
and the plan view Fig. 80. O O are the piercing dies, N N the
cutting and bending dies for the wings, and M the blanking
die. When laying out, spacing and finishing these, great care
was taken to space them correctly and finish each in the proper
relation to the others. Very little clearance was given, finishing
them almost straight. As the two wings a a of the blank, Fig.
78, are cut and bent into the dies N N, the gage plates I I of
the die are required to be of unusual height to allow of the
stock being fed along with ease. The holes in the stripper
plate for the two piercing punches are finished dead in line
with the die O O, so as to be a tight fit for the punches, which,

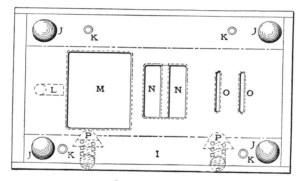

FIG. 80.—PLAN OF DIE.

being rather frail, would not stand up well if they were not
strengthened in this manner. The insides of the die were all
finished as smoothly as possible and polished before and after
hardening. After hardening the face of the die was ground,
after which it was drawn and then oilstoned to a keen edge at
all cutting points.

The construction of the punch is clearly shown in the cross-
section, Fig. 79, and requires no description to be understood.
The dotted lines within the dies N N show clearly the manner
in which the wings a a of the blank are cut and bent. At a a the
punches have commenced to cut and bend the wings; c c show
the faces of the punch when they have entered the dies the
full depth, and d d the wings as bent and finished. All of the
punches were hardened. The blanking punch D and the two
piercing punches F F were drawn to a dark blue temper. The

cutting and bending punch G G was tempered differently. It was first heated, and hardened in clear oil, dipping it from the back, and thus preventing as far as possible the two legs G G from crawling in toward each other because of the channel between them. By dipping from the back this was overcome, as by the time the cutting face was immersed the back was hard and set. It was then polished and tempered by drawing from the back to a dark blue to within $\frac{1}{4}$ inch of the cutting faces and quenched when these portions were a dark straw.

Dies of the design and construction described in this chapter should always be used when the articles required are desired in large quantities, as their use will allow of the attainment of results in one operation which would otherwise require more to produce. For the production of sheet metal novelties in large

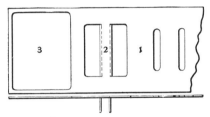

FIG. 81.—SECTION OF STOCK.

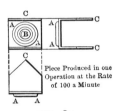

Piece Produced in one Operation at the Rate of 100 a Minute

FIG. 82.

quantities it is possible to design a die that will accomplish in one operation that which usually requires two or three, and as the saving of even one operation in the production of sheet metal parts, which are often turned out to the million mark, adds considerable to the margin of profit, the dies which will produce them in the shortest time are the ones to use.

A "Follow Die" Which Draws, Pierces, End-Finishes, Cuts Off and Bends in One Operation.

The "follow die" here shown was used for producing parts of sheet tin of the shape shown in the three views of Fig. 82. These pieces were required in large quantities, and were used for fastening the corners of thin wooden boxes, such as grape crates, baskets, small packing boxes, and so on. As the number of these tin fasteners required every season exceeds twenty millions, the necessity for producing them as rapidly and as cheaply as possible is at once obvious. We may say before describing the die that the shop in which it was made and used makes a specialty of sheet metal articles for which the demand is enormous, and that their chief concern is to produce these articles as cheaply as possible. Expense in the constructing of a die means very little to them if it will reduce the number of operations in the production of the part required. In this establishment dies of every type imaginable have been improved in every manner possible, so that sheet metal articles, which in numbers of other shops would require two or more operations to produce, are here produced in a single operation. The types of dies which have improved the most, and from which the best results have been secured, are of the "gang" and "follow" types,

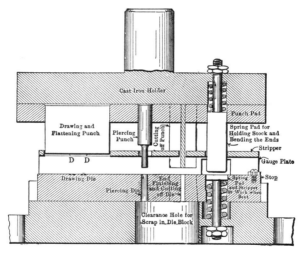

FIG. 83.—"FOLLOW DIE" COMPLETE.

numbers of which work upon a strip of stock from five to eight times before the finished piece drops off the die.

To produce the fasteners as shown it is necessary to draw two rings at A A, pierce the central hole B, finish the ends C C to angles of 45 degrees, cut off the blank and then bend it to the shape shown. In Fig. 83 the manner in which these separate workings of the metal follow each other can be clearly seen. The punch, or male die, consists of the usual cast iron holder, and the machine steel pad in which the punches are located and secured. The first punch is that which draws the two rings

A A and at the same time flattens the stock; the second is the piercing punch which pierces the hole B; the third punch is the end-finishing and cutting-off punch, while the last acts in the double capacity of spring pad and bending punch. The construction and relative position of the punches require no description.

The die is in one piece, made in the usual manner, except

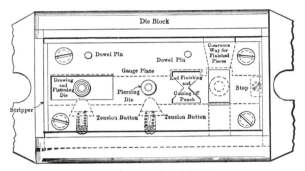

FIG. 84.—PLAN OF DIE.

for the bending die, which consists of a square milled channel across the face to the depth shown, and which is equipped with a spring pad for holding the metal while it is being cut off by the end-finishing punch, and for stripping the finished work from the die as the punch rises. As shown in the plan of the die, Fig. 84, the gage plate is located by two dowel pins, and

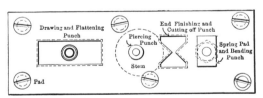

FIG. 85.—PLAN OF PUNCH.

has a clearance channel let through it in line with the bending die as an exit for the finished work, which, as the press is inclined, drops out at the back as soon as it is stripped from the die. As shown, the die is equipped with two tension bottoms which keep the strip of stock against the gage plate and in line with different dies. When in use the punch and die are in the relative positions shown in Fig. 83. The drawing and flattening punch is the shortest, this being necessary to allow the other punches to do their work.

The metal is fed by an automatic roll feed. At the first stroke of the press the two rings A A are drawn and the stock is flattened; at the next hole B is pierced and one of the ends C trimmed; at the third stroke the bending punch, acting as a spring pad, holds the metal while the other end is being finished and the piece cut off, the punch continuing to descend until the bending punch strikes the face of the holder, when the metal is bent into the bending die. As the punch rises the bending punch is forced outward by the spring at the back and the finished work is stripped from the die by the spring pad. This die produced 75,000 of the pieces shown in a working day of ten hours.

A Complete Set of Dies for the Manufacture of Sheet Metal Hinges.

The set of dies here described was made in one of the largest sheet metal goods establishments in New York. The dies were

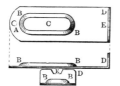

FIG. 86.—LATCH PORTION.

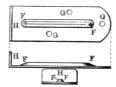

FIG. 87.—ATTACHABLE PORTION.

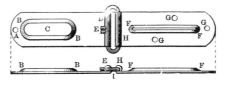

FIG. 88.—HINGE COMPLETE.

used for manufacturing sheet metal hinges and latches for grape crates, and they represent the highest attainment in the adaptation of different types of dies for the production of sheet metal parts at a minimum cost. There is a demand for over 8,000,000 of these hinges and latches annually.

Six dies are required to produce the hinges, and, as the illustrations have been made as clear as possible, their design, con-

struction and operation will be clearly understood with a very
slight description.

There are three different parts to be made—the latch portion,
Fig. 86; the attachable portion, Fig. 87, and the hinge proper,
I, in Fig. 88. Fig. 86 is of cold rolled stock, about 1-32 inch
thick. As this stock comes in rolls of the required width, it
is not necessary to do any blanking. The operations to produce
this part are the piercing of the small hole A and the long one
G, drawing and forming the margin around it at B B, rounding
one end and notching the other at E, cutting off the piece, and,
lastly, bending the notched end to a right angle, as shown at
D. All this is accomplished by a gang of punches and dies of

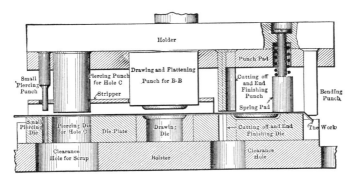

FIG. 89.—"FOLLOW DIE" COMPLETE FOR PRODUCING
THE LATCH, FIG. 86.

the "follow" type. The metal is fed through the die automatically, and as the press is inclined the finished work drops
off into a receptacle at the back.

The die is shown complete in Fig. 89, while Fig. 90 shows a
plan of the punch and die. The die plate in which are contained
the entire gang of dies (the drawing die being separated and
inserted to allow of grinding) is hardened and drawn very little,
while all the punches, except the drawing and bending punches,
are left soft. When the face of the die plate is ground the drawing die also is removed and ground on the bottom.

The manner in which the stock is fed through this die, and
the various operations performed until the finished piece drops
off at the back, can be understood from Fig. 89, in which is
shown a strip of stock lying along the die plate. First, the

small hole A and the long one C are pierced. At the next stroke the margin B B is drawn and formed, and end D is notched at E by the cutting-off and end-finishing punch. At the next stroke the punch descends and the spring pad holds the metal securely while the notched end is being bent by the bending punch and the finished piece cut off.

For producing the part shown in Fig. 87 a die of the same type and design as the one shown in Fig. 89 is used, the only difference being in the construction and arrangement of the

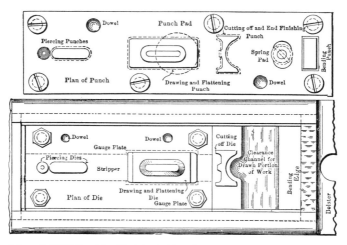

FIG. 90.—SHOWING ARRANGEMENT OF PUNCHES AND DIES FOR THE DIFFERENT OPERATIONS.

punches and dies for piercing the three holes G G G, drawing the rib F F and bending the end H.

As shown in the finished hinge, Fig. 88, the two ends of the wire are formed so that they will project about ⅛ inch beyond the side. This is done so that when the end D of the part shown in Fig. 86 is curled over the wire, the projecting ends of the wire will locate within the notch E, Fig. 86. The piece will thus be fastened permanently to one portion, and the other will turn on the wire.

The result of the first operation in the production of this wire, here called the hinge, is shown at the right of the top view in Fig. 91.

In this figure are also shown two views of the punch and

die used to produce this result. In this die the wire is fed automatically from a reel, and a piece is cut off and bent to the
shape shown at the right, at each stroke of the press. In the
die, L is the bolster, G the bending die, I the cutting die, and
K the stripper, while H is the plate beneath which the wire
is fed. In the punch, A is the holder, B the bending punch, E
the spring pad which holds the wire tightly upon the die while
it is being cut and bent, and C the spring. The lower figure,

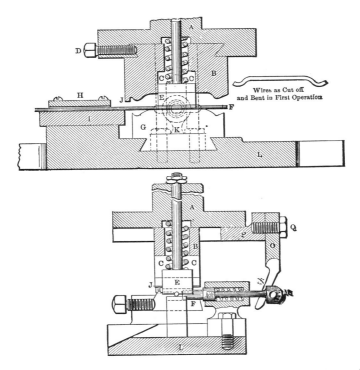

FIG. 91.—PUNCH AND DIE FOR FIRST OPERATION ON WIRE HINGE.

an end cross-section of the punch and die, shows the stripping
arrangement. As the punch descends the stripper or knock-out
R is drawn backward by the inclined figure N engaging the pin
M. As the punch ascends the knock-out pin R plunges outward, and, as the press is inclined, the work is thrown off the
punch and falls down the inclined way into a box. The rapidity
with which a punch and die of this type can be worked, when

equipped with an automatic stripper or knock-out of this construction and an automatic feed, is astonishing.

The second operation on the hinge is by the punch and die,

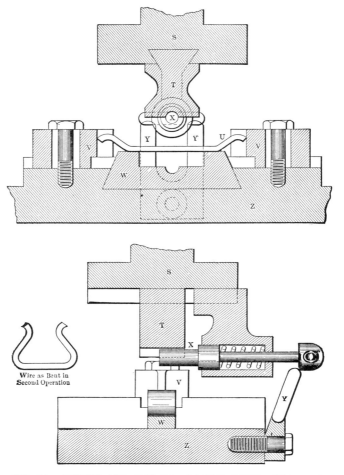

FIG. 92.—PUNCH AND DIE FOR SECOND BEND, SHOWING
AUTOMATIC STRIPPER.

Fig. 92. A stripper of the same construction as in Fig. 91 is used, but, as will be seen, conditions are reversed, and instead of the stripper being fastened and located upon the die it is upon the punch, while the inclined finger by which it is worked is located

upon the back of the die bolster. The punch consists of the
holder S, the bending punch T and the stripper X. In the die,
Z is the bolster, W the bending die, V V the two adjustable
gage plates, between which the work U is located, and Y Y the
inclined fingers which work the stripper.

When in use the wire as bent in the first operation is placed

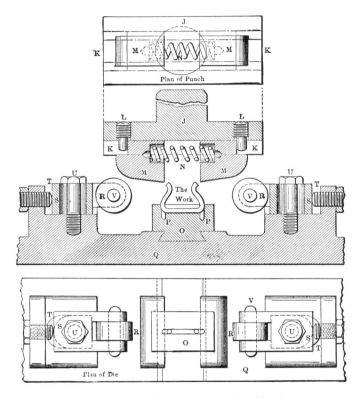

FIG. 93.—LAST BENDING OPERATION.

between the gage plates V V. The punch descending strikes
the wire and bends it into the die, while the ends spring upward
and hug the punch, thus producing the shape shown at the left.
As the punch ascends the knock-out pin X hits the work and
it is thrown off the punch.

The means used for the third operation on the wire hinge
are shown in Figs. 93 and 94. In Fig. 93 the work is in position

as it appears before the punch descends. In this figure are also shown plans of the punch and die. Fig. 94 is a cross-section of the working parts of the punch and die as they appear when the punch has descended and the work is finished.

The punch consists of a machine-steel holder J, the face of which is dovetailed at K K to admit the two tool-steel forming slides M M, which have a stiff spring between them at N. L L are the stop screws for the slides, which are forced against them by the spring at N. The slides are hardened and tempered.

In the die Q is the bolster in which the tool-steel locator O is fastened, and the adjustable roller brackets S S are located. The rollers R R are of tool steel, hardened and ground. The work is fed to the die and removed when finished by a fork in the hands of the operator.

For the last operation in the production of these articles,

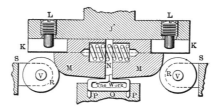

FIG. 94.—SHOWING COMPLETION OF THE BEND.

that of "wiring" the bent ends of the sheet metal portions around the wire hinge, a punch and die of a decidedly novel design are used, shown in Fig. 95. This is a heavy bolster with a standard at each end as bearings for the shaft of an octagon die, which is made with eight locating surfaces for the work to allow the press being run continually and the work being located upon the surfaces by the operator without the danger of clipping his fingers. The die is rotated automatically by a combination of an index wheel, a pawl and connecting rod, one end of the rod being attached to an adjustable stud in the T-slot in the press shaft, and the other as shown. The manner in which the work is located and finished can be seen in the front view, in which are shown three hinges in position, the lower one being the one last located by the operator and the top one as being "wired" and finished by the punch. As the octagon die is rotated the finished work is carried away from the die and drops off at the back, while the next one is then ready and fed to position directly beneath the punch.

By the use of this set of dies hinges of the type shown are

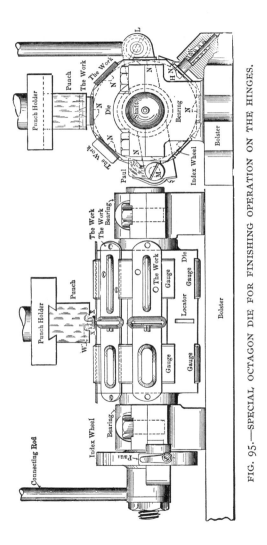

FIG. 95.—SPECIAL OCTAGON DIE FOR FINISHING OPERATION ON THE HINGES.

produced to sell for one cent apiece. Twelve sets, each set consisting of a hinge, latch and hasp, are sold for thirty cents.

*An Automatic Combination Piercing, Bending and Twisting Die
for Box Corner Fasteners.*

The pieces shown in half-tone, Fig. 96, are sheet metal box
corner fasteners. They are produced at a cost so small that
they are used instead of nails or screws. The manner in

FIG. 96.—BOX FASTENERS.

which they are used is shown in Fig. 97. The fastener is
held against one side of the box by hand and points are driven

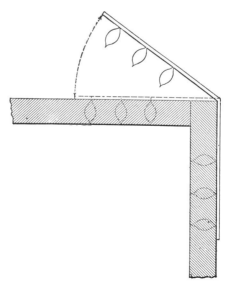

FIG. 97.—HOW THE BOX FASTENERS ARE APPLIED.

into the wood. The fastener is then bent at right angles and
the points in the other end are driven into the other side of the
box.

The half-tones show fasteners of two different types. The longer one has three prongs projecting straight at each end, while the short one has four prongs at each end, and where in the longer one the prongs are straight, in the other they are twisted to an angle of 45 degrees. Fasteners of this last type are used for heavier boxes than the others, the greater number of prongs and the twist in them making it a much stronger fastener.

The die here shown is used for making the short fasteners

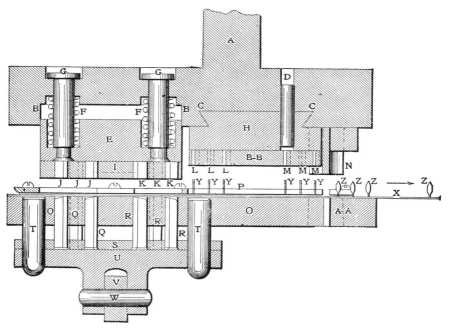

FIG. 98.—COMBINATION PIERCING, BENDING AND TWISTING PUNCH AND DIE.

direct and complete from a roll of metal. The various operations are accomplished in the "follow" order. That is, first the holes are pierced and the prongs are bent up, then the prongs are twisted to the angle required, and, lastly, the ends are rounded and a finished fastener is cut off. The manner in which these different operations are accomplished and the relative location of the means used for each can be seen in the sectional view, Fig. 98. In this die the usual conditions are reversed, and the "punch" as usually applied is the "die" and the die the punch; so instead of calling them by their usual names we will refer to them as the upper and lower sections respectively, the section in the press bolster the lower section.

In the upper section A is the holder, of machine steel. A forging E is the holder and carrier for the piercing and bending die plate I, in which are located the eight piercing and bending dies J and K. The construction of this portion of the upper section is such as to allow the die to descend and strike the metal and then remain stationary while the holes are being pierced and the prongs bent up into the dies by the gage of

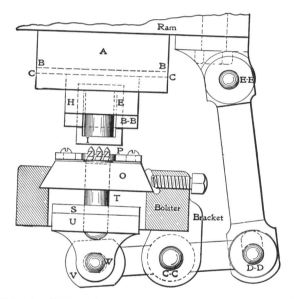

FIG. 99.—END VIEW SHOWING SUB-PU: C I MOVEMENT.

punches in the lower section, at the same time the rest of the upper section continues to descend and perform the other two operations on the advanced sections of the stock. The portion H, in the upper section, is the holder proper for the die plate B B, in which the eight twisting dies L and M are located and the end finishing and cutting-off punch N. The holder H is held in a dovetailed channel and permanently located in alignment with the lower section by a large taper pin D.

In the lower section O acts as the die plate for the cutting die A A, and also as the stripping plate for the eight piercing and bending punches Q and R. These eight punches are located in what might be called a sub-punch holder located under O in a large hole in the bolster and worked up and down automatically on two hardened and ground steel studs T T at a set of connecting levers, as shown in the end views, Fig. 99. All the parts used in this arrangement are of steel, the holder U and the three levers and bracket (which is fastened to the back of the ram) being forgings. The punch plate or pad S is fastened upon the sub-holder U by two dowels and four flat-head screws, as shown

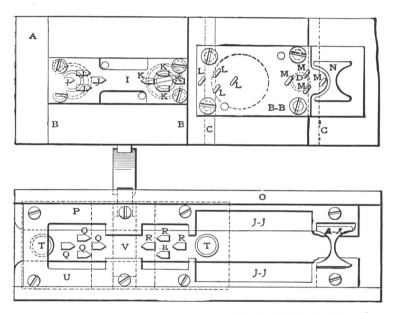

FIG. 100.—PLAN OF UPPER AND LOWER SECTIONS OF FIG. 98.

in the plate Fig. 100. The die plates I and B B also are fastened upon their respective holders in the same manner. The eight piercing and bending dies are finished with about .003 inch clearance, and the die plate is hardened and drawn to a light straw temper. The eight twisting dies are simply eight narrow slits which are let through the die plate B B at an angle of 45 degrees with the front of the plate. The edges of these dies are slightly rounded so that the points of the prongs will enter them with ease. The die plate B B is hardened and drawn slightly, so as to leave it as hard as possible. The end-finishing and cutting-off punch N is let into the holder H and upset and riveted at the back. The eight piercing and bending punches Q and R are inclined slightly on the cutting face and the back ends are rounded so that they will bend the prongs up into the dies; the faces of the punches are one thickness of metal shorter than the dies, so as to allow for bending.

The manner in which this die is used for the production of the fasteners with the twisted prongs is as follows: The strip of metal is shown at X, Fig. 98. At the first stroke of the press the eight prongs are pierced and bent upward by the sub-punches Q and R. The strip of metal is then fed along until the eight prongs are in the positions shown at Y, and at the next stroke they are twisted, and the first end of the fastener is rounded and trimmed by the punch N. At the next stroke the finished part is cut off and at each succeeding stroke a complete fastener is produced. A die of the same design as this is used to produce the long fastener. It differs from it only in that there is no twisting operation provided for. The end view, Fig. 99, shows the automatic arrangement by which the sub-punches are worked.

CHAPTER IV.

THE ADAPTATION AND USE OF SIMPLE DIES AND PRESS FIXTURES

FOR THE ECONOMIC PRODUCTION OF SHEET METAL PARTS.

The Power Press in Agricultural Machine Work.

To anyone who has had the privilege of going through one of the various shops devoted to the manufacture of agricultural machinery, or of working in one for any length of time, the fact is evident that in them machine manufacturing has reached a

FIG. 101.—PRESS FOR PUNCHING 68 HOLES.

point far ahead of the general run of machine practice. In mowing and reaping machines a majority of the parts are of flat or round stock, fastened and assembled by riveting, as in the case of the wheels for such machines, the only cast part of which is the hub.

During the summer of 1901 the author had the good fortune to spend some time in the shops of one of the largest agricultural manufacturing establishments in the United States, and while there he was struck by the methods of manufacture; so much so that he made note of a number of things which were interesting. The thing which impressed him the most was the rapidity with which the work was handled, sent through the different operations and assembled. Strange as it may seem the quickest and most satisfactory results and the most ingenious attachments and fixtures for the production of the parts were accomplished by and used in the power press.

Take, for instance, the wheels for the mowing and reaping machines. The tires for these wheels are of ribbed soft iron. They are first cut off to the required length, and then have the holes for the spokes, straps and fastening rivets punched in them. This in itself is an interesting operation and goes to

FIG. 102.—PRESS FOR PERFORATING HARVESTER TIRES, PUNCHING
OVER 100 HOLES.

show the large scale on which press work and punching is carried on in these shops. The tires before being rolled are almost 10 feet long by 7 inches wide and $\frac{3}{8}$ inch thick, and the number of holes runs from eighty-one to ninety-three, all punched at one stroke of the press. The design and construction of the punches and dies for these tires entail a lot of accurate work, the punches being so placed and finished as to make the punching of the holes successive. The diameter of the holes is usually $\frac{3}{8}$ inch, and when it is considered that ninety-three of them are punched through $\frac{3}{8}$-inch stock at one stroke of the press the size and construction of the press can be imagined (see Fig. 102). In this operation on the tires there was one little kink which was particularly novel and labor-saving. The holes in the tires, into which the spokes are to be entered and riveted, are so punched as to be larger on one side than on the other; so that when the spokes are upset and riveted, the larger portion of the hole will be on the outside of the tire, and when the spoke is upset it fills in the hole and is finished flush with the tire, thereby fastening it permanently without the possibility of pulling out, and doing away with the necessity of countersinking, which would require another operation. This peculiarity of the

FIG. 103.—RIVETING CLEATS ON HARVESTER WHEEL TIRES.

holes is accomplished by making the dies somewhat larger than the punches.

After the holes have been punched in the tire it is rolled to the required radius and the ends are brought together and fastened by riveting a wide strap on the inside. The spokes are then entered into the holes, the two sections of the malleable iron hub are trued and fastened to them, and the ends of the spokes riveted within the tire (see Fig. 103). The cross straps are then fastened to the outside of the tire, the hub is set and riveted and the wheel is complete. The different operations on the parts (except the hub) and the assembling and fastening of them together are all done in the power press, no screws being used, all parts being riveted throughout. The foreman of the department in which the wheels were constructed told the author that the capacity of the department was 200 wheels for a day of ten hours, making the time for the complete finishing of each wheel three minutes, which is, to say the least, rapid production indeed, and to those who have never seen it done well-nigh impossible, while to those standing by and watching them being manufactured it is wonderful.

Punching a Mild Steel Strap.

As a simple instance of the use to which the power press is put in these shops we show in Fig. 104 two views of a mild steel strap finished complete to the shape shown, i. e., piercing the hole A at either end, cutting off to the required length and finishing the ends to the radius shown in one operation. These straps are used, when finished, on the wheel tires, there being sixteen to each tire; the straps after being punched being formed

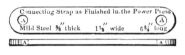

FIG. 104.

in a separate operation to conform to the curve of the outside of the tire in such a manner as to allow of their being fastened at an angle of 45 degrees with the sides of them. The straps for the tire are finished to 6¾ inches long, but as a number of different lengths of straps, with holes in the same position and of the same size, are required for other parts of the machine, the one punch and die is constructed to allow it to be used for all of them. The design and construction of this punch and die are clearly shown in the vertical cross-section and in the plan of the die, Fig. 105. The steel used for the die T is of the half-iron and half-steel brand, and, as shown, is quite heavy. The use of this composite steel and iron for dies for punching heavy stock tends to the longevity of the die, and also gives better results when hardening, reducing the shrinkage to the minimum, and overcoming as far as possible the tendency to warp or crack. The stripping plate S is of heavy mild steel and is fastened (together with the gage plate O) to the die by means of two cap screws M M, and located by the two dowels N N. The holes in the stripper for the two piercing punches are countersunk, as shown, to allow the piercing punches to be as short as possible. The gage plate is of 7-16 stock, planed on all sides and long enough to extend out from the left end of the die 13 inches. It has a slot cut down through the center at P, to admit the sliding stop R, which is fastened by the cap screw Q, thus allowing of adjusting the stop for different lengths of straps.

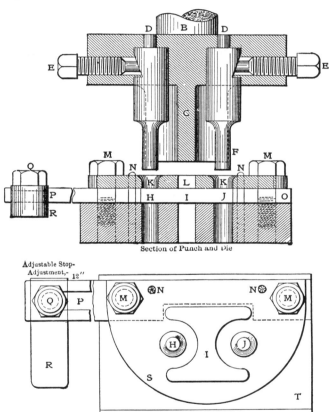

Section of Punch and Die

Adjustable Stop-
Adjustment,- 12"

FIG. 105.—DIE FOR PIERCING AND CUTTING OFF HEAVY STOCK.

The punch shown in Fig. 105 is made as rigid as possible, the cutting-off and finishing punch C, and the holder B, being a forging, the punch proper of tool steel and the holder of mild steel. The two piercing punches G and F respectively are of ⅞-inch round annealed tool steel, let into the holder as shown and fastened by the set screws E E and the little inclined faced plugs which bear against the angular notch in the side of the punch. All punches for heavy stock, of the construction shown, should be fastened in this manner, as it is impossible for them to pull out. The small holes D D, in the back of the holder, are let in to allow of removing the piercing punches with ease. The two piercing punches are made one thickness of metal longer than the cutting-off and finishing punch C, so that the holes in the work will have been pierced, and the punches entered the dies, before the cutting-off punch performs its operation. This insures the rigid holding of the metal and the accurate sizing of the straps, and, also, as it makes the punching of the work successive, the strain on the press and the tools is reduced. The punches are made so that the cutting-off punch is a trifle loose in its die and the two piercing punches very much so. This leaves the two holes in the strap considerably larger on one side than on the other, this being necessary in order to allow of the rivets filling out and finishing flush with the strap when they are fastened to the tires.

When the die is in use the adjustable stop R is set to take in the length required, and the metal to be punched (which comes in 20 foot lengths) is fed along a guide-way, under the stripping plate S, and held snugly against the gage plate O, allowing the end to project half way over the finishing and cutting-off die. At the first stroke of the press, the end of the stock is pierced and then trimmed and finished. It is then fed along and against the stop R, and at each succeeding stroke a complete strap is produced. Before punching, both sides of the stock are "slushed," which makes the cutting clean and leaves the ends of the straps without burrs.

Seeing Power Presses at Work.

To the practical man, the sight of parts (of which the above is a sample) being produced by punching, starts him wondering why this machine tool, the power press, has not been adopted more extensively, not only in the manufacturing shops but in the jobbing shops. When it is considered that tools and fixtures are being constantly designed and constructed for the finishing of parts by milling and drilling, which could be accomplished in the power press in half the time by dies of the simplest and most inexpensive construction, the failure to do so is astonishing. In fact there are any number of parts for various machines and at-

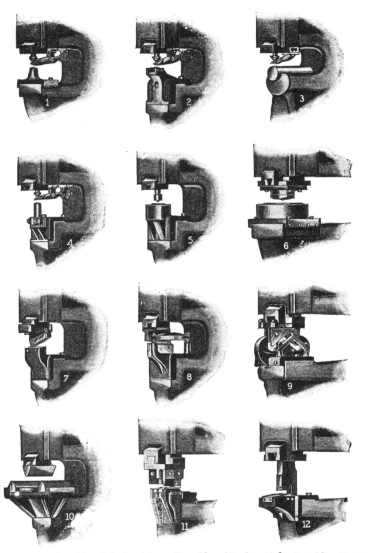

1.—Regular Punching Attachment. 2.—Punching Attachment for Punching Beams, Channels, etc. 3.—Stake Punching Attachment for Punching Flanged Heads. 4.—Stake Punching Attachment for Punching Angles. 5.—Flue and Hand-hole Punching Attachment. 6.—Man-hole Punching Attachment. 7.—Plate Shearing Attachment. 8.—Bar Shearing Attachment. 9.—Angle Shearing Attachment. 10.—Bending and Straightening Attachment. 11.—Coping Attachment. 12.—Slotting Attachment.

Attachments for Cleveland Punch and Shear Works Co. Presses.

FIG. 106.—ATTACHMENTS FOR HEAVY PRESS WORK.

tachments which are used in large quantities being manufactured by other means, which could be produced at half the cost, and to a finer degree of interchangeability, by means of simple dies and fixtures in the power press. The lightness and fine finished appearance of sheet-metal blanks, and the strength and stiffness of formed-drawn or bent blanks add greatly to the beauty of the machines or appliances to which they are affixed, and in many cases improve the working qualities as well.

It is really too bad that business reasons and certain secrets of manufacture make it almost impossible for a stranger to get the privilege of going through establishments devoted to the manufacture of agricultural machinery, and that they are so conservative about admitting anyone to their plants, as, were it otherwise, it would pay anyone who is interested in the manufacturing of machinery to pay them a visit; for in them modern manufacturing is carried on in a manner which is far ahead of other lines, both as to cheapness in production and as to the efficiency and working qualities of the output.

Piercing, Forming and Punching Heavy Blanks in One Operation.

The punch and die shown in Figs. 107, 108 and 109 are used

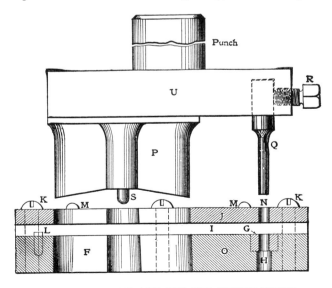

FIG. 107.—PUNCH AND DIE FOR HEAVY STOCK.

for producing pierced blanks from heavy sheet metal, piercing, forming and blanking them to the shape shown in Fig. 110, in one operation. The principle is the same as shown in Fig. 26, except that it is adapted for the working of heavy stock.

The blank, as shown in Fig. 110, is of ¼-inch cold-rolled

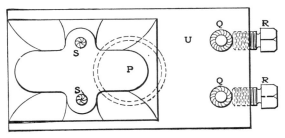

FIG. 108.—PLAN OF PUNCH.

stock with holes pierced at C C. The construction of the punch and die is shown clearly in the engravings and very little description is necessary. As shown, the die is of the usual construction except for the two piercing dies G G, which are hard-

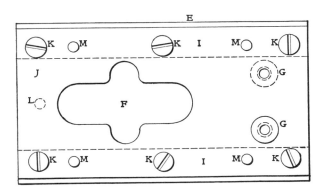

FIG. 109.—PLAN OF DIE.

ened and ground steel bushings forced into counter-bored holes in the die plate O, as shown.

When punching heavy stock it is necessary to have all punches secured in the holder as rigidly as possible. The best way is to have the stem or holder and the blanking punch in one; that is, a forging of mild steel with the portion for the punch of tool steel, as shown at U and P, Fig. 107, and the piercing punches let into holes and fastened with set screws as shown at R R. By allowing the piercing punches Q Q to fit tightly within the stripper they are strengthened and held rigidly while piercing the metal.

This principle of bending blanks by beveling the face of the punch to the shape desired, is practical for producing blanks

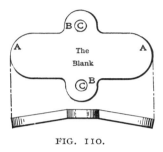

FIG. 110.

which are to be bent and formed to simple shapes, and eliminates the necessity of a second operation. The shearing of the punch also helps the die as it reduces cutting surface and strengthens it. When heavy stock is to be punched and the blanks are desired to come out flat, it is necessary to reverse matters and shear the die, as the blank will always follow the face of the punch. When shearing either punch or die, it should always be done so as to allow the extreme ends of the punch to enter the die first. In shapes where this is not possible, allow the center to enter first.

Making Pinions and Racks by Punching.

The pieces shown in Figs. 111 and 112 are a small brass gear and a rack respectively. The gear was made from sheet brass

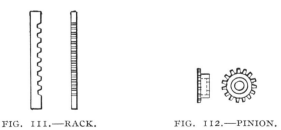

FIG. 111.—RACK.   FIG. 112.—PINION.

5-64 inch thick and was to be drawn to the shape shown, cupped ⅛ inch deep, with a ¼ hole punched in the center for the shaft. The rack was also of sheet brass of the same thickness 3-16 inch wide by 1⅝ inches long. The pitch of the rack was to be the same as that of the gear, and they were to be used on a small automatic music box. They were both made and finished in the power press.

As shown in Fig. 113 the punch and die for the pinion are of "gang" type. In the die N is the cupping die, M the piercing die and J the blanking die. In the punch, A is the holder, B the punch plate, C the cupping punch, D the piercing punch and E the blanking punch. The construction is plain and requires no description.

Fig. 114 shows the punch and die for the rack. In the punch, P is the holder, Q the punch plate and R the punch, with the face sheared as shown at S. The punch was hardened and drawn high. The die is shown in two views below the punch. It consists of the die proper T, which, after being roughed out, was broached and finished by the punch. It was also hardened and tempered. U is the gage plate, which was worked out so as to just accommodate the blank, as shown, leaving it projecting about .002 above the gage plate. V is the lock or binding strap, which swings on the shoulder screw W. When in use, the blank is placed in the gage plate U, the binding strap V is swung and hooked on the screw X, causing the blank to be held flat and firm while the punch de-

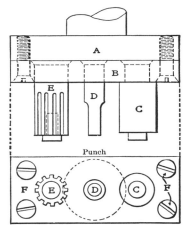
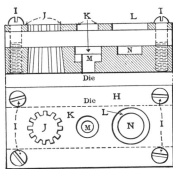

FIG. 113.—PINION DIE.

scends, shearing and cutting, gradually, thereby producing a rack with clean teeth of the proper shape, and leaving no burrs.

This is a very rapid way of doing such work, and the tools are easy to set up and easy to operate. Making the rack punch shearing, causes it to cut gradually; in fact, if the punch had been left straight, the result would have been different. Instead of the teeth of the rack being flat and nearly square at the edge, they would have come out half-round and ragged. This type cf die has been found to give very good results in a large variety of work where the edges were desired to be anywhere near square, and where the stock punched was over 1-16 inch thick. There is

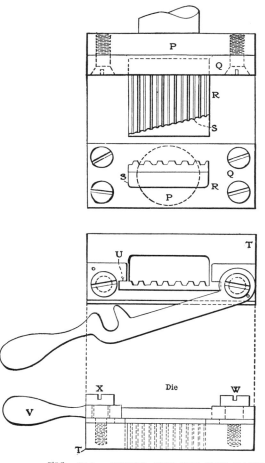

FIG. 114.—PUNCH AND DIE FOR RACK.

a lot of small work of this kind being done in the milling machine, which could be done better in the press with better results and at one-fifth the cost.

A Set of Dies for a Funnel Ended Tube.

The finished product of this set of dies is shown in Fig. **115**.

It is of a rather intricate and novel shape, necessitating care and skill in the finding and finishing of a perfect templet or master blank, and in the construction of the piercing and blanking die.

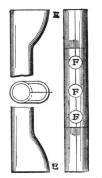 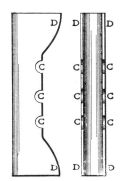

FIG. 115.—LAST OPERATION.   FIG. 116.—SECOND OPERATION.

Here is a tube with two funnel shaped ends which swell out at one side at E E. It is in the perfect closing in and forming of these funnel ends that the real work in the finding of the blank comes in, as there should be a perfect joint along the entire

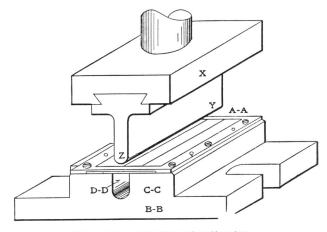

FIG. 117.—DIE FOR FIRST BEND.

length of the tube. When finished there were required to be three holes F F F in the body of the tube, each a perfect circle and all of the same diameter. To attain these results the piercing and blanking die must of course be perfect, and the blanks produced in it interchangeable. It is in the construction of this die that particular attention is called to the various practical points which are necessary for its successful working.

In sheet-metal work of this type, the first things to be settled are the thickness of metal to be used and the shape and size to which it is to be formed. We are then ready to go ahead with the forming dies, leaving the piercing and blanking die until these have been finished. The forming of the blank is accomplished in two operations, both of which are simple. The first consists of forming the blank to the shape shown in Fig. 116, throwing up the sides D D and forming the bottom of the entire length to a perfect half-circle of 3-16 inch radius. The punch

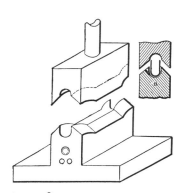

FIG. 118.—DIE FOR LAST BEND.

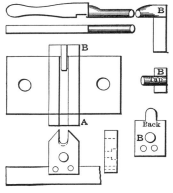

FIG. 119.

and die for this operation are shown in Fig. 117, and those used for the finishing operation in Figs. 118 and 119. As they are of the simplest design and construction, very little description is required.

In the punch for the first forming operation, X is the holder and Y the punch. This punch is of tool steel, with the face finished to a half-circle of 3-16 radius. It is hardened and drawn from the back, leaving the face very hard ⅜ inch from the edge, the remaining portion a dark blue. It is driven tightly within the holder, which tapers about one degree, thereby holding the punch tightly without set-screws.

The die is a forging, the base of mild steel and the face C C of tool steel, the forming portion of the die proper being finished as shown at D D in width and diameter two thicknesses of metal larger than the punch. The working portions of both punch and die were lapped smooth and highly polished after hardening to avoid marking the work. A A is the gage plate for locating the blank. As this punch and die can be finished without trial formings and with the certainty that they will perform the operation required, they can be laid aside until the punch and die for the last operation has been finished.

The stripping arrangement for this punch and die (not shown in the engravings) consists of the usual spring shoulder pins, there being three in the die and two in the punch, all being let in from the back and the faces finished to coincide with the circular portions of the punch and die respectively, and hardened.

By finishing the sides of the die D D slightly taper, so as to be larger at the top, thereby causing the sides of the blank to hug the punch, the work when formed rises with the punch, and as it gets above the stripper pins of the die it is stripped from the punch by the two stripper pins in the face.

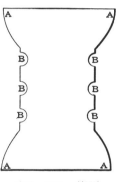

FIG. 120.—THE BLANK.

The punch and die for a finishing operation on a piece of this kind is shown in Figs. 118 and 119, and for it the author is indebted to an article by Mr. B. J. Dougherty, of Brooklyn, N. Y., in the American Machinist. As the engravings explain themselves, a bare description of the principal parts will suffice. As shown, the tools are made on practically the same lines as those for the first operation and, except for the horn, consist of but two parts, the die and the punch. This die requires no gage plate as the shape of the article to be formed, because the flat spots on the sides of the funnel-shaped ends give excellent opportunity to gage and support the metal while being formed in the die itself, and also prevent the work from turning or shifting in the die while the finishing is being accomplished. The perspective drawing of the tools shows the construction of the punch and die, while the section at the upper right hand corner shows the work located and the punch descending. The other drawing shows a detail of the parts. A is the front gage to

support the loose part of the horn, and B is the short part of the
horn secured to the back of the die. With one end of the horn
fastened to the die, as shown, and the other held all the time
in the right hand, the left hand is free to pull the finished tube
off, and put another blank in the die.

The finding of the correct blank for the piercing and blanking die, was successfully accomplished by making a number of
templets and forming and finishing them in the two dies, and

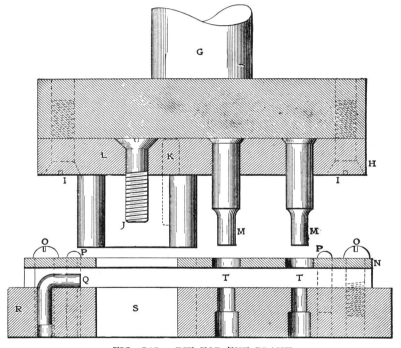

FIG. 121.—DIE FOR THE BLANK.

noting where there was excess metal or not enough. When finding the blank the locating of the circular portions at B B B was
not bothered with, finishing the blank or master templet perfectly
straight at these points and leaving the locating until the blanking die was finished.

Usually when a blank of the type shown is required—that is,
one in which the surface of the blank is left intact and without
holes—a plain blanking die is used, but in this case, as the six
half-circular portions B had to be all of the same radius, the

most expedient and accurate method was by a punch and die of the construction shown in cross-section in Fig. 121, which is of the combination piercing and blanking type. By noting the design and construction of this die, its superior working qualities over the plain die, in regard to the interchangeability of the work produced, will at once become apparent. The blanking die portion S and the six piercing dies T are all finished straight, thus allowing the die face to be ground without changing the shape of the blanks produced. The six piercing dies T are counterbored at the back to half of the thickness of the die. Great care was exercised in the laying out of the blanking die portion, and in the locating of the piercing dies and gage plates. The construction of the punch requires no description, except that the blanking punch instead of being let into and riveted in the punch plate, is located by two dowels K and fastened by two flat head screws from the back as shown.

As in order to produce blanks which are required to be per-

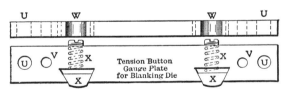

FIG. 122.

fect in every way, especially when the blank is produced in two operations, one operation following the other in the same die by the combination method, it is absolutely necessary that the stock to be punched shall be kept against the back gage plate all the time, and as it is not practical to feed it through a tight channel, other means are required, one of the best and most practical of which is shown at Fig. 122, and is known as a tension button gage plate. The spring buttons W W keep the stock as it is fed along snugly against the back gage plate, which is of the regular type, keeping it there with an equal tension at all times, and eliminating the necessity of the press hand forcing and holding the stock against the back gage plate. By the use of a gage plate of this type for accurate blanking dies, the best results will be obtained and the production brought up to the maximum.

A Set of Dies for a Sheet Metal Bracket.

The four dies shown here were used to produce the sheet-metal bracket shown in Figs. 123 to 125. The die and punch used for the first operation are shown in Fig. 126 and are of the "gang" type. The stock used for the brackets was cold-rolled sheet steel 3-32 inch thick and ⅝ inch wide, coming in strips of the width required. The work accomplished in this first die was the piercing of the center hole J and the two holes I I at the ends, trimming and cutting the ends H H to the shape shown and cutting off the piece as shown in Fig. 123. The construc-

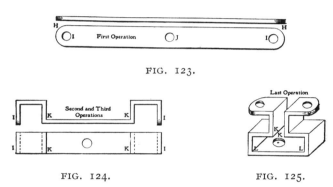

FIG. 123.

FIG. 124.   FIG. 125.

tion of the punch and die for this operation can be understood from the engravings and no description is necessary.

When in use, a strip of metal was entered beneath the stripper and pushed in against the stop-pin S. The punch descending, the three piercing punches O O O pierced the strip and entered the die first and before the trimming punch R began to cut, thus preventing the stock from shifting. After the end of the stock was trimmed, it was moved along until the hole pierced at the right hand end was in line with the pin S, over which it was slipped, thereby locating and centering it correctly for the finishing of the other end and cutting off the piece. At the next stroke of the punch the finished piece was cut off and the front end and the holes pierced in the second piece. The finished pieces were removed from the pin S with the left hand while the metal was fed with the right. As shown, the die is equipped with a tension button gage plate to insure the alignment of the stock with the dies.

The punch and die for the first bend, Fig. 124, are shown in

Fig. 127. They bend the work at K K. This same die is used for the second bending operation. One punch holder also sufficed for the three bending operations, as did one bolster or die block

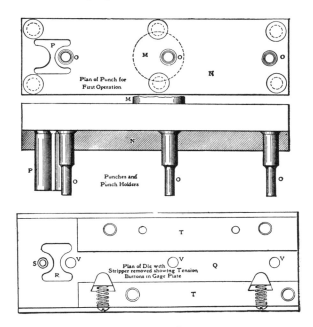

Plan of Punch for
First Operation

Punches and
Punch Holders

Plan of Die with
Stripper removed showing Tension
Buttons in Gage Plate

FIG. 126.

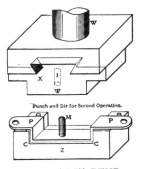

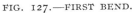

Punch and Die for Second Operation.

FIG. 127.—FIRST BEND.

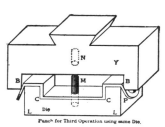

Punch for Third Operation using same Die.

FIG. 128.—SECOND BEND.

for the two bending dies. The construction of this punch and die requires no description.

For the second operation, that of bending the ends of the work as shown in Fig. 124 at I I, the same die as used for the first bend and the punch shown in Fig. 128 were used, the operation being accomplished in the manner shown.

For bending at L L and causing the work to assume the final shape shown in Fig. 125, the punch and die, Fig. 129, were used.

Punch and Die for Third Operation

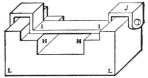

FIG. 129.—THIRD BEND.

The design and method of constructing this punch and die can be understood from the engravings and a very slight description will suffice. The work J was located on, and within, the die at points I I. The die was hardened and drawn slightly, leaving it very hard at the working points. The width of the punch at F F is two thicknesses of metal less than the die at H H. The punch was hardened and drawn, leaving the points F F very hard and the rest a dark blue.

When in use the punch and die were set up in the press and the work, Fig. 124, was placed in position on the die as shown at J. The punch descending strikes the work in the center and causes the two ends to spring upward and inward, hugging the punch, which, continuing downward, forces it into the die at H H, strikes the bottom with a good hard blow, and completes and finishes the work to the shape shown in Fig. 125. The finished work is slid off the punch by hand.

A Double Blanking Die. A Piercing, Cutting-Off and Forming Die, and a Large Double Blanking Die.

The punch and die shown in Fig. 130 was used to produce two blanks at each stroke of the press, the blanks being used when drawn and finished as the shield portion of a large "safety" pin. With this punch and die an automatic feed was used. In the die, E E are the blanking dies, C the gage plate, G the stripper, while I I are the cap screws and H H the dowels respectively for locating and fastening the stripper and gage plates to the die. In the punch, C is the holder, D the punch plate and A A the two punches. The punch plate is fastened to the holder by four flat-head screws, as shown. The construction of this die requires no description. Its type should be adopted whenever possible as the product is doubled.

The article shown in the top left hand corner of Fig. 131 is of flat cold-rolled stock 3-16 inch thick, and is finished to the shape shown in one operation, by means of the combination die shown in Fig. 131. As shown, it was necessary to pierce the four holes, cut off the blank, and bend it to the required shape. As the stock to be worked was quite heavy, it was required that all parts of the punch and die should be as rigid and strong as possible. The construction of the tool is shown plainly and

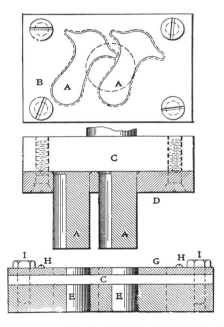

FIG. 130.—A SMALL DOUBLE BLANKING DIE.

only a description of its operation and use is necessary. The stock to be worked was cut into strips in the shear to the proper width. A strip of metal was fed in beneath the stripper V, far enough to allow the end to project slightly over the cutting edge of the die B. The punch descending, the end was trimmed first, and then the four holes pierced. At the next stroke the stock was fed up against the stop G and the blank cut off to the proper length and bent over and formed by the pads R and F, and the

four holes pierced in the next piece. As the punch rises, the
spring L causes the stripping pads J J to strip the finished work
from the die F and lifts it to the surface, from which it drops off
at the back—if the press is inclined.

This principle of construction can also be used to advantage
for cutting off and forming sheet-metal blanks in which it is not
necessary to pierce holes, as it is far preferable to the means

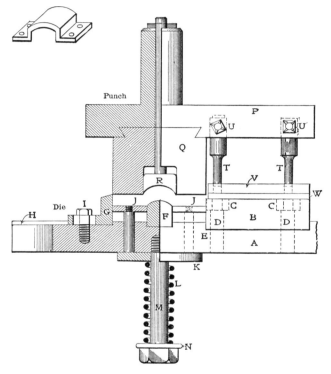

FIG. 131.—A PIERCING, CUTTING-OFF, AND FORMING DIE.

usually employed, of first cutting off the blanks in one operation
and then forming them in another. This method is both cheaper
and more conducive to the production of parts of a uniform size
and quality. Some die-makers use a separate pad for fastening
the punches to the holder, but this will not answer for heavy
stock, as the punches are not so rigid. In fact, the fewer parts
used in the construction of punches and dies of this class, the better the results and the longer the life of the tools.

The punch and die shown in Fig. 132 are of a different type from the one shown in Fig. 130. It is a double blanking die, but instead of producing two blanks of the same size, it produces one blank which is punched on the outside and inside both, as shown at the left of Fig. 132. Its construction can be understood from the engraving. When it is in use, the strip of metal is fed

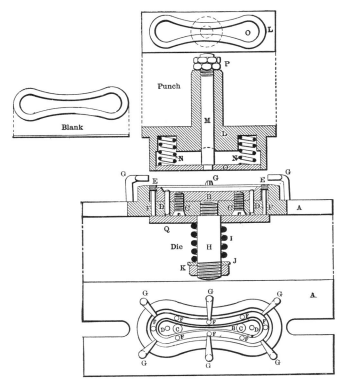

FIG. 132.—A LARGE DOUBLE BLANKING DIE.

in under the stripping pins G, and the punch L blanks the outside of the work into the die A, while the internal punch B punches the inside up into the internal die L. As the punch rises, the spring pad O within the punch L, by the action of the two springs N N expels the waste, while the pad E E within the die A, in conjunction with the pins F, the pad Q and the spring I, strips the finished blank from the die A, thereby producing a blank of the shape shown in Fig. 132. In this die the principles and method of construction are adaptable for the production of a large variety of parts of which large quantities are required, as the cost of the tools will be quickly made up in the time and operations saved in the production of the parts. For small quantities of blanks, dies of a simpler and less intricate as well as cheaper type are preferable, producing at a greater cost work of just as good a quality.

Punches and Dies for Producing Parts of an Electric Cloth-cutting Machine.

The punches and dies shown in Figs. 135 to 140 were designed for and put into successful operation in the manufacture of an electric cloth-cutting machine, the general features of which

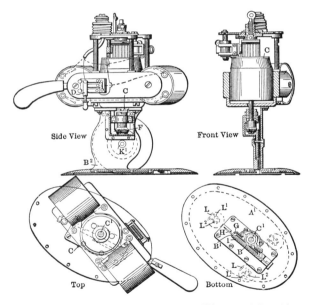

FIG. 133.—ELECTRIC CLOTH-CUTTING MACHINE.

are shown in Fig. 133. It will not be attempted here to describe the machine. In Fig. 134 are shown engravings of the roller plate and parts for the base of the machine. A is the roller plate, $1\frac{1}{4}$ inches in diameter of 3-32 inch cold-rolled stock, with four holes pierced in the positions shown. E is the roller bracket of the same stock as the plate, pierced, blanked and formed to the shape shown, F being the result of the first operation. B is the small stud for fastening it to the plate and C is the

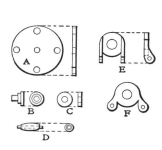

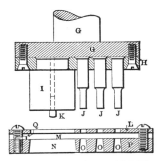

FIG. 134.—PARTS OF ROLLER BRACKET.   FIG. 135.—BLANKING DIE.

washer. All the parts are assembled when finished as shown in the bottom view of the machine in Fig. 133.

The punch and die shown in Fig. 135 is for producing the

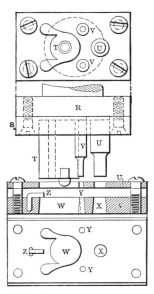

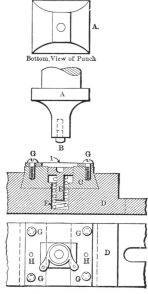

FIG. 136.—BLANKING DIE.   FIG. 137.—BENDING DIE.

roller plate A. P is the die plate, O the piercing dies and N the blanking die. The other parts are clearly shown and require no description.

Fig. 136 shows the punch and die, plan and side views respectively for producing the blank F for the roller bracket E. The manner in which the piercing and blanking punches and dies are laid out and finished and the blank produced can be intelligently understood from the engravings. The tools used for the bending operation are shown in Fig. 137, and are sufficiently clear to make a description superfluous.

The punch and die shown in Figs. 139 and 140 respectively, were used to produce the piece shown in Fig. 138, which was used as a shoe for the base of the cloth-cutter. The blanking, both inside and outside, was all done in the one die; the piercing of the holes was another operation. The die consists of the outside die A, the internal punch B, the spring pad or stripper C and the

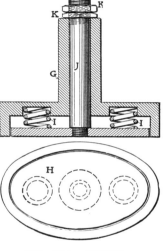

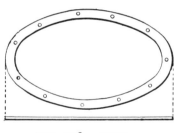

FIG. 138.—SHOE.   FIG. 139.—PUNCH.

bed plate. The punch and holder are all in one; and are constructed as shown with a spring pad to strip the scrap from the internal die. The operation and use of this die requires no description.

The die for piercing the eleven holes shown in the blank, Fig. 138, was made in the following manner: A bolster of cast iron was got out, and one of the blanks drilled, the holes being transferred from the jig used to drill the base plate. A gage plate of ⅛ inch flat stock was made so that the blank would just fit it. It was then fastened to the face of the bolster with screws and dowels, the blank laid within it and the holes transferred through it to the face of the bolster. These holes were then enlarged for bushings of tool steel, ⅜ inch diameter, which were turned, drilled and reamed to the size of a clearance drill for a 6-32 screw, hardened and drawn, the face and outside ground and then driven into the holes. The .die was constructed in this manner to facilitate grinding, and, in case of chipping or shearing, to enable replacing with others. The holes for the punches were then transferred through these bushings to the face of a cast

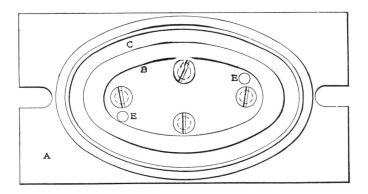

FIG. 140.—DIE.

iron holder; the punches were made and hardened and fastened within the holder with set screws; then a spring pad was fitted over them, and working up and down on two studs, equipped with strong springs, which acted to strip the blank from the punches after the holes were pierced.

An Armature Disk Notching Die With a Dial Feed.

The die and attachments shown in Figs. 141 and 142 were used for notching armature disks. It requires very little attendance while in operation and can be used for punching a number of different sizes of disks. It can be used in any single-acting power press to which a connecting rod for operating the feed can be attached. The sheet-iron blanks used for the disks

were irregular in shape, and it was necessary to finish them to
the correct radius while punching the slots. The die D was made
first. The best way to finish the templet was to solder it to the
face-plate of the lathe, when it was turned to the exact radius required, both inside and outside. The die was then worked out
and finished to it at M and Z, taking care to get it central in the
die. The bolster A is of the regular type, only heavier. It was
dovetailed crosswise for the die and left large enough for the key
X also. It was then dovetailed on the front for the cast iron ex-

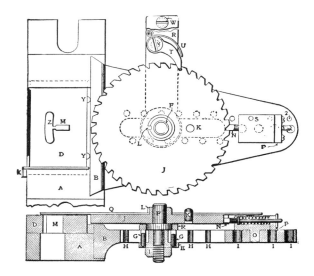

FIG. 141.—ARMATURE DISK NOTCHING DIE.

tension plate B. This was strong and heavy and perfectly rigid.
It drove tightly into B, and a set screw was let into each side
afterward to permanently locate it. We were then ready to lay
out the slot C and the holes H, by first striking a line from the
center of the die M down the entire length of the plate. The
distances between the holes H were one-half of the differences in
the diameters of the disks to be punched.

The bushing E and the stud F are both of tool steel, the bushing being fitted to the slot C with a wide shoulder at E, the top
coming a trifle below the face of plate B. A reamed hole
through the center admits the stud F, with the nut I on one end
and the other fitting the hole in the index plate J. Drilling the

holes in the bushing for the dowel-pins G G required accurate work, as the finished radius of the disks depended on their location. The method used for gaging it correctly is of interest. A piece of cast iron about 1 inch wide and in length about ¾ inch longer than half the diameter of the smallest armature blank, with a lug at one end projecting from the face, was strapped on the face-plate of the lathe with one end central. A hole was let into this end and reamed to the size of the stud F. The inside of the lug at the other end was then turned to exactly the same radius as the die D at Z, which was that of the next to the smallest disk. The outside of the lug was turned to a radius sufficiently small to allow of its entering the die freely. This gage or templet was set with the end with the hole over the stud F. The nut I was loosened, and the stud and bushing moved forward until the locating end of the gage entered the die Z, with the turned face of the lug resting snugly against the inner side. The nut T was then tightened and the holes for the dowels G G were transferred through the plate B to the bushing E. The dowels were then made and driven in. This method of locating holes is somewhat similar to the "button" method used in drill jigs, and is just as reliable and accurate.

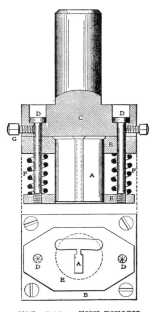

FIG. 142.—THE PUNCH.

The index plate J was of cast iron, with a hub on one side the same diameter as the hole in the armature disk blank. A keyway in the hub allows of the small key punched in the disk to enter and locate. As most disks have from three to five holes punched in them to lighten them, one is utilized to secure the blank and carry it with the index plate, the dowel K fitting the hole snugly. The index plate rests on the collar of the stud F. The two pins Y Y are positive stops for the die D. The ratchet lever R fits the collar of the stud F and rests between the face of the extension plate B and the index plate J, with the ratchet pawl T and a flat spring to keep it against the index plate. The screw W is for fastening the link by which it is connected to the adjustable feed rod at the side of the press.

The positive stop for the index plate is located at the end of the extension plate. A projecting pin fits the holes I in the extension, and a dowel S entering the holes 2 locates it permanently. The punch is shown in two views in Fig. 142, and requires no description to be understood.

When in use, a blank Q, ready to be notched, is placed on the index plate J, the pin K entering one of the holes. The feed is then adjusted and the press is kept running continually until the entire disk is notched. When the punch descends the blank is held securely between the pad E and the die. The notch is then punched and the edge of the blank trimmed to the proper radius. As the punch rises, the metal is stripped and the index plate revolved one space, leaving the blank in position for the punching of the next notch.

To change the die for punching another size, the bushing E is moved forward or backward and the dowels G G entered into another pair of holes. Another die finished to the proper radius replaces the one shown and another punch is also used. If necessary a different index plate is substituted.

Dies for Switchboard Clips.

The set of dies shown in Figs. 143 to 145 were used for producing clips of sheet copper, which were used in large numbers for electrical switchboards. Fig. 148 shows the finished clip, with a 7-32 inch hole in the bottom to admit a screw for fastening it to the board. The ends of the clip were rounded to a 9-32 radius. The metal used was sheet copper 1-16 inch thick, in strips 7-16 inch wide.

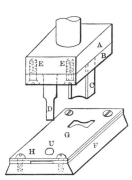

FIG. 143.—FIRST DIE.

The first operation, that of piercing the hole, rounding the ends and cutting off the piece, was accomplished with the punch and die shown in Fig. 143, while the second operation, that of bending the blanks to the shape shown in Fig. 147, was done with the punch and die shown in Fig. 144. Neither of these operations requires a description, as the engravings show clearly all that is necessary.

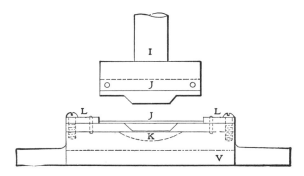

FIG. 144.—SECOND DIE.

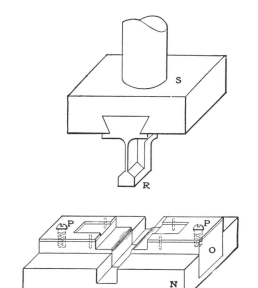

FIG. 145.—THE BENDING OPERATION.

FIG. 146.—FIRST
OPERATION.

FIG. 147.—SECOND
OPERATION.

FIG. 148.—THIRD
OPERATION.

The arrangement for the third and last operation, as shown in Fig. 145, consists of the die O, the gage plates P P to locate the second operation on the die, and the die block N. The punch consists of the holder S and the punch R, the construction of which is shown clearly. When in use the work, Fig. 147, was placed in position on the die and the punch descending causes the two sides to spring up and hug the punch which continues downward until it strikes the bottom, drawing the corners square and producing the shape shown in Fig. 148. The work is re-

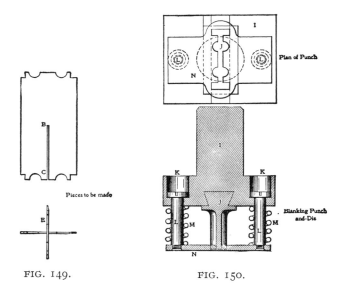

FIG. 149.   FIG. 150.

moved from the punch by hand, coming off easily, the punch itself being finished as smoothly as possible.

A Cutting Off and End Finishing Die, and an Accurate Sectional Die With a Chute Feed, and Finger Stripper.

The punches and dies shown in Figs. 150 to 157 produce the blank Fig. 149, from a strip of sheet tin 1-32 inch thick. The blanks are assembled as in the lower view, Fig. 149, so that they will be at right angles, to serve as a compartment skeleton for a tin chemical box.

The metal for the blanks came in long strips of the required width, so it was only necessary to finish the ends and cut them off. The die for this is shown in Figs. 150 and 151. O is the bolster and P the die, worked out at Q to the required shape. U is the adjustable stop bracket, fastened to the end of the die and R the gage plate located as shown in Fig. 151.

The punch is of the usual type, except that the stripper is located upon it instead of on the die. The holder has a dovetailed channel for the punch J. This punch, after being fitted to the die, is hardened and drawn to a dark blue. The stripper N is located by means of the two studs L L, which screw into and shoulder against the face. The studs L L and the stripper move up and down, the two springs M being strong enough to strip

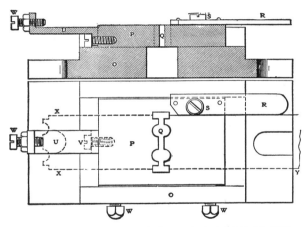

FIG. 151.—VERTICAL SECTION AND PLAN OF DIE.

the metal from the punch instantly. The stripper is worked out to fit nicely around the punch so as to prevent the edges of the stock, after being cut off and finished, from bending or burring inward. The press in which the punch and die are used is tilted backward to an angle sufficient to allow the blanks to drop off through gravity into a receptacle at the back. The metal punched is first held against the gage plate R and the end allowed to project a slight distance over the die. This end is then trimmed by the punch, after which, the stop-screw W is adjusted to get the blank to the required length. The stock is then fed against it, and, as the punch descends, the first blank is cut off and the front end of the next one trimmed. The rapidity with which the blanks can be produced by this die should commend the principle for the production of parts of the type shown in Fig. 149. The application of the stripper to the punch, and the use of an inclinable press wherever possible, will increase the output two-fold without effecting the duplication of the parts.

For the second operation, that of piercing the long narrow slot B C, the punch and die are shown in Figs. 152 to 157. The

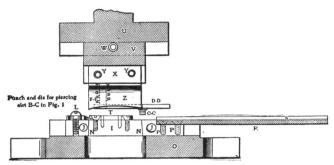

Punch and die for piercing
slot B-C in Fig. §

FIG. 152.—VERTICAL SECTION OF PUNCH AND DIE.

piercing of a slot 1-32 inch wide to the length shown requires a die of sectional construction, as it would not only be impracticable to make a solid die, but it would be impossible to accomplish accurate results with it. As by the use of this die the blanks are automatically fed to the face of the die with great ra-

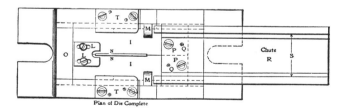

Plan of Die Complete

FIG. 153.—PLAN OF SLOTTING DIE.

pidity, and after being pierced are successively picked up to make room for the next, a description of its construction is presented.

The die was made first of a single piece, two holes were drilled as shown for the dowel pins J J, and the bevel shown planed on the sides, allowing one side to taper lengthwise one degree. The end at K K was milled down 3-16 inch from the face as a locating face for the feed chute R. The holes P P and Q Q were drilled straight through, as were the two L L for the stop-plate. A narrow cutter was then used to cut the die in two, and the inner edges were finished. These sections I I were clamped

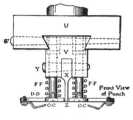

FIG. 154.

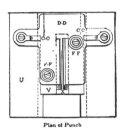

FIG. 155.

together face to face with all sides coinciding, and a sharp square edge milling cutter was used to mill a flat square ended channel .0163 in depth through both of them at N N, about ⅛ inch longer than necessary. The depth of the channels, .0163,

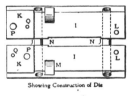

FIG. 156.

FIG. 157.

exceeded that required by .0065, which was to allow of grinding after hardening. After the notches M M had been milled in, as clearance for the stripper fingers, the two sections were hardened and drawn to a light straw. The face of each was then ground until the channel N of the die portion was 1-64 inch deep. The two dowels were then entered as shown at J J. The bolster O was now machined, with a dovetailed channel finished so that the die would drive in. The die was entered, the face ground and oil-stoned and the stop fastened by the screws L L. The feed chute was made of ¼-inch flat brass, with a channel S slightly wider than the blanks to be pierced, the portion on which the blanks were to slide level with the die face. T T, the two gage plates for locating the blanks, are fastened to the bolster instead of the die.

The punch consists of the following parts: The holder U,

the punch pad V, the punch X, located by the taper pins Y Y; the stripper plate D D, to the face of which are fastened the flat spring fingers C C, C C, and the stripper studs and springs F F, F F. The necessary points in construction may be seen and understood from the different views of the punch in Figs. oo, oo and oo. The small spring fingers for picking up the blank after piercing are made from light flat spring steel and are bent to the shape shown and located on the stripper plate. The ends of these fingers project beyond the face of the stripper far enough to allow of them, when the punch descends, to be forced upward, encountering the blank and then slipping under it, and as the punch rises they carry the blank with them, and as the press is inclined it falls off at the back.

When in use the punch and die are set up in the press as follows: The press is tilted backward and the die bolster O fastened to it by bolts through the ends, so that the mouth of the feed chute R will be directly in front of the operator, and slanting downward toward the back of the press. The punch is then set and the chute filled with blanks, the first one resting on the die between the gage plate T T and against the stop-plate L, the next against the end of the first and so on up the chute. As the punch descends the stripper holds the blank tightly to the die face and the two spring fingers C C, C C, slip under it. As the punch begins to rise the blank is stripped from it by the stripper plate D D, and it is raised from the face of the die by the fingers C C, C C, and as the punch reaches its highest point the blank slides off at the back.

Using this die the press was run at a high speed, and the blanks were pierced as rapidly as the operator could feed them into the chute. There is a large variety of second operation work which can be produced rapidly, accurately and at a minimum of cost by dies of this design, with punch, stripper and spring fingers for removing the blank. The face of the piercing punch Z is sheared so as to relieve the strain on it as much as possible.

The twenty-four dies shown and described in this chapter should suggest to the practical man a large variety of work for the production of which they can be adapted, and we will now turn our attention to the class of sheet-metal tools which are next in order of prominence and which come under the head of "Bending and Forming Dies."

CHAPTER V.

Bending Dies—Simple and Intricate.

In tools for the ordinary bending of sheet metal parts it is necessary to combine simplicity in design with durability and cheapness; and one of the things that makes a die-maker valuable is his ability to devise simple and effective means for producing in the fewest number of operations the article required, and constructing the tools so as to allow of their being set up and operated by unskilled help. Very often it is possible to design a die that will accomplish in one operation that which usually requires two or three to produce, being, of course, of a more complicated and accurate construction and requiring more skill and intelligence to operate. On the contrary, it is often preferable to increase the number of operations (by adopting simple methods) in dies that will stand rough usage. The bending and forming dies illustrated and described in this chapter are of both classes.

Dies for Making Large Safety Pins.

In Figs. 159 to 162 are shown a set of dies and fixtures used in the manufacture of the universally known "safety"

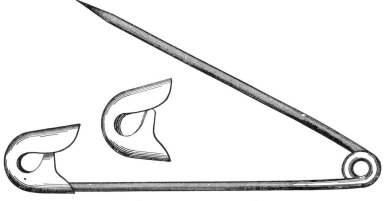

FIG. 158.—LARGE "SAFETY" PIN.

pins, and the ones produced by the particular set of tools here shown are of the largest size made, as shown in Fig. 158. The pin consists of two parts—the head, or shield, which is blanked and drawn from sheet brass, and the pin proper of brass wire. The number of operations required to produce **pins** of this size—which, by the way, are used principally for horse blankets —are seven: The blanking of the piece for the head, the draw-

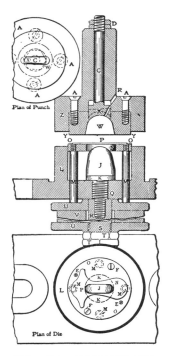

Plan of Punch

Plan of Die

FIG. 159.—DRAWING DIE.

ing and forming of it, the cutting and pointing of the wire, the bending of the end which is fastened in the head, the forming of the spring portion, the wiring and fastening of the pin within the head, and, last, the closing down of the head so as to make the pin "safety." The means used and the **manner** in which all this is accomplished can be clearly understood from the cuts, and very little description is necessary, except as to the methods of constructing some of the tools.

For the first operation—that of punching out the blank for the head—the punch and die shown in Fig. 130, Chapter IV., are used. The second operation, that of drawing and forming the blank as shown in Fig. 158, is accomplished by the drawing die, Fig. 159, the construction and action of which will be understood from the description given of "Drawing Dies" in a chapter further on in the book.

The operations on the pin portion are three. The wire is straight and 10 inches long, and is required to be pointed at one end and bent to conform to the radius of the inside of the head at the other. The first operation, that of pointing and cutting off, is accomplished in the screw machine, the pointing being done with a special box-tool. The second operation, of bending the end to the shape shown at the end, is done by means of a simple punch in the foot press. The last operation on the wire is to bend and form the spring portion as shown at K. This is accomplished by the fixture shown in the two views, Fig. 160. The bent end G of the wire is entered and located

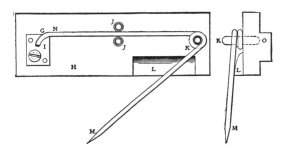

FIG. 160.—BENDING AND FORMING SPRING PORTION.

to gage within the plate I, with the length of wire lying between the pins J J and against the forming horn K. The wire is formed around the horn as shown in the two views. The inclined surface of the body H is necessary, so as to have both ends of the wire in line with each other when fastened within the head. This fixture is used in the vise, gripping it at O as shown in the end view.

The next operation is that of inclosing the end G of the pin within the head. This is done in the foot press by means of the tools shown in Fig. 161, and as the sketches show clearly the manner in which it is accomplished very little description is necessary. V is the die, of tool steel; W the locating or

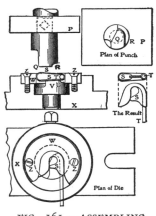

FIG. 161.—ASSEMBLING OPERATION.

gage plate for the work, and X the bolster or die block. The punch consists of two parts—the holder P, of cast iron, and the punch Q, of tool steel.

The last operation is the closing in of the head of the pin so that the points S will act as a guide for opening the pin.

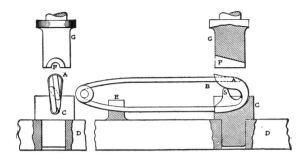

FIG. 162.—LAST OPERATION.

This operation and the simple tools used are shown in Fig. 162, and require no description to be understood.

Forming a Funnel Ended Tube.

The dies shown in Fig. 167 and one of the construction shown in Figs. 118 and 119, Chapter IV., were used to form a blank of cold-rolled sheet steel .048 inch thick to the shape shown in the two views, Figs. 164 and 165. The finished piece was used

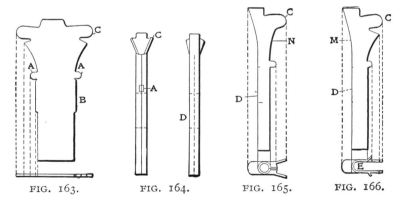

FIG. 163.   FIG. 164.   FIG. 165.   FIG. 166.

SUCCESSIVE OPERATIONS IN TUBE MAKING.

as a funnel on a box-nailing machine, the nails entering at the opening at the top and dropping into a tube at the bottom. The piece was to finish to 4⅝ inches long, in the shape of a tube 13-32 inch in diameter starting from the bottom. There was also a flat surface at the back at D 1 inch long and 13-32 wide, to keep the funnel from shifting when in place on the machine.

There were two lugs at A to act as a gage in setting it to the proper height. The upper part was formed in the manner shown, with an open space in front and two wings extending out.

The construction and use of the dies used to accomplish the desired results can be understood from the engravings of the

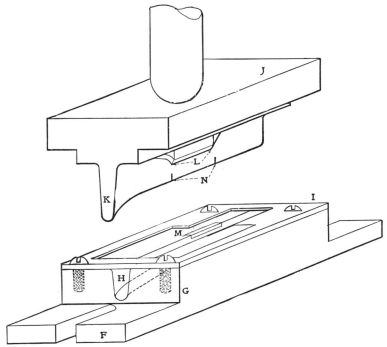

FIG. 167.—FIRST FORMING OPERATION.

forming dies and the diagrams of the blank and its forming shown in Figs. 163 to 166. Fig. 163 shows the blank as punched in a plain blanking die, Fig. 166 the result of the first forming operation, and Figs. 164 and 165 the result of the last operation.

The manner in which the bending and forming of this funnel is accomplished and the tools used, should suggest simple means for the forming of a variety of work.

Bending Dies for Wire Lock Clasps.

One of the uses to which forming and bending dies are

often put is the production of bent and formed wire parts from
either slender or heavy stock. As an instance of what can be
accomplished in the bending and forming of comparatively heavy

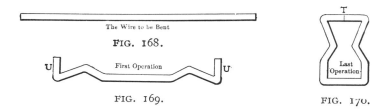

The Wire to be Bent

FIG. 168.

First Operation

FIG. 169.

Last Operation

FIG. 170.

stock in two operations by the use of simple dies, we show in
Fig. 168 a length of wire and the result of two operations on
it in Figs. 169 and 170. The stock used was 5-16 thick Bessemer
rod, and the parts as finished were used as clasps on patented
locks.

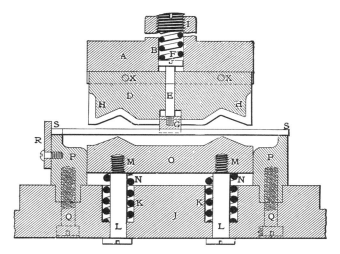

FIG. 171.—FIRST BEND.

Before starting on the dies it was necessary to determine
the exact length of wire required. As shown, the die for the
first operation is made so that the bending of the work will be
progressive. The bolster J was first planed and two square-
bottomed channels let in crosswise for the pieces P P. These
pieces were of tool steel and were worked out and finished to

the shape shown—that is, to a snug fit within the channels in the bolster and with about .007 inch surplus stock on the inside face of each. The tops of these pieces had a half-round groove let in at S to act as locating points for the work. Holes were let into the back for fastening screws Q Q, two to each. After these holes were tapped and a hole let into one piece for the stop-piece screw R, the pieces were hardened and tempered, leaving the portions which were to do the bending very hard and the rest a blue. The pieces were then fastened in, and the inside face of each ground until the distance between them was exactly as required—that is, the same as between the points U U, Fig. 169, after the first operation.

For the part O, which is the bending die proper, a piece of well-annealed tool steel ⅞ inch wide was planed and squared and the ends finished so that it would fit nicely between P P, as shown. This part O was then clamped to the face of the bolster resting between the pieces P P and the two holes for the stripper screws L L were let in. The piece O was then removed from the bolster and the forming and bending face finished to templet, first in the shaper and then with a file, all points as smooth as possible. The two holes M M were tapped, and

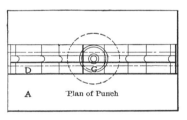

FIG. 172.

the die was hardened and only slightly drawn. The stripper screw holes in the bolster were then counterbored to admit the stripper springs N N. The springs had to be very stiff, to allow of the progressive bending and forming of the work. After polishing all working parts and surfaces and fastening on the stop-plate R, all parts were assembled and were ready for the punch.

The holder A is of cast iron. After turning the stem to fit the hole in the press ram, a hole B is bored completely through it, tapping it at the upper end for the stripper spring adjusting screw I. The punch D, of tool steel, is first planed, fitted to the holder A, driving tightly into the dovetailed channel in the face, and left long enough for fitting it into the die. The punch is driven into the holder and the holes are drilled and reamed for the two taper locating pins X X X. The center for

the hole for the stripper screw E is then located through the
hole B in the stem of the holder, drilled and reamed. The locating pins are then removed, the punch driven out and the
square channel for the stripper G milled in across the face. The
face of the punch is then finished to fit the die and polished.
It is then set up in the milling machine, and, by using a butt
mill, the cutting edges of which are of the same radius as that
of the stock to be bent, a groove H H   milled into the face
and the ends in depth the same as the diameter of the stock to
be bent. This channel is then finished smooth and symmetrical

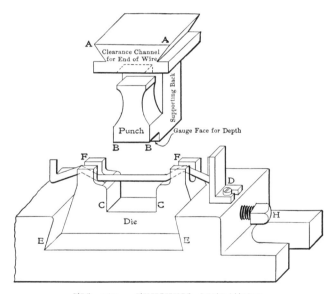

FIG. 173.—FINISHING OPERATION.

at all the corners and angles with a riffler and polished with
oil and emery to as good a finish as possible. The punch is
hardened at the bending face and the ends, and tempered to a
very light straw.

The stripper G, of tool steel, is made and fitted to the slot
in the punch face and finished with a groove in the center to
coincide perfectly with the one in the punch face when resting
in the bottom of the slot. A hole in the center is tapped for
the stripper screw E, the spring F is made and also the adjusting screw I and all parts are assembled.

The length of wire to be bent is rested in the locating grooves S S and endways against the stop plate R. The punch is set to just bottom in the die. As it descends the tension of the springs N N is sufficient to allow of the angular bending being accomplished without the die descending. As the face of the punch strikes the die O the ends of the wire are bent up into the grooves H H in the ends of the punch, which continues to descend until the die strikes the face of the bolster. As the punch rises the die rises with it, and the work clings to the punch until it has risen above the die face, when it is stripped by the stripper G, and, as the press is tilted, it drops off the die into a receptacle at the back of the press.

For the finishing operation the punch and die shown in Fig. 173 are used. The die is finished from a good-sized solid block of tool steel to the shape shown—that is, to dovetail into the bolster at E E and the part C C finished to templet, rounding off the corners, as shown, with a groove along the top faces at F F as locating and centering points for the work. A stop-plate fastened at one end of the bolster acts as an endwise locator. The die is hardened and drawn, driven into the bolster and located by the set screw H. The construction of the punch requires no description. The punch and die are set up in the relative positions shown, the work is located within the groove F F and against the stop-plate D. The punch strikes the work in the middle and bends it into the die, which causes the ends to spring up and form around the punch, the ends coming together tightly at T, Fig. 170. As the punch rises and the work with it, it is stripped off by hand.

These two dies were designed for the production of parts which were required in large quantities, and we believe they are both in design and construction about as substantial and simple as could be devised, as the work is produced in exact duplication and free from marks or bruises, and results are attained in two operations which, as a rule, require three to produce.

A Bending Die for Wire Staples.

In Figs. 174 to 176 are shown different views of a punch and die for bending staples of Stubs wire, so that they can be entered into reamed and accurately spaced holes in a separate piece. As the holes into which the ends of the staples were to be entered were reamed to the exact diameter of the wire, it was necessary to employ accurate and reliable means for the bending. The punch and die shown was constructed to accomplish this result, and the results attained were in every way satisfactory. The staple as finished and bent from the straight wire is shown in Fig. 177. The first part made was the die N, which was of tool steel finished to the length and height shown, and in width

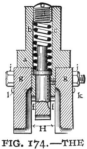

FIG. 174.—THE PUNCH.

to exactly the same as the distance between the inside edges of the holes into which the staples were required to fit. To get this exact distance, the following method was adopted: A piece of Stubs wire of the same diameter as the holes was forced into each and allowed to project out about ¼ inch. The distance between them was then secured by means of a Brown-Sharpe "Vernier" caliper, getting the exact distance. The holes for the dowel pins, and screws for fastening the gage plates O O to the face of the die, were then let in, and also the holes for the screws P. The die was then hardened and slightly drawn, after which it was located and fastened within the bolster, as shown, by the screws P.

The punch proper, as shown in the cross-section view, was

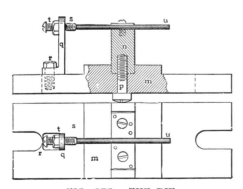

FIG. 175.—THE DIE.

FIG. 176.—PLAN OF PUNCH.

FIG. 177.—STAPLE.

made in three parts, of which those at the sides G G are the "benders" and A the "sizer." The part A was finished at B to fit the ram of the press, while the "sizer" portion was finished in width to the exact width of the die. A hole was bored straight through the punch for the stripper E and spring C, and tapped at the upper end for the spring adjusting screw D. A slot was let into the side of the stripper to admit the point of a small set screw, as shown. This was to prevent the stripper from turning while the punch was in action. A groove was let into the face of the stripper stud and also into the "sizer" at E E, in depth the same as the diameter of the wire to be bent with the bottoms rounded to the same radius. The two side pieces, or "benders," were then made of tool steel and finished square and smooth on all sides. Holes were drilled through them and the "sizer" A, to admit the bolts I I and the dowel pins K and L. Grooves were then let into the inside faces of the "benders" at H, in depth so that the wire when bent would fit snugly within and between them and the sides of the die N. These grooves were lapped smooth and rounded at the face of the "benders" so as to not scratch the wire while bending it. The "benders" were then hardened and drawn to a light straw temper and the parts assembled as shown.

To operate the die, the bolster is fastened to the press and the punch lined up with it by setting it on the die with the "benders" over the sides and then fastening it. The stroke of the press was then set so that the "sizer" would just touch the face of the die when the ram had reached the full length of its stroke. The wire was then located on the die face, as shown in the sectional view and bent and finished to the shape shown in Fig. 177. As the punch rose the stripper E forced the finished work from the punch.

By the use of a punch and die of the construction shown and described herein, wire can be bent to exact dimensions, and each piece produced will be an exact duplicate of the one preceding it. The grooves in the benders should be finished very smooth, as it is necessary to do this in order that the wire when bent shall present a smooth and shining appearance. When this is done, no difficulty will be encountered in entering the projecting ends of the staples within their respective holes. The "benders" should be left as hard as possible at all wearing points, as the bending of the wire is apt to wear them considerably when they are drawn to a temper above a light straw. When the projecting ends of the staples are required to be of a length exceeding one inch, all parts of the punch and die should be left with excess stock at all points which are required to be finished. They should then be hardened, after which they can be lapped and ground to the exact size required. By constructing them in this manner all possibility of error in size will have been overcome and the work produced will be perfectly interchangeable.

An Automatic Wire-Bending Die.

In Figs. 181 to 183 are shown views of a wire-bending and forming die which, although of a rather intricate design and expensive construction, produces results in one operation which would by simpler means necessitate two or more to accomplish. This die is used to bend and form the wire handle A of the metal bottle stopper shown in Figs. 178 to 180. The handle was made of round brass rod, ⅛ inch thick, cut into 3⅛-inch lengths and the ends turned down in the monitor, leaving square shoulders as shown.

In the punch, A was the holder, a machine steel forging turned and finished with a hole straight through the shank to

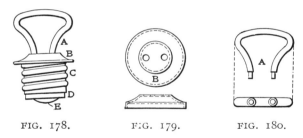

FIG. 178.   FIG. 179.   FIG. 180.

admit the stem C of the forming punch. It was also counter-bored, as shown, for the spring D and then milled across at E. The forming punch B was of tool steel, first turned so that the stem C would fit the hole in the holder, and threaded for the two adjusting nuts shown at the top. It was then chucked in the miller and the forming bending face milled and finished to templet, and the upper portion milled flat on the sides to fit the channel in the face of the holder at E. The inclined faced studs F F were then got out and finished, as shown, and let into the holder in the relative position shown. The forming and bending punch was polished and hardened and drawn to a blue at the back. The spring D was then made from heavy steel wire; the parts assembled, and the punch was complete.

The die consists of the bolster G of cast iron, planed and

milled to the shape shown and dovetailed to admit the two forming slides H H and the gibs K K.   It was also milled straight across to admit the die J, which was of tool steel, worked out, finished and hardened, inserted and held in position by the flat-head screws N N.   The slides H were of tool

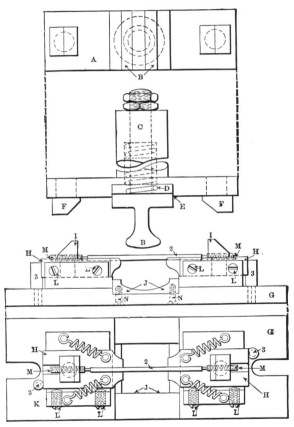

FIGS. 181 TO 183.—AUTOMATIC WIRE BENDING DIE COMPLETE.

steel, worked out to the proper shape and fitted to an easy sliding fit within the bolster. They were inserted and set in the proper position and the holes laid out for the inclined faced pieces I I. The holes were drilled and the slide hardened at the forming faces. The pieces I I were of tool steel and finished, as shown, with a hole drilled through each for the adjusting screws M M;

they were forced into the holes in the slides. After the slides were put in position and the gibs K adjusted by the screws L L, the stop-pins 3 3 were made and riven into the bolster and filed back until the slides would come back just the distance required when drawn by the springs shown on each.

We neglected to state that a half-round groove was let into the top of each slide, as a form or seat for the work to locate in. After all parts were assembled, as shown, the punch and die were set up in the press and the work 2 placed in position as shown, the screws adjusted correctly, and the press stepped. The punch descends, striking the work in the center, and causes it to spring up and hug the sides of the punch, which, continuing down further until within $\frac{1}{8}$ inch of the bottom, when the inclined faced punch studs and the die studs come in contact, causing the forming slides to move inward, the punch continuing down until the work is entirely formed and finished. As the punch ascends the springs carry the slides back to the stop-pins 3 3, and the work is removed from the punch by hand. The spiral spring D in the punch is to allow the forming punch to remain stationary while the work is being formed at the sides by the slides.

Cutting, Perforating and Shaping at One Operation.

Fig. 184 shows an open back press equipped with dies for cutting, perforating and shaping at one and the same handling the lock-cases used on satchel frames. It will be understood from the engraving that the operator pushes the metal strip into the die against an automatic finger gage, which permits of running the press continuously. After the piercing and punching, which are done in a double die, the blank is automatically moved sideways into the forming die, which finishes it and drops it out of the press at the rate of about 60 to 80 a minute. Presses of this type equipped with the "punch feed" and "finger-gage" are used extensively in the manufacture of belt hooks, tobacco tags, staples, etc. Sometimes a roll feed is used in addition for feeding in the stock.

Blanking and Stamping in a Press with Automatic Slide Feed and Ejector.

The engraving, Fig. 185, illustrates an inclined press fitted with a blanking die set in front of a stamping die for making

FIG. 184.—PRESS EQUIPPED WITH PUSH FEED, FINGER GAGE AND DIES FOR CUTTING, PERFORATING AND FORMING AT ONE AND THE SAME HANDLING LOCK CASES FOR SATCHEL FRAMES.

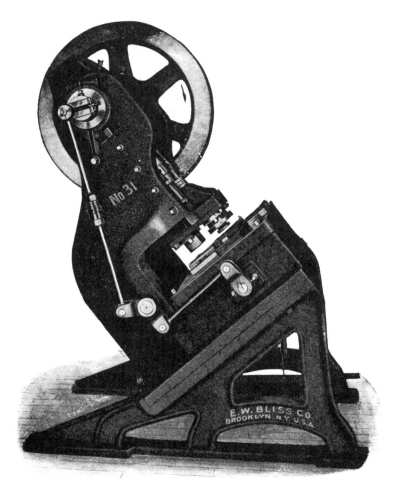

FIG. 185.—INCLINED PRESS WITH SLIDE FEED AND EJECTOR,
EQUIPPED WITH A BLANKING DIE AND A STAMPING DIE.

covers for key-opening sardine boxes. The press is set on inclined legs and the blank naturally drops back to the stamping die through gravity, but a cam-actuated slide feed is provided to insure its proper locating on the stamping die, from which, after being stamped, it is automatically ejected by a device not shown. Articles of this general character may be cut from the strip and stamped at the rate of about 50 to 60 pieces a minute.

Two Bending Dies for Flat Stock.

In Figs. 186 and 187 are shown two bending dies for bending and forming the sheet steel pierced blank shown in Fig. 188 to the shape shown in Fig. 190. As the engravings show

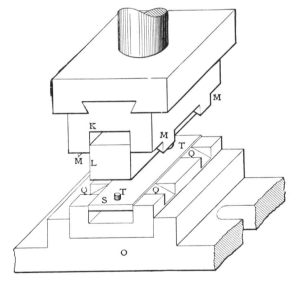

FIG. 186.—BENDING DIE FOR OPERATION, FIG. 189.

clearly the design and construction of both dies no detailed description is necessary. The first operation is the bending of the blank to the shape shown in Fig. 189, with the four wings B B B B bent to an angle of 45 degrees with the sides E E and the top A A. The punch and die used are shown in Fig. 186. The blank is placed on stripping plate S, and located by the two gage pins T T entering into two of the pierced holes D

in the blank.   Springs within the bolster keep the stripper S
at the face of the die, and strip the work when bent.   The punch

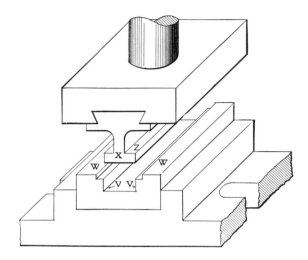

FIG. 187.—BENDING DIE FOR OPERATION, FIG. 190.

L for the bend at E is also equipped with springs which are
strong enough to allow of the punch bending the blank at this

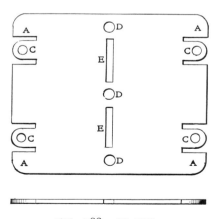
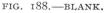

FIG. 188.—BLANK.

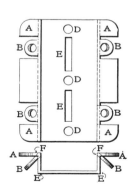

FIG. 189.—FIRST BEND.

point before it bottoms at K.   M M M M are the punch portions
for bending the wings, and Q Q Q Q the die portions for the

same. The appearance of the work after passing through this
die is shown in Fig. 189.

For the finishing operation the die, Fig. 187, is used, the
work being located at W W and as the punch
descends it is formed into the die at V V, which
causes the ends of the work to spring up and
hug the punch at X and Z, the result being the
shape shown in Fig. 190. All wearing surfaces
of both punch and die used for the two operations are draw-filed and polished smooth, after
which they are hardened and drawn slightly,
leaving them as hard as possible without danger
of cracking. The manner of fastening the
punches within the holders by dovetailing them
is far preferable and more reliable than by the
use of screws.

FIG. 190.
SECOND BEND.

An Automatic Slide Forming Die for a Sheet Metal Ferrule.

The punch and die shown in Figs. 192 to 195 are used to form
the sheet steel blank produced in the die shown in Figs. 79
and 80 Chapter III., to the shape shown in Fig. 191. As this
punch and die is of a rather intricate and elaborate type, and
as there are a number of practical points in its construction
which are essential to the successful production
of the work, it is of sufficient interest to warrant
a detailed description of its principal working
parts.

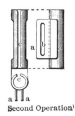

Second Operation.

FIG. 191.

The punch and die as used when in operation
are shown in Fig. 192, which shows a longitudinal cross-section of each, with the blank in position for forming. The die consists of a heavy
cast iron bolster R, which is finished with a
dovetailed channel running down its entire
length, and with a central channel at right angles to
the first to admit the forming die N. This die is of
tool steel and is shown in a plan view—as are all the other
working parts of the die—in Fig. 193. It is finished on the
face in a half-circle of the radius to which the blank is to be
formed, and has two narrow slots sunk in it to accommodate
the wings of the blank, as shown at N. It is hardened and
drawn and ground to a nice fit in the channel. Before hardening

a hole is let into the center of the bottom to accommodate the
adjusting stud V, Fig. 192. A hole is drilled straight through
the bolster at this point and enlarged and tapped at the back
to admit the spring case screw T and the spring S. By using
these parts as shown the tension of the spring can be regulated,
as can the height of the punch N also.

The two forming slides K K are of flat tool steel of the thickness shown and are finished in the following manner: A piece

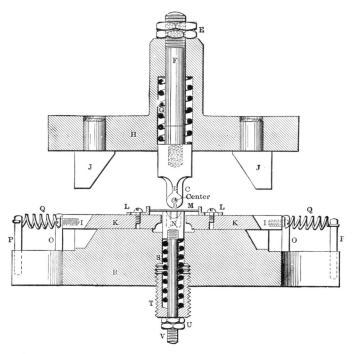

FIG. 192.—DIE FOR FORMING A SHEET METAL FERRULE.

of steel, long enough to form both slides, is first planed all over
and fitted to the dovetailed channel in the face of the bolster,
fitting it tightly. It is then strapped to the table of the milling
machine, with the sides at dead right angles with the cutter,
and a half-round groove of exactly the same radius as that in
the face of the die N let in, using the graduated dial on the
table feed screw to get the correct depth, and feeding very
slowly with a good flow of oil on the cutter, to get as smooth a

finish as possible. This done, the forming cutter is removed and a sharp saw 3-32 inch thick substituted in its stead, setting it in the dead center of the half-round groove in the work and feeding it through to within a shade of the table of the miller. The work was then removed and the two sections separated. The faces of each were then finished and polished. This method of finishing the forming faces of the slides insured their alignment with the forming portions of the die, and with each other. The angular inclined cam portion in each end was finished as shown at I I, to templet, finishing the faces to an angle of 25 degrees with the slide face and polishing them as smooth as possible. The slides were hardened at the working surfaces and drawn to a light straw, leaving the remaining portions soft. The construction of the remaining portions of the die requires no

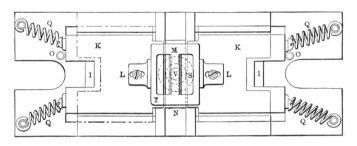

FIG. 193.—PLAN OF DIE.

description as they are simple and are shown clearly in the engravings.

The punch, as shown in Fig. 192, consists of seven parts— the holder, or body H, forged from mild steel, the two slide cams J J of tool steel, the forming punch K of the same material, the punch stud F, the adjusting nuts E, and the spiral spring G. The holder H after being chucked and faced, and the hole for the spring G and stud F let in, was strapped to the lathe face-plate and the stem trued with the hole, then turned, as shown, and the back faced. It was then set up in the miller and the sides and ends milled, and a channel let into the face to admit the forming punch K. The finishing of this punch was a nice milling job, as it serves when finished as the punch for forming the bottom of the blank and also as the horn for the sides. The method of finishing was as follows: A piece of

annealed tool steel, large enough all over to allow of finishing
it to the shape shown in Fig. 194, was first centered and placed
on the lathe centers and a narrow shoulder turned at each end
in diameter exactly one thickness of metal less than that of the
die. We now had two reliable points to work from. The punch
was then set up on the miller centers, jacked up from the bottom,
and the portion D finished with a narrow mill to the same

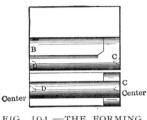

FIG. 194.—THE FORMING
PUNCH.

radius as the ends before mentioned,
finishing the punch in a perfect radius
to within 3-64 inch of each side of the
center, and ending in a stout wall at
the back C, running out and ending
in a fillet as shown. It was necessary
to have this wall at the back, because
of the frailness of the central wall B.
By moving the punch around on the
miller centers and locating and fasten-
ing as required, the back of the punch was milled true with the
circular face. The punch was then held in the miller vise and
the sides milled to fit the channel in the holder, finishing both
sides equidistant from the center of the punch face. As will be
seen, this was about as accurate and expeditious a method of
finishing of the punch as could be adopted. The circular portion
of the punch was then draw-filed, taking off all high spots, and
giving the surface a perfectly symmetrical appearance. The two
ends were then milled down and squared with the back and sides,
the hole for the punch stud F let into the center of the back
and tapped, and the punch hardened, polished and drawn to a

FIG. 195.
GAGES.

dark blue and laid aside until the other portions
were finished. The construction of the other parts
of the punch and die can be clearly understood
from the engraving without a description.

The action of this punch and die may be understood from Fig. 192. The blank is placed on
the die as shown at M, and the punch set.
As it descends the blank is formed into the die N, the
spring S being strong enough to allow of this being done
without moving the die. As the punch forms the blank, the
die descends until it bottoms. The forming punch now remains
stationary, and as the holder continues to descend the slides
commence to move in, by means of J J, until the sides of the

blank have been formed around the punch, and the face of each slide presses tightly against the wall B.   As the punch rises all parts return to their respective positions, and the finished work is slid off the punch by hand.

When dies for producing work of this type are designed and constructed in this manner, the results will be all that can be desired.   They will work well and rapidly and, what is more, turn out the maximum amount of work before requiring repairs.

A Press with Automatic Device for Tube Forming.

Fig. 196 shows a press equipped with lateral slides and movable mandrel for forming sheet-metal tubes in one operation, forming a tube 8 inches long, either straight, taper, round, oval or square, at one blow.   The toggle slides, which operate from right to left, are cam-actuated and easily adjusted for different shapes.   The mandrel, over which the tubes are formed, first descends upon the blank, bending it into a U shape and carrying it against the lower die, whereupon the forming tools attached to the lateral slides complete the operation.   Presses equipped in this manner are used extensively in the manufacture of bicycle parts, such as hubs, pedal centers, etc., also spouts, penholders, small can bodies, either round or square.

Bending and Forming Dies for Round Work.

The dies here shown and described are known as circular bending and forming dies, and are very suggestive of ways and means for upsetting and forming the edges of circular-drawn shells into a variety of difficult shapes.   The piece of work shown here in the different operations, running from Fig. 197 to 203, was used as a part of a patent fruit-jar cover.   The first operation, Fig. 197, was to blank and draw a shell of the size and shape required.   After this it was necessary to upset, bend and form the upper edge to the shape shown in Fig. 200, for which three operations were necessary.

The first, Fig. 198, was to upset or start the upper bend. The punch and die are shown in Fig. 204. A, the bolster, is of cast iron and B the die, for holding the shell, of tool steel. The construction of the parts of both punch and die can be clearly understood from the engravings.   The metal used for the shells was sheet tin .01 inch thick.   The shell C being placed

FIG. 196.—A PRESS EQUIPPED WITH LATERAL SLIDES AND MOVA-
BLE MANDREL FOR FORMING SHEET METAL TUBES IN ONE
OPERATION, FORMING A TUBE 8 INCHES LONG, EITHER STRAIGHT,
TAPER, ROUND, OVAL OR SQUARE, AT ONE BLOW.

in the die B, the punch descending causes the edge to collapse to the shape shown in Fig. 198.

For the next operation a bolster H, which would answer for all the bending operations, was made as shown in the cross-section in Fig. 205, with a plan of it in Fig. 210. It was first bored ¼ inch deep to just fit the outside of the shell at J J for a gage point in setting the punches, and then planed on the top and the two gibs L L finished and each fastened by three screws, as shown. A slide M of flat cold-rolled stock was then fitted to slide freely within L L and to locate itself against the stop K. It was bored out to just strip the work from the

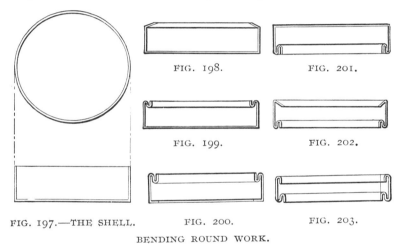

FIG. 198.

FIG. 201.

FIG. 199.

FIG. 202.

FIG. 197.—THE SHELL.

FIG. 200.

FIG. 203.

BENDING ROUND WORK.

punch, the round-head thumb-screw being used as a handle to slide it back when locating the work. The action of the punch and die for this operation is plain, as shown in Fig. 205. The punch G is worked out and finished to templet to the shape shown at K, and hardened and polished. In descending the central portion projects further, and enters the shell I before the forming commences, thereby holding the outer edge while it is formed and bent to the shape shown in Fig. 199. The operation of finishing the upper bend was done by the punch N, Fig. 206, tapering slightly, as shown, entering the work and gradually forcing it inward and finishing the bend as shown in Fig. 200. The upper bend finished, we were ready for the lower, which required three operations to complete it.

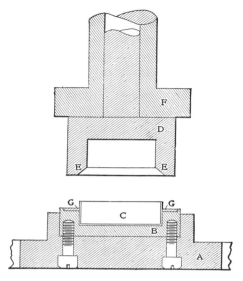

FIG. 204.—FIRST OPERATION.

The first was to blank the hole in the bottom, as shown in Fig. 201, which was done by the punch and die shown in Fig. 207. T is the bolster, U the die, inserted at T and held down

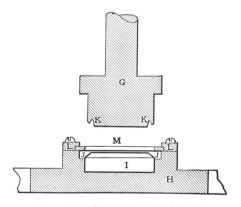

FIG. 205.—SECOND OPERATION.

by the gage plate V, which is located on the face of the bolster in a recess sunk true with the die. The work W is shown just fitting within Y. The punch X is the ordinary blanking punch, equipped with the spring rubber Z, a stripping plate Y, and O O the two screws or studs for the plate to move on. The blanking punch descends and punches the hole, and as it rises the plate Y strips the work from the punch.

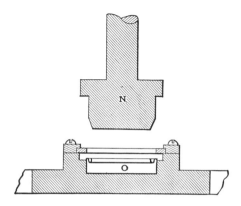

FIG. 206.—THIRD OPERATION.

The first bend is shown in Fig. 208, the punch tapering sufficiently to allow it to enter the hole in the work Q while the taper part forms it to the shape shown in Fig. 202. The next and last operation is shown in Fig. 208, the punch, taper-

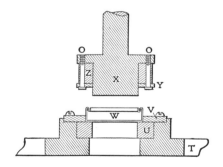

FIG. 207.—CUTTING THE HOLE.

ing slightly and then left straight, descending and finishing the bending and leaving the work as shown in Fig. 203.

It was necessary to have some means for setting the punches central with the work, and to do this the piece, Fig. 211, was made, the upper part fitting around the punch and the lower part in the recess J J in the bolster. This proved an easy and reliable means of locating them. In making the punches, templates were necessary in order to get them the proper shape

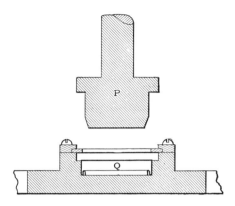

FIG. 208.—FIFTH OPERATION.

and size, as in work of this kind it is very easy to start a wrinkle, which increases with each operation and spoils the work. All the working parts must be well finished and polished

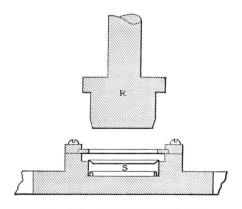

FIG. 209.—SIXTH OPERATION.

and left very hard, as the bending of sheet metal in this manner wears the punch rapidly.

Although the work looks simple enough, considerable skill

is required with the hand tool to get the proper shapes and sizes, first working down, and then trying and easing the tight spots, until the exact shape required is produced.

Of two styles of bending round work the one here described, that of decreasing from a larger diameter to a smaller, is easier than the other. This form of bending is used quite extensively in the manufacture of tinware and metal lamps, and it is sur-

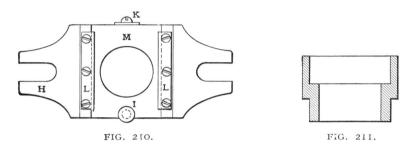

FIG. 210.   FIG. 211.

prising the variety of work and the symmetry of form that is attained when the simplicity and cheapness of the tools used are considered. The extensive use and improvement of such tools has been the chief factor in the unusual cheapness of sheet-metal ware, as formerly all this was done by spinning. The adoption and use of such tools has also increased the usefulness of the die and toolmaker. And so it is in all lines of sheet-metal work, the power press being used to-day to accomplish results that were not thought possible a few years ago.

Bending and Closing-in Dies for Round Work.

The punches and die shown in Figs. 216 and 217 are of a type in general use for bending and closing-in the rim of a drawn shell. It is of a type which is adaptable (with slight

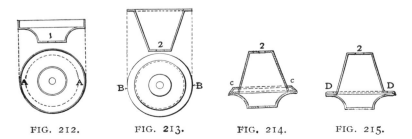

FIG. 212.   FIG. 213.   FIG. 214.   FIG. 215.

changes which readily become apparent) for a considerable number of different shapes in bending and forming round work.

As can be seen from the engraving, this particular punch
and die are used for joining the two drawn pieces, Figs. 212 and
213; that is, enclosing the drawn shell, Fig. 213, at B B within

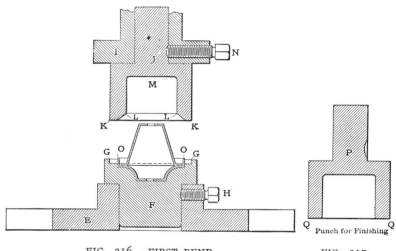

FIG. 216.—FIRST BEND.   FIG. 217.

Fig. 212 at A A, first starting or upsetting the edge A A as
shown at C C, Fig. 214, and then finishing it as shown at D D,
Fig. 215. Although these tools are of a very simple design, it
is necessary to exercise care in the finishing and sizing of the
parts, as, wherever a good job in the product is desired, close
and good work is necessary in the tools.

*Foot Presses and Outfit of Dies for Producing Five-Gallon
Petroleum Cans.*

In Figs. 218 to 223 are shown a number of foot power presses
as equipped with punches and dies for the different operations
necessary in the production of five-gallon petroleum cans. As
the half-tones show clearly the construction of the dies and the
manner in which they are located, fastened and used, no description will be attempted.

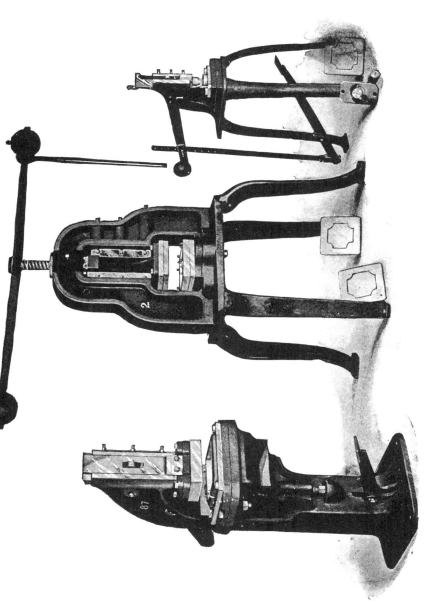

FIG. 218.—BLANKING OPERATION.

FIG. 219.—BENDING AND FORMING OPERATION.

FIG. 220.—PIERCING OPERATION.

FOOT POWER PRESSES AND OUTFIT OF DIES FOR PRODUCING FIVE-GALLON PETROLEUM CANS.

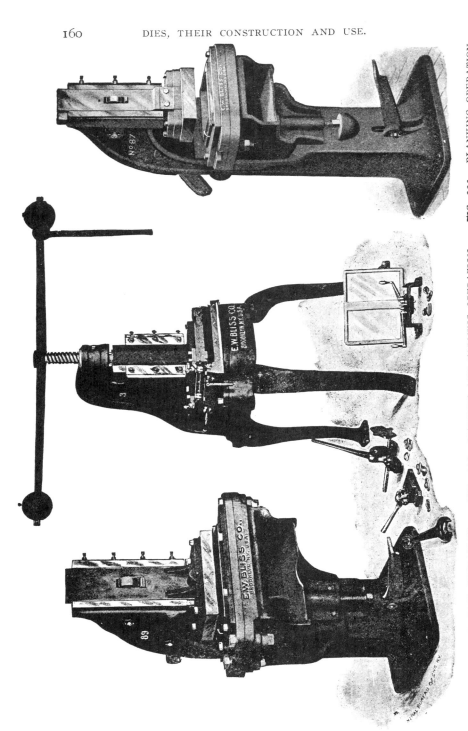

FIG. 221.—BLANKING OPERATION.   FIG. 222.—BENDING AND FORMING OPERATION.   FIG. 223.—BLANKING OPERATION.

FOOT POWER PRESSES AND OUTFIT OF DIES FOR PRODUCING FIVE-GALLON PETROLEUM CANS.

A Double Crank Press and Outfit of Bending Dies.

The press shown in Fig. 224 is a double crank press and the "horns" and "forces", with which it is equipped are used for setting down the inside corner seams of even bodies. Presses of this type and fixtures of the class shown are used to the best advantage for operations in the manufacture of heavy pieced iron ware, such as setting down lock seams on very heavy stock.

A Pick-Eye Forming Press with Dies in Position.

The press shown in Fig. 225 with a set of dies in position is used for the manufacture of such articles as hammers, axes, pick-axes, adzes, mattocks, hoes, etc. A series of dies of the type shown is set side by side, and the article is forged in one or several heats by passing it through from one die to another. The slide or ram of the press can be quickly and accurately raised and lowered by means of an adjustment which is arranged to operate both crank connections simultaneously.

Four "Follow" Bending and Forming Dies.

The dies shown in engravings herein, while not exactly "bending" dies in the proper sense of the term, may be shown and described in this chapter because of the fact that the work principally accomplished by their use is bending. The construction of dies of this class is similar to that followed out in "gang" dies, and as the operations on the work as it passes through them are progressive they are known as "follow" dies. The dies shown here show four adaptations of the "follow" principle for articles or parts of sheet metal to be pierced, bent, formed or drawn and finished complete in one operation or handling.

The punch and die shown in Figs. 227 and 228 produce the formed and pierced blank shown in two views in Fig. 226. This blank has two holes B B, the ends are trimmed and the center is bent and formed to the shape shown at A. The metal used came in strips or rolls of the required width. As first inserted within the die it fitted between the gage plates and against the stop-pin T. At the first down stroke of the ram the forming punch M encounters the metal and bends and forms it into the die R, and, bottoming there, remains stationary while the two

FIG. 224.—DOUBLE CRANK PRESS AND OUTFIT OF DIES FOR BENDING
DOWN CORNER SEAMS OF SQUARE BOX WORK.

FIG. 225.—PICK-EYE FORMING PRESS WITH DIES IN POSITION.

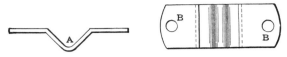

FIG. 226.

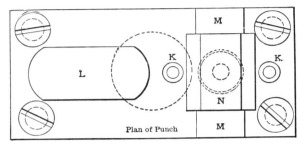

FIG. 227.

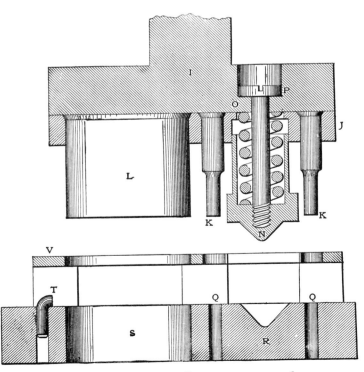

FIG. 228.—' FOLLOW " DIE FOR FIG. 226.

holes B B are pierced by the punches K K and the end of the
stock is trimmed by the punch L. At the next stroke the
metal is held against the stop-pin and the formed and finished
blank is punched out. The position of the stop-pin T must
be accurately located, as the metal is first forced against it by

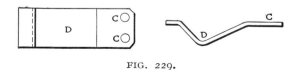

FIG. 229.

hand and then drawn away some distance by the action of the
forming punch N.

The punch and die, Figs. 230 to 232, for producing the bent
flat spring shown in Fig. 229, are more simple than the first.
They pierce the holes C C, make the bend at D, cut off the
piece and trim the corners. G G are the piercing dies, H the
forming or bending die, and X and I the trimming and cutting-
off dies. For the forming die H the shape required is milled
across the face of the die. The trimming die I is also made
wider than necessary, as shown, and is made to allow the back
end of the work to be cornered and the front end to be cut
off square. The stop K, of flat cold-rolled stock fastened to

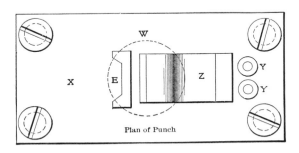

FIG. 230.

the end of the die, is made adjustable to allow of using the one
die for producing springs of different lengths. The punch is
simple, consisting of the two piercing punches Y Y, the bending
punch Z and the trimming punch E, all fastened in the pad X.
The bending punch Z is shorter than the piercing punches and

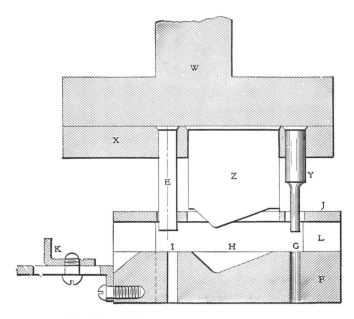

FIG. 231.—"FOLLOW" DIE FOR FIG. 229.

cut-off punch. This is done so that the two holes will have been pierced and the finished piece cut off before the next one is bent. When the die is in use the strip of metal, which is the

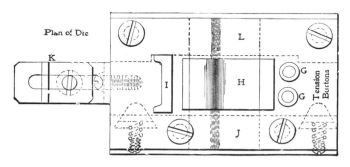

FIG. 232.

exact width required, is inserted beneath the stripper and against the stop K. As the punch descends the two holes are pierced first and the end of the strip is trimmed, and the work bent. At the next stroke the finished piece is cut off.

The only bad feature in a die of this construction is that it does not easily allow of frequent grinding. To compensate for this defect it is best to leave the die as hard as possible and to

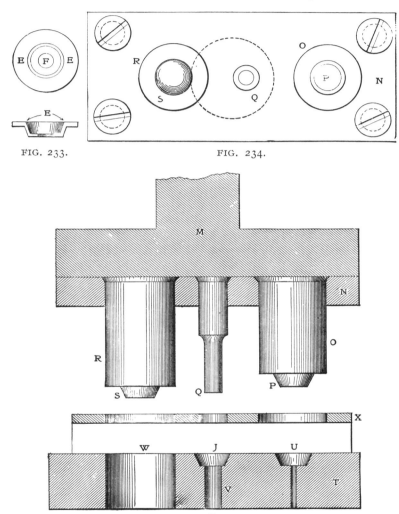

FIG. 233.   FIG. 234.

FIG. 235.—"FOLLOW" DIE FOR FIG. 233.

exercise care when setting it up in the press. We have seen dies of this type which have produced from seventy to eighty thousand blanks without requiring grinding.

The punch and die, Figs 234 to 237, produce the piece shown in Fig. 233. This die instead of bending the work draws and forms to the shape of a shallow shell, pierces the hole in the center E and punches out the finished piece. The die comprises the drawing die U, the piercing die J and the blanking die W. When laying out the centers for the three dies the distances between them had to be determined according to the amount of

FIG. 236.

metal required to form the shell portion of the work. The length of the drawing punch P is just sufficient to draw the shell and flatten the rim on the face of the die. The pilot pin S in the punch R is to locate the work central within the blanking die after the hole has been pierced. The blanking punch is left the longest for reasons which will be understood from the description of the operation of the die.

After the punch and die are set up the strip of metal to

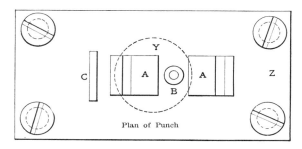

FIG. 237.

be worked is first entered beneath the stripper, far enough to allow the first shell to be drawn at the first stroke. The metal is then moved along and the shell drawn at the first stroke is centered and located within the locating portion of the piercing die. At the next stroke the hole is pierced and a second shell drawn. The stock is then fed forward another space, and, the punch descending, the blanking punch R enters the die first, thereby allowing most of the stock for the shell to be drawn from

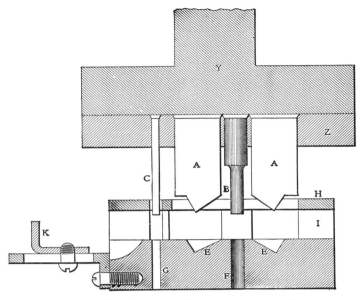

FIG. 238.—"FOLLOW" DIE FOR FIG. 236.

the sides. Punch P and punch O are in separate pieces to facilitate grinding, so that when the piercing and blanking punches
are ground the face of O may also be ground so as to keep it
the proper length in relation to the other two.

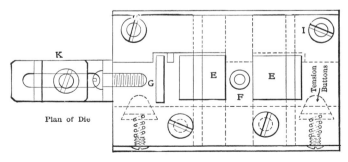

FIG. 239.

The die, Figs. 237 to 239, differs from the other three, as
it has to bend and form at two points H H, pierce a hole in the
center at F and cut off the finished piece, thus necessitating
drawing the metal for the bends from both ends. D is the die

proper, E E the bending dies, F the piercing die and G the cutting-off die. K is the adjustable stop, I I the two gage plates,
and H the stripper plate. The punch consists of the stem or
holder Y, the pad Z, the bending and forming punches A A and
the cutting-off punch C. The bending punches have the piercing
punch let into the center between them. The cutting punch C
and the piercing punch B are left ⅛ inch longer than the others,
so that the forming punches A A will accomplish their work
after the others have entered the die.

The stock to be worked is inserted far enough for the end
to project slightly beyond the edge of the cutting die G.   As
the punch descends the piercing punch pierces the hole and the
cutting-off punch trims the end of the stock. The punch continuing downward, the forming punches A A form the work
into the dies E E, while the piercing punch having passed
through the stock and into the die, holds the metal true and
central while the bends are being accomplished.   At the next
stroke the stock is pushed against the stop K and a finished
piece is cut out and dropped.

A Special Forming Die.

In Figs. 240 and 241 is shown a special forming die for forming the piece shown "before" and "after" in Figs. 242 and 243.

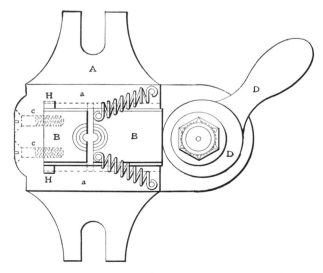

FIG. 240.—PLAN OF SPECIAL FORMING DIE.

The piece X was made in the screw machine from round brass rod, with a neck turned smaller than the body, and, as it was impossible to form the head in a solid die, the laterally opening and closing die here shown was made.

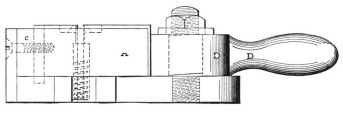

FIG. 241.

The base of the bolster A was ½ inch thick, and the central portion a, 1 inch thicker, this portion being planed dovetailing for the die to slide in. The casting has openings provided at H H for the tool clearance when planing the die channel. The two halves of the die are machined together in a single piece, and

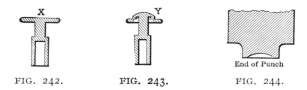

FIG. 242.   FIG. 243.   FIG. 244.

after fitting into the bolster, are cut apart with a narrow milling saw. One half of the die is fastened securely to the back of the channel in the bolster by the flat-head screws C C. The other half of the die is to slide in and out, being forcibly closed by

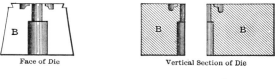

FIG. 245.   FIG. 246.

the handled eccentric D, and pulled open by the springs on each side. When the dies were properly fitted and closed tightly, the bolster was strapped on the face-plate of the lathe, the hole for the neck of the piece drilled, and the shape for the under side of the head worked out on the face of the die with hand tools, after which it was lapped smooth. The larger portion of the hole is counterbored from the under side. The depth of the smaller hole in the dies, which clamps the neck of the piece to be headed, is shorter than the length of the neck, so that the piece to be formed will rise slightly above the face of the dies before the lateral movement of the half die in opening occurs. A hole is drilled in the bottom of the bolster concentric with the finished hole in the die, and a pin is driven in with a loosely fitting spring around it to serve as a knockout for the finished work. A section of the end of the punch is shown, the finishing of which was a job of simple lathe work, requiring no special mention.

Two Can-Body Bending and Forming Machines.

The machine shown in Fig. 247 is used for forming the

FIG. 247.—CAN-BODY FORMING MACHINE, FOR BENDING AND FORMING THE BODIES OF SQUARE, OBLONG, CONICAL AND PYRAMIDAL CANS, ALLOWING SIDE SEAM TO BE SOLDERED WHILE BODY IS CLAMPED IN FORMING PARTS.

bodies of square, conical and pyramidal cans and to allow of soldering the side seam while the body is securely clamped in the forming fixtures. When the hand levers of the outside forming parts are thrown back the horn or inside former contracts, thus permitting the easy removal of the finished body. The con-

FIG. 248.—CAN-BODY FORMING MACHINE FOR CANS WITH LAPPED OR LOCKED SIDE SEAMS.

struction and arrangement of the working parts are such as to insure uniformity of size and rapidity of production.

The machine shown in Fig. 248 is very extensively used when equipped with fixtures of the type shown, for forming the bodies of square, oblong, conical and pyramidal cans, which are to be finished with either lapped or locked side seams. The manner in which the work is accomplished in these machines can be intelligently understood from the illustrations.

An Inclined Press Equipped for Stamping and Bending Body
Blanks for Petroleum Cans.

In Fig. 249 is shown an inclined press equipped with a set of
dies for the production of petroleum can-body blanks.   The
blanks as produced are shown on the floor at the back of the

FIG. 249.—INCLINED PRESS WITH PANEL-PRESSING DIE, HOOK-FORM-
ING ATTACHMENT, AUTOMATIC TRIP-GAGE AND BENDING DEVICE.

press.   With a press of this type equipped as shown, an experienced operator can feed the blanks, stamp the panels, prepare
the hooks and bend 1,400 body blanks per day.

A Novel Bending and Forming Die.

The punch and die shown in Figs. 250 to 253 was used to

bend and form the two extensions A A of the blank shown in Fig. 59, chapter III., to the circular shape shown in Fig. 60 of the same chapter, and also to bend the end C C at right angles with the body in one operation, and as it shows a novel and rapid method for accomplishing the results desired it is worthy of attention. It is no simple job to bend and form a blank to the shape shown in one operation, but by means of the die shown it was accomplished with ease. The principle of constructing the

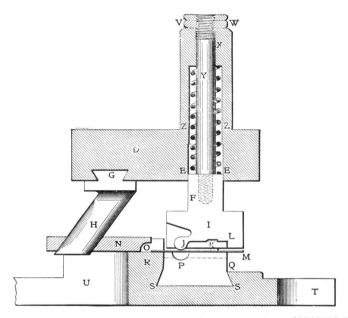

FIG. 250.—VERTICAL CROSS-SECTION OF BENDING AND FORMING DIE.

parts for forming the circular parts is somewhat similar to that of another die shown in this chapter, but the application of it is entirely different. As the engravings show all that is necessary in order to clearly understand the construction of the parts, we will confine ourselves to the description of its operation and use.

The manner in which the forming and bending of the blank is accomplished can be understood from the sectional view of the punch and die in Fig. 250, which shows the blank in position at M on the die P, it being located by the locator K. The inclined stud is within the slide and as the punch descends, the portion J bends the two ends A A of the blank into the die P, which causes them to spring clear of the forming slides N and

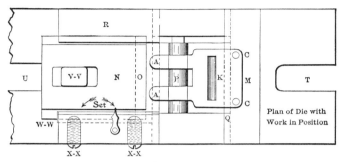

FIG. 251.

O, at the same time the portion L of the punch bends the opposite end of the blank down over the edge of the die at Q. As the punch I bottoms on the die, it remains stationary while the holder continues to descend, and with it the inclined stud, which

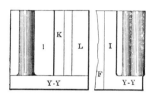

FIG. 252.—THE PUNCH.

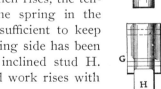

FIG. 253.

causes the forming slide to move inward and form the ends A A over the punch at J, thereby finishing the ends to the shape required. As the punch rises, the tension of the spring in the holder is sufficient to keep the punch I stationary until the forming side has been moved back out of its way by the inclined stud H. The punch then rises and the finished work rises with it and is slid off by hand.

This punch and die can be operated very rapidly, and when once it has been set correctly, it is impossible to produce anything but good work in exact duplication. We do not think that the results accomplished by this die in one operation could be attained by any other means in as simple, practical and inexpensive, as well as rapid manner, and as such we think the design and method of construction could be adopted to advantage for the rapid production of a large variety of bent and formed blanks of the type shown, which it is impossible to produce in one operation by dies of simpler construction.

CHAPTER VI.

The Use of Perforating Dies.

The construction of punches and dies for piercing or perforating sheet metal is comparatively simple and, as no intricate methods are involved, we will confine ourselves to describing a few sets of dies and to the setting forth of the most approved means for the accomplishment of the desired results, from the punching of a single hole to the multiple punching of any number of holes. The construction of the dies is usually similar to that of the "gang" type, and they are used for operations on work ranging from ornamental thin sheet metal articles to the punching of holes in steel beams and boiler-plates. The holes pierced may be of any shape and spaced as desired. Often a number of small blanks are produced at each stroke of the press by dies of this class, a sheet of metal of the required width being fed to the dies automatically. Perforated sheets of different metals are now in great demand and are used for a variety of purposes too numerous to mention.

The Construction of a Simple Piercing Punch and Die.

In Figs. 254 and 255 respectively we show a sectional view of a piercing punch and die and a plan view of the punch. This die was used for piercing the six holes R and the large one in the center of the drawn shell shown in Figs. 256, 257. The die B made of tool steel with a hole bored through the center was set upon the dividing head of the miller and the six holes were indexed, centered and drilled. The die was then hardened and drawn and the holes ground and lapped to size—grinding the large one and lapping the six small ones. The bolster A was bored to admit the die B with a clearance hole in the base, two holes E E being drilled in the ends and one bored at the top to admit the gage plate C. This was fastened to the die B and within A by six round head screws D D, the face of B was ground, the various parts assembled and the die was complete.

The punch consists of a cast iron holder F, turned and finished, and of the hardened and ground central punch G, which was let into a hole in the center shouldering against the face of the holder, as shown, and fastened by a large set-screw, not

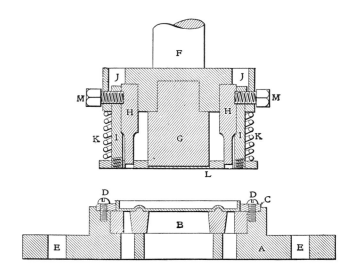

FIG. 254.—SIMPLE PIERCING DIE.

shown. The holes for the six small punches H were transferred through the die B to the face of the holder F and drilled and

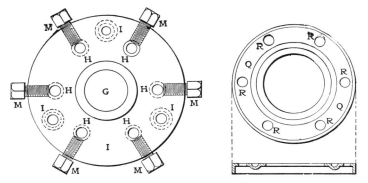

FIG. 255.—PLAN OF PUNCH.   FIGS. 256 AND 257.—THE WORK.

reamed to size, after which the hardened and ground punches were let in and fastened by the set-screws M.

Now came the stripper plate L, for stripping the work from the punches, which fitted over them freely. See Figs. 254 and 255. The studs I I I with heads 3-16 inch larger in diameter than the bodies were screwed into the plate L; three holes J J J were drilled in F to allow them to move up and down freely, and

Fig. 1—Steel Range Front

Fig. 2—Colander

Fig. 3
Milk
Skimmer

Fig. 4—Flat Skimmer

Fig. 5—Pepper Top

Fig. 6—Colander

Fig. 7
Gasolene Burner Shell

Fig. 8
Burner
Gallery

Fig. 9—Can Top

Fig. 10
Can Top

Fig. 11—Steamer Bottom

Fig. 12—Grater

Fig. 13—Strainer

Fig. 14
Perforated Strip

Fig 15
Perforated Sheet

Trade No.	Hole Diameter	Stubs Drill Gauge	Holes per Inch	Holes in 2 Rows 20-in. Sheet	Approx. Value per Hole	Approx. Value Complete Die
0	.024	72	20	800	......	......
1	.031	67	18	720	......	......
2	.037	62	15	600	......	......
3	.052	55	12	480	......	......
4	.070	50	9	360	......	......
5	.070	50	7	280	......	......
6	.1015	38	7	280	......	......

Standard Perforations for Tin Plate

FIG. 258.—SAMPLES OF PERFORATING DIE WORK.

were counterbored half-way down to allow the heads I I I to shoulder and to keep the plate L even with the face of the punches. The three spiral springs K K K were slipped over the studs I and the tools set up in the press. The work was now placed within the gage plate C, the punch descending, the large punch G blanking the center hole and entering the die first, and continuing down until the small punches had pierced the work. On the up stroke the work was stripped from the punches by the stripper plate L actuated by the springs K K K.

Piercing Two Holes on Opposite Sides of Drawn Shells.

In Fig. 259 is shown a horizontal two-slide foot press equipped with die and punches for punching simultaneously two holes or

FIG. 259.—HORIZONTAL TWO-SLIDE FOOT PRESS.

slots on opposite sides of drawn shells. As the half-tone shows everything plainly, very little description is necessary. The die is located in the center and is made with cutting edges on opposite sides and a clearance hole through the bottom as an escape for the scrap or punchings. The punches are of steel rod and are located and fastened in punch holders or chucks which are adjustable and mounted on slides which are provided with adjustable gibs. Each slide, as shown, is equipped with an adjustable stop to allow of piercing shells of different diameters. Dies of this type when used in a machine of the class shown are very convenient for rapidly and accurately piercing shells for lampburners, satchel locks, and a variety of other shells requiring holes punched on opposite sides.

Fixtures for Perforating Burners and Other Shells.

Figs. 260 to 264 show five different sets of perforating fixtures in position on presses for perforating burner shells, etc. Fixtures of this type are used very extensively for work which it is desired to perforate all around. The construction of the punches, dies and fixtures used requires little description as the half-tones show nearly all that is necessary for an intelligent understanding of their adaptation and use.

These attachments shown here represent only a few of many perforating devices which are used for sheet metal shells of various shapes. The attachments shown in Figs. 260 and 261 are made for taper and crowning shells, which necessitates the setting of die holder and rotating device at an angle to the lower face of the slide. The other attachments are for perforating cylindrical work. For perforating special shapes of shells special attachments have to be devised. The number of holes perforated at each stroke depends upon the shape of the shell operated upon.

In attachments of the type shown the perforating die, with a chuck of suitable shape, is mounted on a die-holder, and a ratchet having teeth spaced to suit the spacing of the holes desired in the shells, is mounted and arranged to rotate the shell at each stroke of the slide. By the use of such attachments perforating may be done at the rate of 150 to 200 strokes a minute, according to the size of the shell and its shape.

The adjustments of the parts of these perforating attachments are easily and quickly made, so that but a short time is required to change the attachments from one style of shell to another. Presses in which such attachments are used are often furnished with a latch lock for the clutch connection, which is automatically released after each complete revolution of the article on the per-

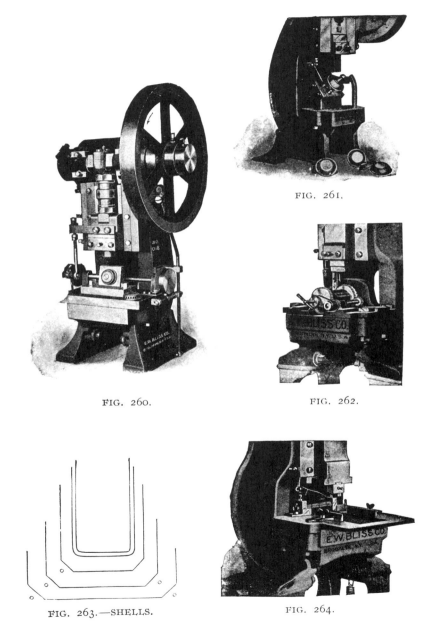

FIG. 261.

FIG. 260.

FIG. 262.

FIG. 263.—SHELLS.

FIG. 264.

FIXTURES FOR PERFORATING BURNERS AND OTHER SHELLS.

forating chuck, thus stopping the press automatically after the requisite results and number of strokes have been made.

Press With Cam-Actuated Stripper for Perforating Sheet Metal.

For perforating articles of considerable size or flat plates which are to be afterward drawn and formed to shape, or left flat as the case may be, dies of the usual construction will not do, as on such dies stationary strippers are used and they are liable to distort the metal punched by them, often to such an extent as to require subsequent straightening.

To overcome this defect, a press with a cam-actuated stripper should be used, especially on accurate work such as parts of clocks, electric instruments, etc. A press equipped in this manner is shown in Fig. 265. As shown, the stripping device is such as to leave a clear space between the punch and die, thus allowing of the operator manipulating and observing the work quickly and accurately. The action of the stripper when the press is being operated is as follows: The stripper plate strikes the blank first, or article as the case may be, straightening and clamping it before the punches enter, and holding it under pressure while the punching and stripping are being accomplished. In this manner the blank or formed piece comes out perfectly straight or true. The punches used in a press of this type may be made considerably shorter than where a die with a stationary stripper is used, thus making them considerably more resistant and durable. Also, in this manner, a smaller hole in proportion to the thickness of stock may be pierced, because of the close support which is given to the punches by the movable stripper up to the point where they enter the stock.

Piercing and Blanking Armature Disks in One Operation.

In Fig. 266 we show a set of dies as located in an inclinable press for accurately piercing and blanking armature disks for small generators and motors. The press is equipped with an automatic knock-out and its inclined position allows of the blank after being punched and pierced being lifted out of the die and sliding off at the back by gravity. The pierced blanks are usually produced by dies of this type from strips sheared to the necessary width. As shown, the construction of the dies is such as to allow of the outside and the inside of the disk being punched simultaneously, after which it is held between the face of the blanking punch and the face of the pad and descends far enough to allow of the piercing punches, which are located around the die, piercing the holes. The finished disks as produced by dies of this construction are shown on the floor beside the press.

FIG. 265.—PRESS WITH CAM-ACTUATED STRIPPER FOR PERFORATING SHEET METAL.

A Quadruplicate Automatic Slide Die for Piercing Conical Shells.

The die shown in Figs. 267 to 271 was used for the economic production of a pierced brass shell which was being manufactured in large lots and which formed the draft regulator of a new burner of the "Bunsen" type. As the chief feature sought in this line of manufacture is the reduction of cost and the elimination of as many operations as possible, a die which allows the

FIG. 266.—INCLINABLE ARMATURE DISK-CUTTING PRESS, WITH POSITIVE KNOCK-OUT DEVICES FOR PUNCH AND DIE.

accomplishment in one that which usually requires three or more operations cannot fail to interest.

The shell to be pierced was of conical shape, as shown in the section P P, Fig. 267, and was blanked and drawn and a hole pierced in the bottom at Q in a previous operation. To finish the shell it was necessary to pierce it at four points equidistant around the conical portion with an oblong slot I and two circular holes J J on each of the four sides. To accomplish this in one operation the die, Fig. 267, was constructed. A plan of the die is shown in Fig. 268, and of the inclined studs and holder in Fig. 269. The die is of the automatic slide type, quadruplicate in action, punching from four sides at the same time by means of four slides, in each of which is located a set of punches, which

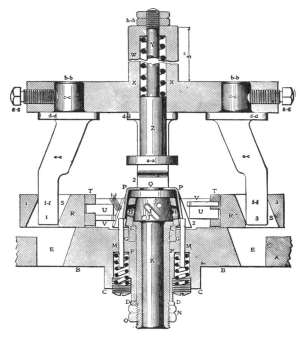

FIG. 267.—VERTICAL SECTION OF DIE.

are worked back and forth by means of inclined studs which are located and fastened within a holder, which is in turn located and fastened within the press ram.

All the parts of the die proper are contained within a holder or base A A. This base resembles the usual die bolster, but instead of being cast iron was a forging of wrought iron, for reasons which are at once obvious. This forging was finished with a circular raised portion and with an extension to the base at each end for fastening it to the press bolster. Before starting to ma-

chine the holder further the piercing die H H was got out. A
piece of round annealed steel about 2 inches long and the same in
diameter was first bored to the shape and size shown, terminating
in a shoulder at L L, and then finished with a hole of smaller
diameter straight through for the clamping sleeve. The die was
then turned outside and the ends were finished to the shape shown

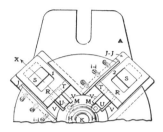 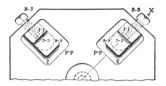

FIG. 268.—PLAN OF LOWER   FIG. 269.—PLAN OF UPPER
SECTION.   SECTION.

in the detail drawing, Fig. 271—that is, to fit tightly the inside of
the shell to be pierced and then reduced for the remainder of
its length to the diameter shown. The outside was then nicely
polished and we were ready to locate and finish the four sets of
piercing dies.

The positions in which these dies are located and the manner in which they were worked out can be understood from Fig.

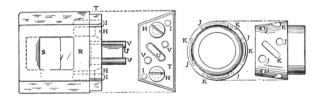

FIG. 270.—PUNCH SLIDE.   FIG. 271.—DIE PROPER.

267. A mild steel stud was turned with a taper stem to fit the
dividing head of the universal milling machine and the other end
to a driving fit within the smallest end of the die blank. The arbor or stud was then driven into the die blank and the taper end
located within the head of the milling machine, which was then
set vertical. The holes for the round piercing dies J were then
located and spotted and drilled by manipulating the feed screws

and getting the distances, which had been previously deter nined, finishing the holes within a reaming size of the diameter required.   The locating of the oblong piercing dies was accomplished in the same manner, they being located directly in the center of the blank in each position.   The accomplishment of these separate results, of course, entailed considerable tin e, patience, skill and a thorough knowledge of the use of the universal miller.

After all the foregoing had been accomplished and the holes being drilled at what were to be the extreme ends of the oblong piercing slot K, the die was removed from the arbor and the round piercing dies were reamed to size, reaming each two holes which were in line with each other at the same time.   A slight clearance was then given these dies by inserting a small taper reamer through the holes from the inside and holding the projecting end in the drill chuck while reaming the holes.   The oblong dies were then worked out in the usual manner, first by hand, with a file, and then finished in line with their opposites and to duplicate size by forcing a broach through them.   The die was then hardened in oil, and drawn to a medium straw temper and the outside ground, which gave all the dies a sharp cutting edge and allowed the shells to fit nicely over it.

The forging A A for the die holder was now machined.   It was first strapped to the lathe face-plate with the bottom up and finished at B B as a locating surface, at C C for the stripper pin adjusting screws and at D D for the clamping nuts M.   A hole was bored straight through for the clamping sleeve K and reamed to size.   The forging was then reversed on the face-plate, a cut was taken off the top, and a seat was bored to locate the die in, as shown at G G, the outside of the round top was turned and the ends A A were faced, this being possible at the one setting as the work was located and fastened to the face-plate by means of screws let in from the back.

We were now ready to mill the four slide-ways for the four punch slides.   This was done by strapping the forging on parallels to the table of the universal miller; milling the slide-ways by means of an angular cutter and the vertical attachment, first locating the work so that the slide-ways would come as central as possible with the die seat at G G, then milling straight across, and finishing the two opposite slide-ways as shown; finishing so as to allow of a gib for each slide.   The two remaining channels were milled by feeding the work against the cutter at right angles to the first two.   Care was taken to have the cutter sharp, and a good flow of oil running on it while cutting, so as to get as smooth a finish as possible.

The hollow clamping sleeve K for locating and clamping the die was of tool steel and was first bored and reamed to the diameter shown, as an outlet for the punchings.   It was then turned on the outside to fit snugly the center hole in the holder at F F, with a head at L L to clamp the die down, and threaded at the other end for the nuts.   Holes were drilled around the inside of the holder on a radius shown in the plan view, Fig. 268, for the four stripper pins M, drilling all holes entirely through, and enlarging and tapping them at the back for the spring adjusting screws.

The four punch slides or rams 1, 2, 3 and 4 were of tool steel, milled all over and fitted to the channels in the holder.   The inclined holes in each slide were then worked out, finishing each to the same angle with the slide face and polishing the wearing surfaces as smooth as possible.   The locating of the punches within the pads T and the locating in turn of the pads on the slide faces were accomplished as follows: Four pieces of mild steel were planed up and milled to the angular shape of the slide face, only smaller all around, as shown at T in the detail, Fig. 270.   The four oblong piercing punches U were finished to fit the die, hardened and drawn to a dark blue temper, and one let into and located in the center of each of the pads, getting them in the approximately correct position; they were then upset or riveted at the back to prevent pulling out when in action.   Next the piercing die H H was located and fastened within the holder and adjusted until the pads would rest squarely against the faces of the punch slides, and the punches enter the dies nicely.   Each of the pads was then securely clamped to its slide face, the slides were removed from the holder and the holes drilled for the two dowels I I in each and into the slide.   These holes were then reamed and the pins driven into the pad, fitting snugly into the holes in the slides.   We now had a perfect alignment of the oblong piercing punches with their dies.   The two flat-head screws were then let into each pad and slide, and the pads were relocated to their respective slides.

The holes for the two piercing punches in each pad at V V were located by entering a slide into its channel and moving it up until the oblong piercing punch had entered the die; then, by using an extra long drill of Stubs wire, the holes were located and spotted in perfect alignment, drilling through the dies and allowing the center drill to enter the hole opposite the proper piercing die and project through the piercing die and spot the pad. This operation was repeated until the holes for all the punches had been located. The holes were then drilled and reamed to the required size, slightly countersunk at the back, and the punches of Stubs wire let in and upset, leaving them somewhat longer than the oblong piercing punches. The stripping pins were then got out, as were also the springs and adjusting screws, and all parts were assembled within the holder A A.

There now remained to finish the four inclined studs 1, 2, 3 and 4, the holder for them and the spring pad Z for holding and locating the work on the die while being pierced. The inclined studs were of tool steel, and a brief description will suffice. The portions f f are straight, so as to move down a certain distance while the work is being secured on the die by the spring pad Z, and are then finished at e e to the same incline as the holes S in the slides. They are finished with a stiff wire shoulder at d d, to locate against the face of the holder, and the end c c is turned to fit tightly. The locating, spacing and finishing of these four stud holes in the holder was accomplished to the desired degree of accuracy, by chucking the holder by the stem in the dividing head of the universal milling machine, indexing for four and spotting the holes and afterward drilling and reaming them to the size required on the drill press.

The drawn shell is slipped over the die by the hand of the press operator and rests on the tops of the four stripping pins M, two of which can be seen. As the operator places his foot on the treadle, the holder, in which are located the inclined studs, commences to descend, all parts of the die remaining stationary until the spring pad a a strikes the work and commences to force it down on the die, when the inclined portions of the slide studs strike the faces of the inclined holes in the slides and commence to move them inward. The spring pad a a having meanwhile forced the shell down on the die remains stationary, while the holder in which it is located continues to descend and the inclined studs move the slides toward the die, all the punches pierce the work and enter the die. The inclined stud holder then ascends and the slides move backward, and, as the piercing punches clear the work, the spring pad a a rises from the shell, which is in turn stripped from the die by the springs under the four stripper pins M, and the spring left in the metal by the piercing is sufficient to cause the shell to spring clear of the die as soon as the stripper pins loosen it, and, as the press is tilted or inclined, the pierced shell drops off at the back and another can be instantly located.

Regular and Staggered Perforating.

In Figs. 272 to 287 are shown a number of samples of perforated metal. As shown, some of the patterns are staggered and others are regular; to produce them a single gang or row of punches or a double row are used. When a double gang of punches and dies are used the metal is usually fed automatically by means of a roller feed to a press of the type shown in Fig. 288. The construction of the punches and dies used in a press of this kind is such as to allow of removing any one of a number of punches or dies without disturbing the others. The punches are usually located in a cast iron holder which is fitted to a dovetailed channel in the face of the press ram. The punches are short and stocky and are fastened by set screws. The dies are tool steel bushings hardened and ground and let into holes drilled and reamed in a bolster of similar construction to that used for the punches. The bushings are also fastened by set screws. The press shown in Fig. 288 will punch one hundred and fifty-four holes in ¼-inch plate at each stroke of the ram. It is provided with a roller attachment consisting of four adjustable rolls, 6 inches in diameter and 54 inches long, which feeds the stock automatically in multiples of sixteenths of an inch up to 4 inches. For heavy work the back gears are used, while for lighter work they are thrown out so as to give a higher speed. The slide adjustment is such as to allow of raising or lowering it to overcome the shortening of the punches through wear.

Perforating Press with Automatic Spacing Table.

Fig. 289 shows another type of press used for perforating flat sheets of metal. A sample of the work accomplished in this press is shown in the same figure. The punches and dies used on this job are shown located and fastened within the press and their construction is plainly shown. The press as equipped punches a row of forty-three ½-inch square holes, 3-16-inch

FIGS. 272 TO 277.—NEEDLE SLOT SCREENS—SAMPLES OF
PERFORATED METAL.

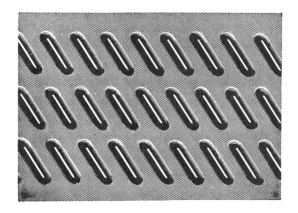

FIGS. 278 TO 281.—SAMPLES OF PERFORATED METAL.

FIGS. 282 TO 287.—SAMPLES OF STAGGERED PERFORATIONS
IN SHEET METAL.

spaces, in $\frac{1}{4}$-inch plate and feeds the plate forward for the next row. When square or irregular shaped holes are to be punched, as shown here, the dies are usually worked out in one long piece of tool steel or a number of segments are used, as it would be impossible to secure a perfect alignment between all

FIG. 288.—PRESS MILL ROLLER FEED FOR PERFORATING.

punches and dies where bushings were used, because of the irregular shape of the dies.

Double Roll Feed Perforating Press Having Lateral Feed for Staggered Patterns in Perforated Metal.

When irregular or staggered patterns are to be produced in perforated metal by means of a single row or gang of punches and dies, a press with a roll feed having a lateral motion must be used. We show a press of this type in Fig. 292. This press equipped with suitable tools will punch 240 $\frac{1}{8}$-inch holes in 1-16-inch plate, staggering the pattern as the metal is fed. It is equipped with a cam-actuated stripper and the feed rolls are provided with a side motion which automatically shifts the metal sideways at each stroke, thus allowing of perforating a staggered pattern, Fig. 290, by means of a single row or gang of dies. This reciprocating motion which shifts the feed rolls can be easily adjusted for different patterns, and should amount in each case to one-half the distance between the centers of the holes in the dies. The expense of constructing dies for use in a press of this type, embodying, as it does, one-half of the holes and punches that would otherwise be required, is about one-half the usual cost. By omitting the intermediate holes in the dies the remaining ones are far enough apart to allow of using steel

FIG. 289.—PERFORATING PRESS WITH AUTOMATIC SPACING TABLE.

bushings in a machine steel or cast iron holder, as shown in Fig. 291, thereby obviating the difficulties of hardening dies made in one piece or segments, and permitting the quick repairing of any damage done to any of the holes by inserting a new bushing, which will amount to no more, in the way of time and expense, than putting in a new punch.

In a press of this kind the feed-roll brackets are so hinged on the frames that they can be easily swung back for the pur-

pose of changing or adjusting any of the tools.   The support
of the stripper is made in sections, each of which can be swung

FIG. 290.—STAGGERED PATTERN.   FIG. 291.—DIE CONSTRUCTION.

forward for removing or replacing any of the punches.   The
punches are backed against a steel bar which is also made in
sections, so that there is no need of disturbing more than a

FIG. 292.—LARGE PERFORATING PRESS WITH DOUBLE ROLL FEED, HAVING
LATERAL MOTION FOR STAGGERED PATTERNS; ALSO EQUIPPED WITH CAM-
ACTUATED STRIPPER.

section of it for the sake of replacing a broken or sheared punch. A press of this type when properly equipped with tools will punch in ten hours forty sheets 50 x 96 inches of No. 16 iron with ⅛-inch round perforations of any ordinary pattern.

For perforating very heavy sheets, or where but a small quantity of the same pattern or design of perforating is wanted, it does not generally pay to make dies for the entire width of the sheet, such as are used in the press shown in Fig. 292, which finishes the whole sheet in one passing through. Instead a press with an accurate sliding table should be used and the dies made to perforate a row of holes in one-half of the width of the sheet, thus necessitating the passing of the metal twice beneath the punches.

The Constructing of a Special Punch Press for Perforating Tin Ferrules.

The press was for punching two rows of holes in tin ferrules

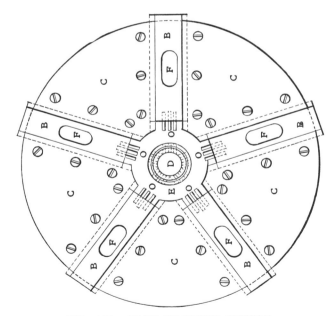

FIG. 293.—PLAN OF LOWER SECTION.

of the shape shown at E, Fig. 295. These ferrules were used as frames and stiffeners for bicycle handle tips, and after being punched were set into a mould and a composition resembling rubber run around them and into the holes.   There were to be two rows of holes, fifteen in number, spaced equally around the outside, five in the top row and ten in the bottom.   As will be seen, it was impossible to devise a practical means for punching them in one operation in the ordinary power press, so the special punch press shown here was designed and made.

At first a circular casting A, Figs. 294 and 295, with a

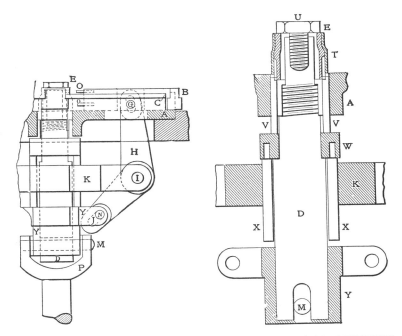

FIG. 294.—LOWER SECTION.   FIG. 295.—STRIPPING ARRANGEMENT.

hub on the back or under side was faced and bored.   A recess was also counterbored for locating centrally the die E.   The casting A was turned and finished on the outside and was then reversed and a hole bored and threaded for the central stud D. After the hub was faced it was ready for the miller.   As shown in Fig. 293 there are five rams, or slides, equally spaced and radial, and equipped with three punches each.   In milling the channels for these slides a threaded arbor, fitting the hub of the casting with a wide shoulder for the hub to rest against, was

made and finished with a taper shank fitting the dividing head of
the universal miller. It was then set up on the table facing the
spindle by using the extension plate. The table was raised and
moved until the work A was perfectly true and central with the
spindle. This was done by using a bent scriber in the chuck and
truing the center hole in the work by it. An end mill of the
size required was used to mill the channels, indexing for five,
starting from the center and running straight through to the
depth shown in Fig. 294.

The five slides B, of machine steel, were then made to fit
the channels in A snugly, leaving a margin on each side even
with the top of A, and 9-32 inch wide for the gibs. These
gibs, or plates, were of 3-16-inch thick cold-rolled stock and
were fastened with six screws each, as shown. The next thing
was to drill the holes in the slides B for the punches. This was
a rather delicate job. The slides were first finished to exactly
the same length as the channels and then located in the channels
in A with their ends even with the outside of A. The plates or
gibs were then tightened, holding the slides fast. The casting
A was now replaced on the dividing head with the work upward,
and the table was raised until the work was high enough for
the top row of holes. A small center drill was then held in the
chuck and the head revolved until the exact center of one of the
slides coincided with the point of the drill. The center was
then carefully spotted and the head moved one-fifth of a turn
to the center of the next slide. This center was drilled, and
the rest likewise. A drill the diameter of the punch was used
and each hole drilled to the desired depth. The table was then
raised for the next line of holes, shown in Fig. 296. As there
shown, there are two holes in each slide 5-16 inch apart, each one
an equal distance from the center of the upper one. The table
was moved along exactly 5-32 inch and the hole centered; then
indexed for five, the holes drilled in the other four slides, and
the starting point was again arrived at. The table was now
moved in the opposite direction 5-16 inch, and the other holes
centered and drilled. We were now sure that the holes were
accurately spaced and correct, and the exact distance between the
two lower holes and the distance between the centers of the upper
and lower lines were noted. The slides B were then scraped
and eased to a sliding fit. They were then removed and a slot,
⅜ inch wide and 13-16 inch long, milled through from the top,

as shown at F, Fig. 296, being sure to get them all the same distance from the faces. A 9-32-inch hole was let through from the side at G and the slides were finished.

The central stud D, the construction of which is shown clearly in Fig. 295, was made—it requires no description. Six holes were drilled through the hub A, equal distances apart, with a 3-32-inch drill, all on a 13-32-inch radius, for the pins of the stripping attachment, which was made as shown in Fig. 295. It consisted, first, of a cast iron collar W, 7-16 inch thick, bored and reamed to fit the stud D nicely. Six equally spaced holes were drilled with a radius sufficient to clear the largest part of the stud, and deep enough to allow six steel pins X, 3-16 inch

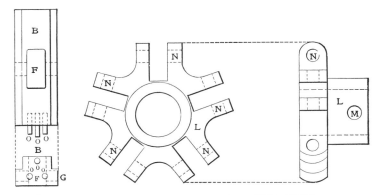

FIG. 296.—PUNCH   FIG. 297.—LOWER LEVER YOKE.
    SLIDE.

in diameter and 1⅜ inches long, to be driven into a shoulder. Six pins V, 3-32 inch in diameter and 15-16 inch long, were cut off and inserted in the holes drilled in A. The collar W, with the pins X, was then slipped onto the stud D, resting on the shoulder as shown. The stud was then screwed tightly into A, the pins V resting on the upper side of W.

The lower lever yoke is shown in Fig. 297, from which its construction can be understood. The slide levers are shown in Fig. 298 and require no description. The other parts of the press require little explanation; a casting with a bearing at each end, being finished and bored to admit a driving shaft, which turned with an eccentric in the center, giving the yoke X a movement of 13-32 inch.

The press complete, the next thing to tackle was the die, which was an accurate piece of work indeed. The manner in which it was made can be seen from the engravings and understood from the description of the die shown in Fig. 267 of the quadruplicate piercing die.

By reverting to Fig. 294, it will be seen that the upper works are fastened to a cast iron frame, which in turn was fastened to the top of the bench in such a way as to be within easy reach of the operator. The lower part was fastened to a

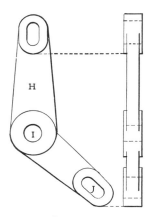

FIG. 298.—SLIDE LEVER.

skid and the skid fastened to the floor. When operating the work a ferrule was placed over the die by hand, as shown in Fig. 294, the yoke Y moving downward causing the levers H to move the slides B inward, thereby punching all the holes at once. On the return stroke, the yoke Y moving upward, until the slides had traveled back half-way, coming in contact with the lower stripper pins X, caused the stripper to move upward and the pins V to strip the work T from the die. The action of the press was very fast, and the spring left in the work by the punching was enough to cause it, when the pins V struck it, to spring clear of the die.

CHAPTER VII.

Defining of the Terms—Use of the Tools.

We will now take up a class of press tools and fixtures which have been adapted to accomplish results in the working of sheet metal parts and articles, which a few years back were attained only by spinning. This class of tools have now been improved to such an extent that they have completely superseded the old methods. The operations in which these tools are used are known as curling, wiring, and seaming operations, respectively. Curling consists of producing a curled edge around the top of any formed or drawn article or part of sheet metal. Wiring is the curling of the top of such articles around a wire hoop, when the vessel or shell requires stiffening. The tools used for both curling and wiring are almost of the same construction. Seaming is the upsetting and joining of two or more parts of an article together, or joining the two edges of a shell, which has been rolled or formed from a strip, together in such a manner as to fasten them permanently.

The use of dies for the operations mentioned above will give satisfactory results in all cases, and the results accomplished by them are not to be compared with those attained by the old methods, as their work is more uniform and the saving of time and labor great. In straight-sided work, and work but slightly flared, the metal will be turned, when wiring, around the wire and under it quite perfectly at one stroke of the press. From 2,000 to 8,000 pieces can be wired per day of 10 hours, according to the size of the work and the skill of the operator. In the following pages are shown various types of curling, wiring and seaming dies and fixtures together with the presses in which they are used, and as the illustrations are very clear only a slight description of the various types of dies and fixtures, the action of the presses and the manner in which the work is produced, will be necessary.

Curling Dies—Fundamental Principles—Action of the Metal.

Figs. 299, 304 and 308 show cross-sectional views of dies which may be used for curling the edges of circular-drawn shells, and as the engravings are very clear, we will dispense with a description of their construction and confine ourselves to the prin-

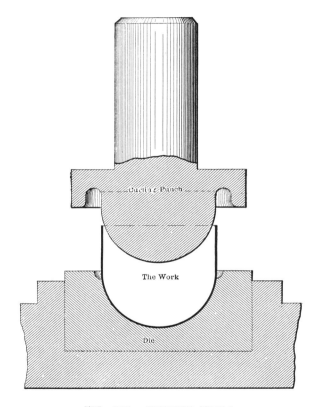

FIG. 299.—CURLING TOOLS.

ciples involved; the action of the metal during the process; and the manner in which work of this kind is produced.

In work of this kind it is not possible to see the action of the metal while the die is working, but by setting the die in the press, locating a shell, and coming down with the ram by hand until the upper die begins to form the metal and then backing the press, taking out the shell and seeing how the curl has commenced, and repeat two or three times until the ram has reached the full length of its stroke, one will be able to see the exact action of the dies and the metal. The groove in the upper die (or lower die as the case may require) must be finished to a perfect half-circle of the radius required, and must be highly polished and free from cuts or scratches. Figs. 300 to 303 show how the upper die forms the edge of a half-round drawn shell, showing

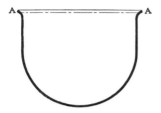
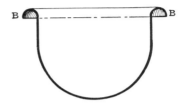

FIG. 300.—CURL STARTED.　　　FIG. 301.—HALF CURLED.

the results accomplished at various stages of the descent of the die. As shown in the first stage A, the metal has commenced to curl; at the next stage B, the metal has curled to a half-circle of the width of the curling groove in the upper die. At C the third stage is shown, the punch continuing to descend, and as the pressure is now on top of the half-circular curled edge it causes the metal to curl further around until the circle is complete, as shown

FIG. 302.—THREE-QUARTER　　FIG. 303.—FULLY CURLED.
CURLED.

at D. As will be understood, only one operation is necessary to curl the edge of a shell of the type shown, as the metal once started around the curling groove of the upper die follows or continues on the same radius as long as the pressure continues; thus a shell may be quarter-curled, half-curled or completely curled by the same die, according to the length of stroke to which the die is set.

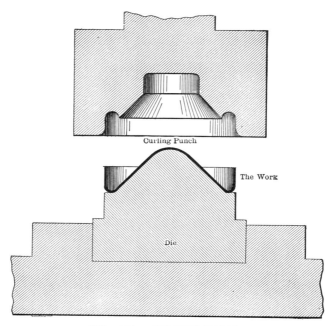

FIG. 304.—CURLING TOOLS.

When it is desired to curl the edges of a shell of the shape shown in Fig. 305 to the shape shown in Fig. 307 two dies are

FIG. 305.

necessary. The first die is a bending die and is used to bend or form the edges to a vertical position as shown. The second die

FIG. 306.   FIG. 307.

used is shown in Fig. 304 and the manner in which the edge is curled will be understood from the engravings. As shown, the

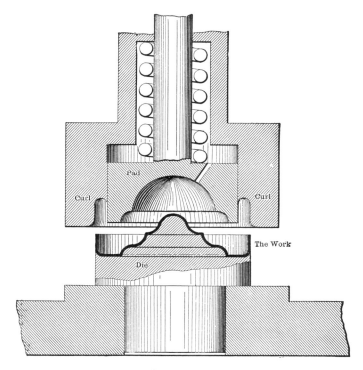

FIG. 308.—CURLING TOOLS.

construction of the upper die is such as to insure the edge of the
shell entering the curling groove, and the parallel part will en-

FIG. 309.—SHELL AS DRAWN.

close the wall of the shell while the edge is curling, so that it
is impossible for it to bulge out, which would be the case were

FIG. 310.—SHELL AS BENT.

FIG. 311.—SHELL AS CURLED.

this portion of the tool finished otherwise: thus, the metal being held securely, and having no place else to go, must follow the shape of the curling curve.

The curling of the edges of drawn shells by means of dies of the above type is done in endless variety, the articles worked upon ranging from shoe eyelets to bath tubs of both round and irregular shapes. The construction of the tools depends upon the shape of the shell, the thickness of metal and the diameter of curl required, but the principles involved are the same in all of them.

The tools in Fig. 308 show how a shell of different shape may be curled. The shell as shown in Fig. 309 is produced in a combination die while the bending as shown in Fig. 310 is accomplished by a bending die. The curling as shown in Fig. 311 is done in the die shown in Fig. 308. This shell differs from the other only in that it has a flange or flat part between the curled portion and the body of the shell. In the upper die a pad is located so as to hold the flange of the shell tightly while the curling is being done, the pressure being exerted by strong springs at the back of the pad. Were no pad used in this manner, the metal, when the pressure is exerted on the edge of the shell, would creep back and buckle.

Wiring Dies for Shell Work.

The manner in which wiring dies are made and used on both large and small work will be understood from Figs. 312 and 313. Dies of this type may be used for real wiring or false wiring on round or oval shells or cylinders. The bottoms of the shells may be any shape as long as they are properly supported during the operation. Fig. 312 shows a tool steel ring at A attached to the punch holder. The inner diameter of this ring must fit accurately the inner diameter of the shell to be wired, so as to prevent buckling of the walls. When a wire hoop is to be inclosed by the rim of the shell the ring B must be used in the die, and should be arranged in such a manner as to return to its proper position after the up stroke, as shown plainly in the engravings.

When in use, a wire hoop, which has been rolled or formed to fit the outer diameter of the shell, is placed in position on the ring B, as shown, the shell being located within the die. The press is then stepped and the result of the stroke is shown in

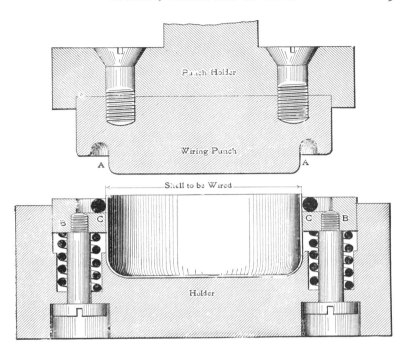

FIG. 312.—WIRING TOOLS, SHOWING SHELL BEFORE WIRING.

Fig. 313, which shows the wire C inclosed within the curled edge of the shell.

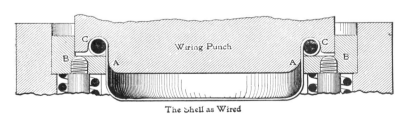

The Shell as Wired

FIG. 313.

A Curling Punch and Die For Milk Pans.

In Fig. 314 are shown a curling punch and die and the article for which it is used. The illustrations show the construction of both punch and die plainly. As shown, the portion of the punch which does the curling is composed of eight segments, so that it shall have a contracting action, which is necessary because of the flared shape of the article to be curled. The action is as follows: The article to be curled is located within the locating seat of the die and the punch descends until the edge of the article strikes the half curve in the curling segments. The punch continues to descend and the metal follows around the curling curves, and, of course, as the diameter of the portion of the metal touched by the punch decreases, the segments contract, the punch descending until the edge of the metal has curled to within a shade of the body of the article. As the punch rises, the article remains in the die and the segments of the punch expand so as to be ready for the next piece.

A Curling Punch and Die for Deep Shells.

A curling punch and die for curling deep shells or articles of thin sheet metal, and the press in which it was used, is shown in

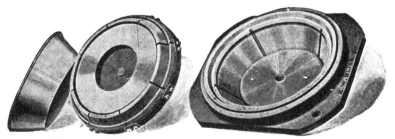

FIG. 314.—MILK PAN AND CURLING TOOLS FOR SAME.

FIG. 315.—ARRANGEMENT FOR CURLING THE EDGES OF DEEP SHELLS.

Fig. 315. The punch is located and fastened within the ram while the die is located on a sliding table which may be pulled back and forth by the operator. The horn or die for locating the work is of a slight taper and consequently a solid one piece curling punch can be used, as the decrease in diameter when curling is so slight that contraction is unnecessary. When in use, the table on which the horn or die is located is pulled out so as to allow of the article to be curled being slipped over it. This is done, and the table shoved back to place against a stop. The punch then descends and the edge of the article is curled. The punch ascends, the table is pulled out, the work removed, another located and the operation repeated. When a press of the type shown in Fig. 316 with an automatically actuated die slide is used, the articles can be wired or curled much faster.

Wiring Large Work.

In Fig. 318 are shown a set of dies for wiring large work. As shown, the dies are located within a press which has an extra long stroke, thus doing away with the sliding table and allowing of removing and locating the articles wired without trouble. As will be seen, the wiring punch is in segments so as to contract when wiring the edge of the work. The die is equipped with a floating ring supported by a number of springs. This floating ring is where the wire hoop is placed before the work is located, and it supports the wire while the punch descends and curls the metal around and under it, the stiffness of the metal being sufficient to overcome the tension of the springs and force the floating ring downward while the metal creeps under the wire, thus enclosing it within the curl.

The dies, press and fixtures shown in Fig. 319 illustrate how large pans of tin are wired. This press is built specially for wiring, by means of dies of the construction shown, the top edges of foot tubs, heavy pails and other large sheet-metal articles. The roller slide shown in connection with this press permits of removing the heaviest wiring dies with speed and ease, while the locking device, also illustrated, makes it impossible to trip the clutch while the die is being returned to its correct position, thus obviating the possibility of costly accidents.

Fig. 320 shows another set of wiring dies as set up in the press for wiring large work. The construction of the dies is on the same principle as those described and shown in Fig. 319,

FIG. 316.—WIRING PRESS WITH AUTOMATICALLY
ACTUATED DIE SLIDE.

FIG. 317.—WIRING PRESS WITH ROLLER BEARINGS FOR
SLIDE, AND LOCKING DEVICE.

FIG. 318.—WIRING PRESS WITH EXTRA LONG STROKE
FOR WIRING LARGE DEEP WORK.

FIG. 319.—GEARED DOUBLE CRANK PRESS WITH ROLLER TABLE AND DIES IN POSITION FOR WIRING LARGE SHEET-METAL GOODS.

FIG. 320.—DOUBLE CRANK PRESS FOR WIRING LARGE
SHEET-METAL GOODS.

the punch contracting as the wiring is accomplished. In the press shown the same attachments as described in the one shown in Fig. 319 are used.

Horizontal Dial Press With Pick-off Attachment.

In Fig. 321 is shown a press which is something of a curiosity. It is used, when equipped with dies of the required construction,

FIG. 321.—HORIZONTAL DIAL PRESS WITH PICK-OFF
ATTACHMENT.

Used for necking-in, curling, rounding, or swaging the top edges of cans or other sheet-metal shells. The operator puts the articles on as the dial revolves. After the punch has performed its work the pieces are automatically picked off by a Gripping Finger Device. From 40 to 60 pieces may be done per minute, according to shape and style of work.

for curling, necking-in, rounding or swaging the top edges of shells or cans. The horns on the dial are made to fit the shell which is to be worked upon, the operator putting the articles on as the dial revolves. After the punch has performed its work, the pieces are automatically picked off by a pair of **gripping** fingers as shown in the illustration. With a press of this type properly equipped with dies, from 40 to 60 pieces may be finished per minute, according to shape and size of the work.

Horning or Seaming Dies, Tools and Presses.

A press specially equipped with an automatic fixture for double horning or seaming is shown in Fig. 326. By means of this machine equipped as shown, the two corner seams on large square cans having round corners with seam in the center may be closed at one blow. Tins with sharp square corners require a coaxing operation on single horn to start the seam over before setting down on double horn press. The "horn" which is movable in ways, has two working surfaces; the upper one is acted on by the "force" bolted to the press slide, while the lower one in descending with the slide acts against a stationary "force" fastened to the bed. It will be understood that the two body-halves loosely hooked together are pushed over the sliding horn, which, by means of the adjustable slide gages shown, secures accurate size and position. By the use of this machine the capacity of the operator is nearly doubled, as compared with what can be done on an ordinary horn press. The press as shown in the illustration, is arranged for seaming five-gallon petroleum cans.

Duplex Folding and Seaming for Locked Seams.

In Fig. 327 are shown the successive stages of a lock seam, and a press equipped with the tools for accomplishing the results shown. In this cut the manner in which both an inside seam and an outside seam are finished is shown, two blows being necessary for each. The first operation is the forming of the hooks, and the second the smashing down and locking together. There is a large variety of work which requires finishing with locked seams of this kind.

Double Seaming of Flat, Round, Deep Bottoms.

For double seaming of bottoms, tops, and parts of round bodies together, the work is accomplished by special machinery and dies are dispensed with. A machine for this work is shown in Fig. 322 and diagrams of the work done on it in Figs. 323 to 325. These machines are used extensively for double seaming "flat bottoms" onto tea kettles, coffee pots, pails and similar goods in the tin and enameled ironware lines.

The lower spindle, carrying the "inside chuck or roller," is mounted on a sliding plate, which is drawn forward for putting

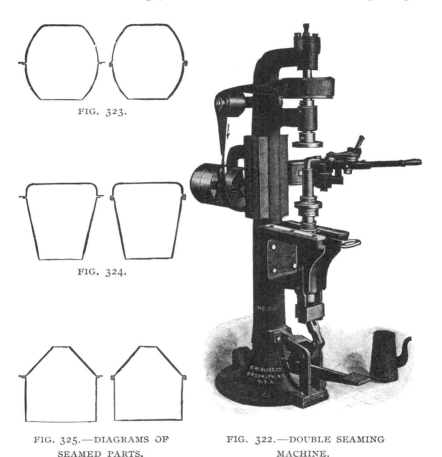

FIG. 323.

FIG. 324.

FIG. 325.—DIAGRAMS OF
SEAMED PARTS.

FIG. 322.—DOUBLE SEAMING
MACHINE.

on and taking off the articles. In the case of flaring pails, dish pans, and other articles which are smaller at the bottom than at the top, the double-seaming is done against a solid plate of the size of the bottom mounted on the sliding spindle. For buckets, cups, and other straight sided articles, collapsible chucks are used. These chucks are so made that they spread so as to fill

FIG. 326.—DOUBLE HORN PRESS FOR CLOSING THE TWO CORNER
SEAMS ON LARGE SQUARE CANS AT A SINGLE BLOW.

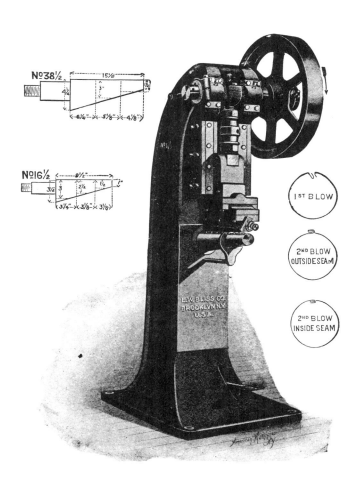

FIG. 327.—DUPLEX FOLDING AND SEAMING PRESS, FOR FORMING
AND CLOSING LOCKED SIDE SEAMS.

along the edge of the bottom, when the article is carried up against the upper chuck, and fold together after the work is done, so as to permit the rapid and easy removal of the seamed article.

A Double Seaming Machine With Blank Centering Device and Collapsible Chuck.

In Fig. 328 is shown a double seaming machine which is equipped with a blank centering device and a collapsible chuck. The chuck is shown in Fig. 330, a diagram of the operation accomplished in Fig. 329, and the work before and after finishing at the lower right.

In this machine the treadle is made with a toggle joint to take the thrust while seaming. The separate view of the chuck shows same drawn forward and in its extended position. In order to collapse it for the purpose of putting on the kettle body to be seamed, it is only necessary to disengage the hinge hook shown at the bottom of spindle bearing, whereupon the chuck draws itself together automatically. It is expanded to fill against the bottom edge of the kettle by raising the spindle until the hook snaps in, after which the flat bottom is laid on and the slide pushed back into working position.

Double Seaming Oval, Oblong, Square Shapes, Etc.

Double seaming machines for seaming articles of irregular shapes differ from others shown herein, in that they are constructed so as to allow the seaming rolls to automatically follow the shape of the can. As they do the seaming at the top of the can, they are preferable for filled cans. In action, the pressure on the foot treadle, which raises the pressure plate so as to clamp the can and the lid against the chuck, also throws in a friction clutch which starts the work. The double-seaming rolls, controlled by a cam made in a piece with the chuck and finished to the shape of the can, follow the shape of the can automatically, while the necessary pressure to form and finish the seam is imparted by the handles. These pressure handles are so arranged as to relieve the hand of the operator from all vibrations due to the irregular shape of the cans. This machine can be readily adjusted for different heights of work by means of a hand-wheel, and for different shapes by exchanging the cam chuck, which can be done in a few minutes.

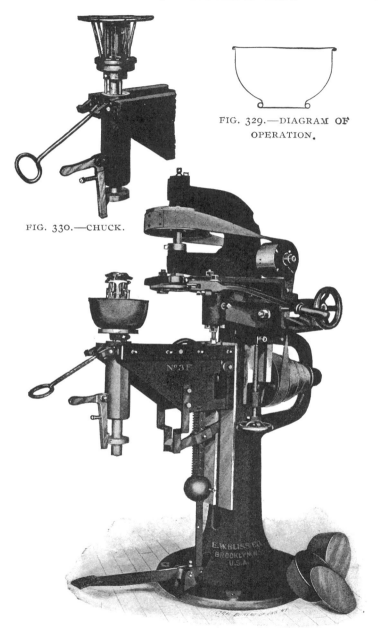

FIG. 329.—DIAGRAM OF
OPERATION.

FIG. 330.—CHUCK.

FIG. 328.—DOUBLE SEAMING MACHINE EQUIPPED WITH BLANK
CENTERING DEVICE AND COLLAPSIBLE CHUCK.

Rolling Seams on Square Cans.

The rolling of seams on square cans is accomplished in the following manner: The can is firmly held between two disks made exactly to fit the heads of the can, the upper disk being mounted on a vertical shaft fastened rigidly to the upper part of the main frame and the lower disk to a shaft passing through the lower part of the frame, and prevented from turning by an arm running in guides, but capable of vertical motion imparted to it by a cam on the treadle shaft.

The steel rolls which operate on the seams at the top and bottom are carried by a frame which rotates upon the upper and lower stationary shafts and around the can. These rolls are mounted on levers pivoted in the rotating frame, the opposite ends of the levers being furnished with rolls bearing against star-

FIG. 331.—HORN FRAME WITH SUNKEN BOLSTER AND SLIDE
FRAME COMBINED.

shaped stationary cams on the two vertical shafts, which give the in and out motion required in passing around the corners of the cams. The rotating frame carries two sets of these rollers, which press on opposite sides of the cam at both the top and bottom, thus equalizing the side pressure and rolling the seams more perfectly than would be possible by the use of a single set of rolls, each seam being rolled twice in each revolution.

There are additional cams provided, which, as the machine comes to a rest, move the roll outward from the surface of the cam, so the latter may be removed from the machine. Attached to the bottom of the rotating frame is a bevel gear meshing with a pinion on the pulley shaft. The pulley is provided with a friction clutch controlled by the treadle.

A can being placed upon the lower disk and the foot pressed upon the treadle, the can is raised and clamped firmly between the upper and lower disks. The clutch is now thrown in, and the roller frame makes one revolution around the can, the latter remaining stationary. After completing one revolution the clutch is automatically released, the rolls are thrown outward, and the

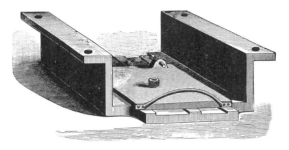

FIG. 332.—SUNKEN BOLSTER WITH SLIDE PLATE FOR
WIRING DIES.

lower disk drops, leaving the can free to be removed. The capacity of these machines is from 9,000 to 12,000 cans in 10 hours, and the saving of solder by the use of each machine amounts to from $15 to $18 per day.

Fig. 331 shows a horn frame with sunken bolster and slide frame combined for horning and wiring, while Fig. 332 shows a sunken bolster with slide frame for wiring and curling dies exclusively.

CHAPTER VIII.

Scarcity of Mechanics Who Understand Drawing Processes.

It is safe to make the assertion that in no line of sheet metal work have dies and press fixtures been adopted more extensively for the production of articles for universal use than in the production of drawn and formed shells, and notwithstanding the universal use to which such articles have been put, the means, methods and processes for their production are not understood as they should be. Although there are any number of establishments which make a specialty of drawn sheet metal work, there is always great difficulty experienced in getting mechanics who understand thoroughly how to design and construct the tools which will produce such parts in the most approved manner. Now while there is no difficulty in finding men who can construct dies for almost any other line of sheet metal work, it is unusual to find an all-around toolmaker who understands the construction of drawing dies. In fact we may say that we have worked with some of the best toolmakers in the country who were capable of making a tool for almost every known purpose, but when they were given a sample of drawn work for which to make a set of dies, they would flounder about and show by their actions that they had not the slightest conception of the principles and rules by which they might construct the proper tools successfully.

Uncertainty as to the Best Means to Adopt.

In view of the uncertainty among mechanics as to the best and most approved means to adopt for the production of drawn sheet metal work, we will describe and illustrate in this chapter the different processes for the production of such articles, including in the descriptions all the kinks, fundamental principles, etc., which we have found to be the best for each type indicated. In arranging this chapter in this manner, i. e., from the view point of a practical man, we are convinced that it will be found the best, for this reason. Now while the student and mechanical expert may desire to know and understand principles of sheet metal drawing processes from a technical point of view and may charge the author with having ignored principles and theories, which, by such men, are considered absolutely necessary to an intelligent understanding of the subject; the author, as a practical man, is inclined to think otherwise, and for that reason we give in the following pages a complete description of how to construct drawing dies for all the different varieties of drawn, formed and embossed sheet metal parts.   For some classes of work two or three different types of dies are shown and described, for the reason that conditions, tool equipment and other circumstances often prevent the adoption of tools of one construction, but make that of another available.   What we recommend is this: When the toolmaker has a set of drawing tools to construct let him adopt the dies described here for the production of a part which is similar to that which he is to produce.   Follow the description of the tools carefully, memorize the little kinks and ways of accomplishing the results, and lastly let him convince himself that perfect and accurate work on all parts is necessary.   When the mechanic has done this, and has acquainted himself with the fundamental principles, which are given here in a simple and concise manner, he will experience no difficulty in attaining the desired results.

Types of Dies in General Use for Producing Drawn Shells.

For the production of drawn and formed shells from sheet metal, the dies in general use consist of four distinct types.   The first is the most primitive and consists of punching out the blank to the desired shape and size in a plain blanking die, and then pushing it through a drawing die or dies, according to the desired length of the shell.   This manner of producing the shells is the cheapest where only a small quantity is required.   The second method is by the use of compound dies and a double acting press, in which the blanking punch descends and punches out the blank and then remains stationary while the shell is being drawn and formed by the internal drawing punch.   The third method is by means of a punch and die of the combination type, in which the punching and drawing dies are combined and are used in a single-acting press. This method is the most popular and generally used one, as well as the most practical for the production of plain or fancy formed and drawn shells which are not required to exceed one inch in height.   The design and method of constructing dies of the combination type differ according to conditions, but the fundamental principles involved are substantially the same in all of them and may be adopted for the production of round shells of any shape which it is possible to produce in one operation in a single acting press. The fourth and last type of dies used for shell work are known as "triple-acting drawing dies," and are used to produce shells which are required to be blanked, drawn and embossed, lettered or paneled in one operation. They are used in triple acting presses.

Combination Dies—Their Use.

Combination dies are used in single-acting foot or power presses. They cut a blank, and at the same time turn down the

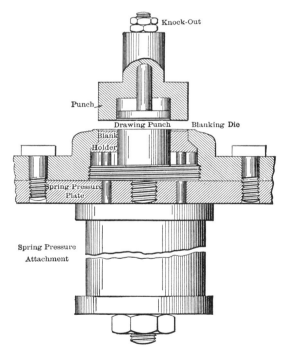

FIG. 333.—A COMBINATION DIE.

edge and form the article into shape. In most cases the articles thus produced are of shallow shapes, their edges frequently not over 3-16 inch deep, as, for instance, can tops and bottoms, pail, bucket and cup bottoms, etc. On the other hand, however, dies of this class are used for making deeper articles, such as boxes and covers for blacking, lard, salve and other goods up to $\frac{3}{4}$ inch deep, or for cutting and drawing burner and gas fixture parts, toys, etc., up to 1 inch in depth. Suggestions concerning a large variety of shapes and styles of work such as can be done in combination dies will be found on the following pages. Most combination dies are so arranged that the finished article is automatically pushed out of the dies by the action of springs. With the press set on an incline, the finished work will therefore slide back by gravity, effecting a considerable saving in labor and greatly increasing the speed of production. An expert operator, with a medium size combination die in a power press, will produce from 15,000 to 17,000 pieces per day of 10 hours.

Spring Pressure Attachment for Combination Dies.

Combination dies are now mostly used in connection with a spring pressure attachment, which is fastened to the bolster plate, projecting downward through the bed of the press. The rubber spring carries a plate which, through pins in the die, holds up the pressure or blank holder ring and keeps the metal from wrinkling or crimping during the drawing operation and also acts as a "knock-out" for the finished work.

Double-Acting Cutting and Drawing Dies—Their Use.

These dies are used in double-action presses. They cut a blank and at the same stroke of the press draw it into shape. The kind and thickness of the metal used determine whether one or several operations are required to obtain the desired depth and shape. The nature of the shaping process which is known as "drawing" will be understood from the annexed sectional views of cutting and drawing dies. These illustrations show two essentially different kinds of drawing dies, viz., Fig. 334, a "push through die," and Fig. 335, a "solid bottom die."

The lower die A is fastened to the bed of the press, while the combined cutting punch and blank-holder B is worked by the outer slide, and moves slightly in advance of the drawing punch C, which is actuated by the inner slide. The outer slide in double-acting presses is so arranged that, after making its stroke, it stops during about one-quarter of the revolution of the crank shaft. The blank having been cut out from the sheet by the cutting edges of A and B, drops into the lower die, and is there held between the annular pressure surfaces O and P during the down "dwell" of the outer slide.   While the blank is thus held under pressure, which can be regulated to suit the special requirements of each case, the drawing punch C continues its

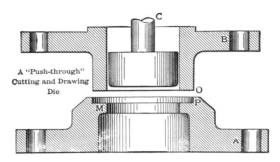

FIG. 334.—DIE FOR DOUBLE-ACTION PRESS.

downward movement, thus drawing the metal from between the pressure surfaces into the shape required.   In this manner the metal is prevented from wrinkling.

For straight-sided, cylindrical, prismatic articles which conform to the shape of the punch without requiring a counterpart

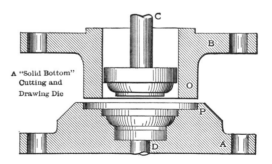

FIG. 335.—DIE FOR DOUBLE-ACTION PRESS.

in the bottom of the power die, tools similar to those shown in Fig. 334 are used.   They admit of pushing the finished article right through the die, it being "stripped" from the punch at the commencement of its up stroke by the action of the "stripping edge" M.   Where a counter pressure in the lower die is required,

⋅dies of the kind shown in Fig. 335 are used. These have in addition to the lower die, blank holder and drawing punch, what is known as a "push-out plate" D. This plate rises at the same time as the blank-holder B, thus lifting the finished article from out of the lower die.

Plain Drawing Dies, and Redrawing Dies.

Drawing dies of the type shown in Fig. 336 differ from the tools shown in Fig. 335 in this, that they draw the article to be produced in them from blanks previously cut, instead of being provided with cutting edges, which punch the blank at the same stroke. They may be made of any style and size, and draw the

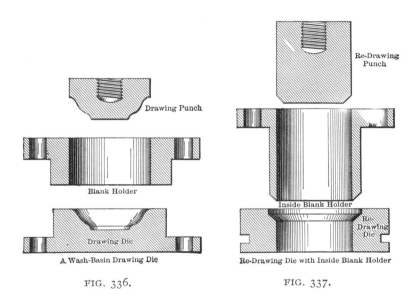

FIG. 336.   FIG. 337.

article at one or more operations, according to the shape and depth to be obtained. In work of considerable taper, such as milk pans for instance, two or more blanks are usually drawn at the same stroke of the press.

Drawing Dies With Inside Blank-Holders.

Drawing dies with inside blank-holders, as shown in Fig. 337, are used for redrawing shells that have been first drawn in dies having outside blank-holders, similar to that shown in Fig.

334. The inside blank-holders hold the partly finished article at its lower beveled edge O, while the punch draws it into a deeper shape of less diameter. These drawing and redrawing dies are mostly made of a special grade of cast iron treated in such a manner as to give a very dense and uniform texture to the metal at the working surfaces. Sometimes, however, steel rings are set into the dies, and the blank-holders made of steel casting, which adds considerably to the durability of the tools. For articles which have to be very accurate in diameter a hard steel "sizing" punch and die are sometimes used after the last redrawing operation.

Triple-Action Drawing Dies.

Triple-action drawing dies are used in triple-action presses. They are frequently used instead of the solid bottom double-action dies shown in Fig. 335. Like these, they cut, draw and stamp at one operation, but they deliver the finished article below the dies, instead of pushing it up, enabling the operator to feed con-

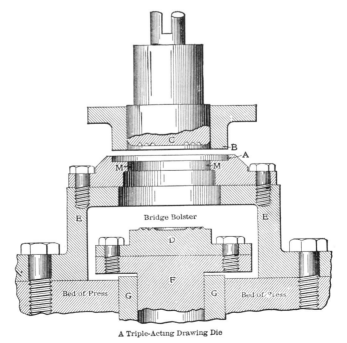

A Triple-Acting Drawing Die

FIG. 338.—DIE FOR TRIPLE-ACTION PRESS.

tinuously, instead of waiting for each piece to come up before the next one can be cut.   Their construction will be understood from the sectional view in Fig. 338, in which A, set on raised bolster E, represents the cutting and drawing die, B the cutting punch and blank-holder, C the drawing and embossing punch, and D the embossing die, which corresponds in its action to the solid bottom in double-action dies.   After the article is cut and drawn

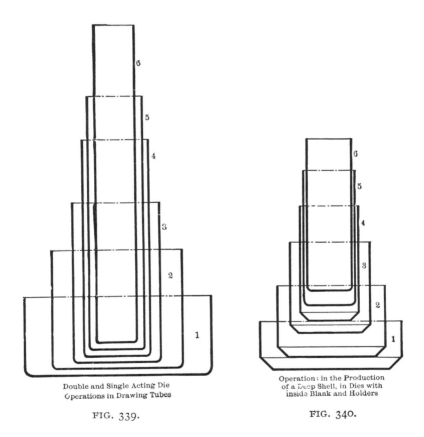

Double and Single Acting Die
Operations in Drawing Tubes

FIG. 339.

Operation; in the Production
of a Deep Shell, in Dies with
inside Blank and Holders

FIG. 340.

by the action of A, B, and C, as explained before, the punch C continues to descend and carries the drawn article down until its lower surface meets the embossing die D mounted on plunger F, working in sleeve G, on its up stroke, where it receives the required impression of beads, fancy designs, or lettering, etc.   On the up stroke of the punch the finished article is stripped from it at the edge M, and the press being set on an incline, the work slides back by gravity beneath the raised bolster E, into a box placed behind the press. In this manner, embossed drawn articles can be produced as rapidly as ordinary plain covers in push through dies.

The Making of a Combination Die, for Blanking and Drawing a Shell in a Single-Action Press.

In the following we show and describe one type of combina-

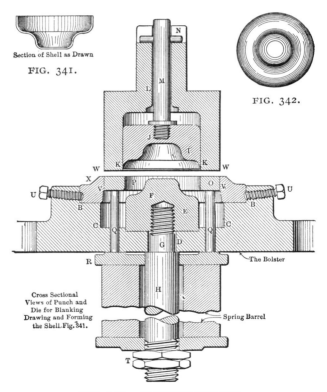

Section of Shell as Drawn

FIG. 341.

FIG. 342.

Cross Sectional
Views of Punch and
Die for Blanking
Drawing and Forming
the Shell. Fig. 341.

The Bolster

Spring Barrel

FIG. 343.—COMBINATION DIE.

tion die, and the way to construct it, and further on in the chapter other types and methods.

In Fig. 343 is shown a cross-sectional view of a combination punch and die, while the shell produced in it is shown in Figs. 341 and 342 respectively. When constructing dies of this class the first requisite is to decide upon the shape and size to which the shell is required to be finished and the thickness and texture of the metal to be used. This being settled the next thing is a pair of templets, and in the working out and finishing of these templets to the desired degree of accuracy, depends the quality of the work produced when the punch and die are finished and operated. These templets, from which this particular punch and die were constructed, are shown in Fig. 344, one for the drawing die and the other for the drawing punch, the difference between the two being exactly one thickness of metal at all points. With the templets finished we are now ready for work.

A piece of tool steel, annealed, and long enough to get both the drawing punch and die out of it, is chucked and the outside of the projecting portion turned to the size of the largest diameter of the templet I shown in Fig. 344, and the end finished or faced. This end is then worked down to the exact shape of the templet, first, by using the compound rest, and then finished with hand tools, getting all curves symmetrical, and the surfaces as smooth as possible, by lapping with a stick, oil and emery. The die is then cut off, leaving it the height shown. The punch E is then worked out and finished to the shape and size of the other templet, in the same manner as the die, and cut off with a stiff parting tool. The tapped holes in both die and punch are then let in, as shown, for the knockout stud, and the spring barrel stud H, respectively.

The bolster is the next thing to finish. This, for a die of this construction, should be of cast iron, cast good and solid. After a cut has been taken of the top and back to take out strain, a finishing cut should be taken off the bottom and also off both ends, as shown in Fig. 343. . It should be then strapped on the face-plate of the lathe and the inside bored out as shown, leaving three shoulders or seats. That is, at B B for the blanking die (which is not worked out and finished until the correct size and shape of blank is found) at C C for the blank-holder ring O, and the last or bottom one for the locating central of the drawing punch E, as shown. The bolster is then removed from the lathe and six equally-spaced holes are drilled around the inside for the tension or blank-holder pins Q, as shown in the sectional view. The drawing punch E is then located and fastened within the bolster in the position shown, by means of the spring barrel stud G, which shoulders against the bottom of the bolster. The

spring barrel is of hard spring rubber about six inches long and
$3\frac{1}{2}$ inches thick, with a clearance hole through the center to allow
of slipping through the stud H, as shown. Two cast iron washers
and two jam nuts complete the arrangement, the washer R being
faced on the side which supports the blank holder ring pins Q,
and both sides of the jam nuts T chamfered.

The blank holder ring O is then machined as follows: A

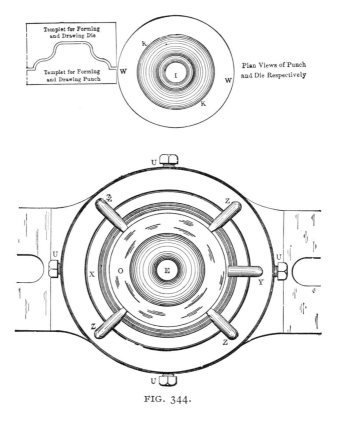

FIG. 344.

piece of tool steel about $\frac{1}{2}$ inch thick, large enough to leave
considerable surplus stock around the outside after finishing the
inside, is first chucked and one side faced, and a hole bored
through the center at P, so as to fit nicely around the forming
punch. It is then placed on a mandrel and both sides faced,
leaving it the thickness shown; the outside diameter is left unfinished until the blanking die has been hardened and ground.

A piece of round annealed tool steel, in size sufficient to form the blanking punch, is then chucked and a hole bored completely through it for the knockout stud M, as shown. It is then worked out to admit the drawing die I, as shown, finishing the inside as smooth as possible.   The punch is then driven onto a man-

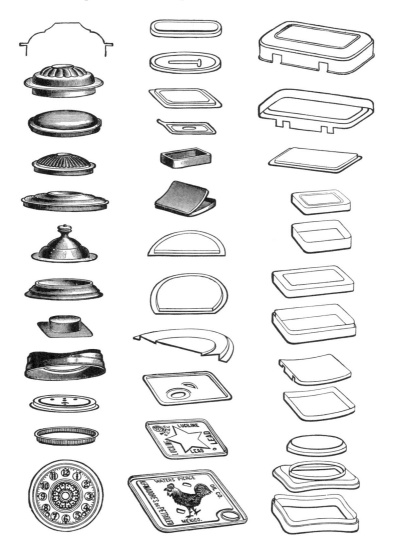

FIG. 345.—SAMPLES OF COMBINATION DIE WORK.

drel and the stem turned and both ends of the punch faced. A slot is then milled into the stem to accommodate the pin N of the knockout stud. Now, to find the blank, the punch and die, which are complete except for the blanking or cutting portions, are set up in the press and a number of trial draws made from templets until the exact size and shape required to form the shell as desired is found. The various parts are now removed, and the blanking die X got out. For this a steel forging is generally used, and it is first chucked and the back faced and the outside turned to within 3-64 of the finish diameter, or the seat for it in the bolster. It is then reversed on the chuck and the face finished to the shape shown, tapering it away so as to leave about 5-32 inch of surface at the cutting edge. The inside is then bored out to within 3-64 of the size of the templet, and the face polished with a stick, oil and emery. The blanking die is now hardened and slightly warmed, and then set up in the grinder and ground on the outside to fit snugly within the bolster and on the inside to the exact size of the templet, giving it about one degree of clearance. The die is then drawn on a hot plate to the temper desired, which in this case—as the stock was a soft brass—was a dark straw. Four setscrews U are then let in around the outside diameter of the bolster—spacing them equally—and notches ground in the die to correspond with them, and the die fastened and located within the bolster as shown.

The blank-holder ring is now finished on the outside to fit within the die, hardened, drawn to a light straw temper, ground on both sides, and located within the die on the six tension pins Q. These pins should be of stiff drill rod and finished so that all of them will be exactly the same height.

The outside of the punch is now turned to within 1-32 inch of the finish size, hardened, and drawn so that the blanking portion W will be a dark blue and the inside or drawing portion a light straw. The punch is then ground to fit the die, by driving it on a mandrel, finishing it so as to fit within the die without play. The stop-pin Y and the four stripper pins Z are then let in at the positions shown, in the plan view of the die, Fig. 344, the stop-pin being so placed as to leave a trifle over a thickness of metal between the punchings, and the four stripper pins so as to project to the edge of the cutting die, and in height sufficient to allow of the stock passing freely beneath them. The punch and die are now complete and ready for work.

The tools are set up in the press in the relative positions shown in the sectional view, Fig. 343, adjusting the stroke of the press so that when the punch has descended to its limit of stroke, the drawing die will bottom within the blanking punch.   The jam nuts of the barrel stud are adjusted so that the blank when punched, will be held with sufficient tension between the faces of the blank-holder ring O and the punch to prevent the stock from crimping or wrinkling as it is being drawn and formed.   The action of this punch and die when in operation can be understood from the sectional views.   The result is shown in Figs. 341 and 342 respectively.

Simple or Push Through Drawing Dies.

As mentioned in the foregoing when describing the combination blanking and drawing die, it is possible to produce plain drawn shells not exceeding one inch in height in two operations by the use of simple dies.   This is always preferable when only a small quantity is required.   The punch and die shown in Fig. 346 is of this class, and was used for drawing the shell shown in Fig. 347.   To operate this punch and die it is necessary to have a

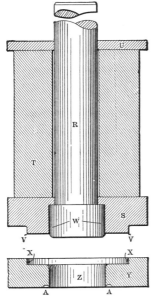

FIG. 346.—PUSH THROUGH
DRAWING DIE.

FIG. 347.—THE
FIRST DRAW.

FIG. 348. — THE
LAST REDRAW.

press with at least an inch and a half of stroke, and one that will take in at least seven inches between bolster and ram. As the majority of power presses of any strength and size will take this, the punch and die shown is the best for the work mentioned, the cutting out of the blank, of course, being done in a separate operation by means of a plain blanking die. In the die shown in Fig. 346 the principle of holding the blank described for the other while it is being drawn is reversed. It will be remembered that the rubber spring barrel was fastened to the bottom of the die, while in this case it is on the punch. The making of a die of this kind is simple indeed, it being a piece of round tool steel turned and faced at X X, in diameter sufficient to allow of the blank to be drawn to rest true within it. A hole is let through the center at Z for the drawing portion, in diameter the exact size of the outside of the shell, Fig. 347. The upper edge of the die is slightly rounded, after which it is highly polished (or when a grinder is handy, it is left .010 small and ground to size after hardening). The die Y is then reversed and an oval groove about 1-16 deep is turned into the back at A A, running out to a dead sharp edge at the die Z. Push-through dies of this class should always be left as hard as possible as they wear fast.

A simple cast iron bolster, with a recess to accommodate the die, is all that is required for the die. For the punch R, a piece of tool steel about seven inches long is first centered and turned to the size shown, to the length of the shank R, to within ⅛ of an inch greater than the depth of the shell to be drawn, Fig. 346, ending in a square shoulder as shown. The end W to form the punch portions is then turned to within .010 of the finish size, that is, exactly two thicknesses of metal less than the diameter of the die. For the blank holder, a piece of cast iron of sufficient size is first chucked and bored out to fit the punch, fitting at R, resting on the shoulder of the punch and fitting the punch proper at W, loosely, as shown. It is also reduced at V V to just fit the die at X X. A cast iron washer faced on both sides and bored to fit the stem R serves as the back plate U for the rubber buffer T, which has a hole through the center, as shown, large enough to leave about 1-16 inch of space all around the stem R of the punch. This is so that when the rubber is compressed it will not choke up around the punch.

In setting up a punch and die of this kind the following way is the best. The stem of the punch is first shoved up into the

ram of the press, which is then brought down until the face of
the blank holder rests on the face of the die and the rubber is
compressed sufficient to allow of there being enough tension on
the blank as soon as the punch starts to draw the metal.   The
punch is then fastened within the ram with the washer **U** resting
tightly against the face of the same.   The punch is then brought
down far enough to allow of the points V V of the blank holder

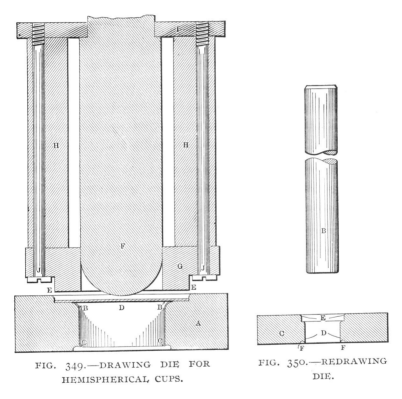

FIG. 349.—DRAWING DIE FOR   FIG. 350.—REDRAWING
HEMISPHERICAL CUPS.   DIE.

locating true within the die at X X, and the bolster is securely
fastened to the press bolster.

In operating a die of this kind a blank is laid within X X of
the die, and the punch descending, it is held tightly between the
faces of the blank holder (by means of the spring barrel T com-
pressing) and drawn through the die Z, the punch descending
far enough to draw the shell completely through the die.   As
the punch ascends, the shell is stripped from it by means of the

sharp stripping edge at A A at the back of the die. One thing in setting dies of this kind is to be sure to have sufficient tension on the blank when the punch starts to draw it, as otherwise the blank will start to crimp or wrinkle, thereby spoiling it. The shell shown in Fig. 347 is the first drawing operation of four necessary to produce the shell shown in Fig. 348. The means used for reducing the diameter and increasing the height was by reducing dies of the type shown in Fig. 350. The two first reducing operations reducing the shell ⅛ inch in diameter respectively, and the last or finishing die 1-16 inch. These dies are known as redrawing, reducing or push through dies, and their design is almost the same as the die shown in Fig. 346. D is the die, F F the stripping edge, and E the gage used. To set the shell to be reduced, it is located within the gage portion of the die at E, the punch descending pushes it through the die D and strips it at the edge F F. This is a type of die most frequently used for producing shells of unusual height. The greater the height desired the greater the number of operations required to attain the result. The finishing die should be hardened and ground and lapped as smooth as possible, and the punch ground to exactly two thicknesses of metal less in diameter in order that a smooth well-finished shell shall be produced.

Drawing a Small Shell from Heavy Stock.

In the production of the shell shown in Fig. 352 a very simple and inexpensive die was used, this being possible as the blank was of comparatively heavy stock. The die, Fig. 351, is a simple drawing die. C is the bolster, of cast iron, bored to admit the drawing die A, and the knockout pad D, the die A resting squarely within it at B and the knockout pad at E. A clearance hole runs down through the bolster for the shank of the knockout. The two setscrews F F were let into the side of the bolster, at an angle as shown, to keep the die A securely in position. The die is finished to the exact size and at the top to the shape of the shell A, with a depression let into the face for the flat blank G, thus serving as a gage. This die was well polished and tapered inward toward the bottom nearly one degree. It was left very hard. In the punch I is the holder and H the punch, the latter being in diameter two thicknesses of metal less than the die. The set-screw J holds it. In operating, the blanks are lubricated by pouring heavy hot grease over them. One is placed in the recess on the die, and as the punch descends it is drawn and formed to the shape shown at A. As the punch ascends, the press knockout device strikes the knockout stud or pad D' and

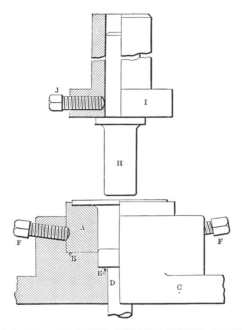

FIG. 351.—DRAWING DIE FOR HEAVY STOCK.

raises it sufficiently to strip the shell from the die. When metal as thick as here shown is to be drawn, neither blank-holder, pad or spring-barrel rubber is required, as the thickness of the blank

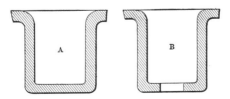

FIG. 352.—SHELL DRAWN FROM HEAVY STOCK.

in proportion to the diameter of the shell to be drawn prevents wrinkling or crimping.

For the hole in the bottom of the shell the punch and die,

Fig. 353, were used. K is the bolster, M the die and N the gage plate. P is the stripper bent to the shape shown and fastened to the back of the bolster. R is the punch and H the holder. The shell A is placed in the gage portion N, and the punch descending blanks the hole; and as it ascends, the shell is stripped from the punch by the stripper P. In drawing the shell and blanking the

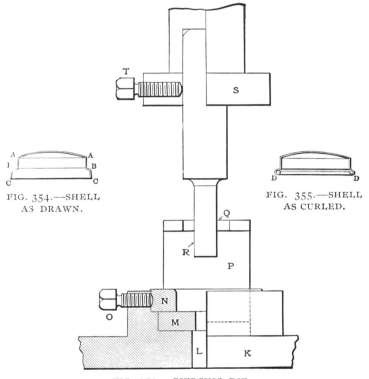

FIG. 354.—SHELL AS DRAWN.

FIG. 355.—SHELL AS CURLED.

FIG. 353.—PIERCING DIE.

hole, stock was left to allow of finishing the shells in the screw machine as they were to form part of tire valves for automobiles.

Making an Accurate Combination Blanking and Drawing Die.

In the following we will describe a practical method, somewhat different from the first, of constructing an accurate combination blanking and drawing die for the production in a single acting press of a symmetrically formed and nicely finished shell of sheet brass, which was to be afterward polished and plated and used as the cover on a piece of table ware. This shell is shown as first drawn in Fig. 354 and the punch and die for producing it in Fig. 356. As these shells were required in large quantities and were required to be duplicates and free from scratches and marks, it was necessary to construct all parts of the die as accurately and durable as possible, and with each working part separate to allow of substituting when any one of them became worn or were broken.

Making the Drawing Punch.

After making a pair of templets of sheet-steel, one the size and shape of the outside of the shell, and the other its exact duplicate, only one thickness of metal smaller at all points, we were ready to start. The drawing punch J was made first. A piece of cold-rolled stock was then threaded to fit the hole in J, which was screwed on to it and the outside turned to within 1-64 inch of the finish size. The curved face of J was then finished to templet to the radius shown, the shape of the inside turned in, leaving enough stock to allow of grinding to a finish after hardening. The punch was then hardened, slightly drawn, and then placed on the threaded arbor and ground to the exact size and shape in the lathe by means of a tool-post grinder. The points requiring the most accurate finishing are at X X, as the shell at this point was required to fit tightly the piece on which it was used.

The Drawing Die.

We now tackle the female die and blanking punch combined, G, which is in fact a compound of a blanking punch and a drawing die. A forging of tool steel is chucked and a hole bored and reamed through it lengthwise for the plunger and knockout F. While still in the chuck, the inside is roughed out and bored as shown, using the compound rest to get the desired angle at I I, and hand-tooling the rounder corners. The straight portion was bored back the distance shown, ending in a square shoulder at the back. The inside was then lapped and polished. The forging was then removed from the chuck and forced onto an arbor, the stem E turned to fit the ram of the press, and the back faced, but the outside of the punch proper was not touched until after the blank was found. The plunger or knockout H was then finished, the face to the radius of the templet. This face acted as the face of the drawing die. An air hole was let through from the back and one let through the blanking punch also. The end of the stem F was threaded for the adjusting nuts and the face H hardened and drawn to a light straw color. The drawing punch and die were now complete and we were ready

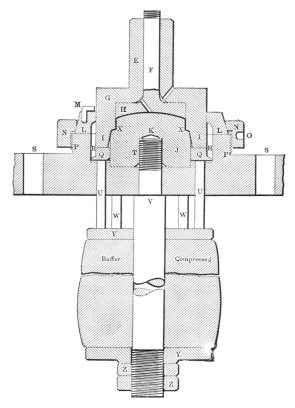

FIG. 356.—COMBINATION BLANKING AND DRAWING DIE.

to finish the other parts, and make the trial draws to find the blank.

The Die Bolster.

The cast iron body of the die, after being planed, was fastened to the faceplate of the lathe by entering screws into four tapped holes in the back. A cut was taken off the face and the inside bored at R R, which had to be somewhat larger than the blank would be. This can be usually determined within ⅛ of an

inch at least. A recess was then let into the bottom of the inside
as a locating seat for the drawing punch J, and a hole bored and
reamed through the center for the spring barrel stud V. The
ends of the bolster at S S were faced and eight 5-16 inch holes
let through around the inside, for the eight blank holder tension
pins U. The blank holder ring Q Q was then got out, and then
the eight tension pins, of 5-16 inch drill rod. All the finished

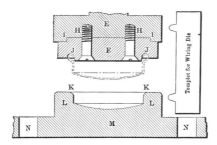

FIG. 357.—DIE AND HOLDER FOR HALF CURL.

parts of the die were then assembled within the bolster as shown,
fastening the drawing punch J down in its seat by screwing the
spring barrel stud V up into it, allowing it to shoulder against the
back of the bolster. The tension pins U were let down into the
bolster and rested on the cast iron washer Y of the spring barrel, while the blank holder ring was placed on top of them. The
edge of the hole in the blank holder was rounded so as to come
down over the drawing easily.

Finding the Blank.

The bolster, with the parts mentioned, was now fastened on
the press, and the punch G, with the plunger H in it, set in line
with it. The nuts Z Z were tightened until the buffer had been
compressed sufficiently to hold the blank tightly between the
blank holder ring Q and the face of the punch G, as soon as the
blank commenced to draw. Now, to find the blank cut out two
or three different sizes of templets and scratch outlines of them
on a sheet of metal, draw up the templets and work from the
outline which proves the nearest to the desired size and shape.
Thus the correct blank will be found in a short time.

Machining the Cutting Die.

As we now have the correct diameter of the blank, we could go ahead and finish the die. The blanking die L L, chucked by the hole, is faced on the back and the outside turned to an angle of ten degrees and then laid aside, and the fastening nut N N is finished.

The bolster is now reset on the faceplate, the blanking die

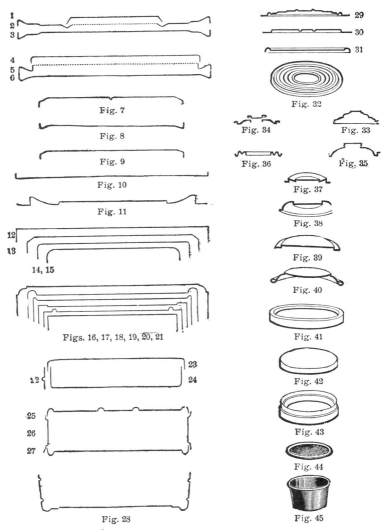

FIG. 358.—SAMPLES OF COMBINATION DIE WORK.

L L is secured by the fastening nut N, after which the outside of this nut is finished and the blanking die bored to within 1-64 inch of the size of the blank templet, and a cut taken off the face. The blanking die is then removed from the bolster, after which it is hardened and drawn to a light straw temper. It is again fastened on the bolster and the inside ground to the size of the templet and the cutting face ground also with a tool-post grinder. The hole for the stop-pin M, as will be understood, is let in before the die is hardened.

Finishing the Punch.

The blanking punch is now roughed down on the outside, hardened and ground to fit the blanking die, the face is ground and the inside polished by lapping with flour emery. The blanking punch temper is drawn from the back, manipulating it so as to get the cutting edge a very dark brown and the drawing portion a light straw temper. All the various parts of both punch and die are now assembled, as shown in Fig. 356, and the stop-pin M let in and also the four stripping pins. These pins are of 5-16 inch Stubs wire, and are bent to project over the face of the die to within a fraction of the cutting edge, thus allowing of the strips of stock being fed beneath them.

Using the Die.

All parts being finished, the die is ready for work. It is set up in the press and the rubber spring barrel is adjusted by tightening the nuts, so that the blank holder ring Q Q will be held level with the face of the cutting die. The manner in which the punch descends and punches out and draws the blank to a finished shell is shown in Fig. 356, the shell being shown by a dark section between the drawing punch and the die. The blanking punch descends until the blank has been drawn from beneath its face and that of the blank holder ring Q Q, the tension for holding the blank being communicated to the blank holder by the compression of the rubber spring barrel. The blanking punch is made longer than necessary, to allow of grinding the face. The cutting portion of the blanking die is finished straight for its entire depth and it also can be ground.

When stock over 1-16 inch thick is to be punched, the die should be ground shearing. Fig. 356 represents the die as it appears when the blanking punch has reached the bottom of its stroke, and shows how the tension pins are forced down by the pressure on the blank holder, and how they compress in turn the rubber spring barrel by means of the washer Y. The locating and fastening of the blanking die upon the bolster by the fastening nut N N is the best of several methods, as it allows of removing and grinding the blanking die and then relocating it in the shortest possible time.

The shell as finished in the second operation is shown in Fig. 355. This operation consists of rolling inward and half-curling the edge. The means used to accomplish this are shown clearly in Fig. 357, and can be intelligently understood with the help of a very slight description. The shell before wiring is placed in the cast iron holder M, the edge of which is rounded to facilitate rapid locating. The curling die F is of tool steel and fits into a depression in the holder E. The face of F is turned as shown and a V-shaped groove with a half-round bottom of the required radius turned into the face, to match the templet. This groove is lapped to a high finish. When half curling a shell, the curling die is set to just descend far enough to curl the edge half way. When a full curl, until the edge meets the side of the shell.

Constructing a Solid-Back Combination Die for Shallow Rectangular Shells.

In the following we will endeavor to show the most practical and expedient method for the construction of a combination

FIG. 359.

die of a generally used type for blanking and drawing shallow rectangular shells, of plain metal of the shape shown in the two views of Fig. 359 and also explain a few kinks which are new and of interest.

The first things to be considered are the same as those laid down for constructing round combination dies, i. e., the thickness of stock to be used, the shape and size of the shell, and the making of the templet. As for finding the blank, although some die makers become so skillful through constant practice that they can find simple blanks without trial draws, there is no reliable formula which will prove correct for any two different shapes or thicknesses of metal, as the conditions under which the metal is drawn and formed, whether in round or rectangular shapes or otherwise, are distinctly different in each case.

Making the Templets and the Drawing Punch.

After the forging for both punch and die (which should be of wrought iron body and tool-steel faced) have been secured, the templets for the drawing portions of both punch and die should be made. These templets should be of stiff sheet metal, and finished all over to the exact shape and size to which the

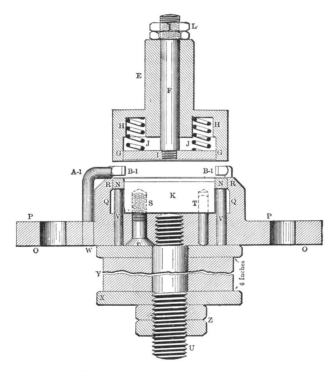

FIG. 360.—DIE FOR RECTANGULAR SHELLS.

shell is to be drawn, the difference between them being exactly one thickness of metal at all points. Then by using the smaller templet the drawing punch K, Fig. 360, should be finished to it. To finish the four corners of the punch another templet, Fig. 362, is required. Take a piece of stiff sheet brass and drill and ream a hole at D to the exact radius to which the inside corners of the shell are required to be, then cut away the stock as shown and finish the two sides C and B to leave a perfect quarter of a circle. We fit all four corners of the drawing punch to it, finishing them smooth and free from lumps. Great care should be taken to get all four corners alike.

Machining the Drawing Portion of the Punch Proper.

Having finished all the working parts of the drawing punch K, we turn our attention to the blanking punch, shown in Fig. 361, the inside of which is to be finished to act as the drawing die. This forging is first chucked and a hole is bored and reamed through its entire length to admit the pad stud F. An arbor is then forced into this hole and run on the lathe centers, and the stem or shank E is finished to fit the ram of the press. Both ends of the forging are then faced, and after the lines have been struck for the drawing die portion the arbor is removed

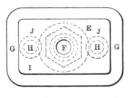

FIG. 361.—PLAN OF
PUNCH.

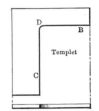

FIG. 362.—TEMPLET
FOR CORNERS.

and the work set face up in the chuck of the universal milling machine, where, by the use of the vertical attachment, the die portion is finished to the lines and templet. First a roughing cutter is used and the inside at G G is roughed out. Then by using a sharp end butt mill, the radius of which is one thickness of metal and .003 of clearance greater than that of the corners of the drawing punch K, and starting from one corner, so as to get a perfect quarter of a circle, the work is fed along one way until the distance from the start of the cut to the finish is exactly two thicknesses of metal longer, plus .003 inch clearance, than the length of the punch K. The cut is then started again at right angles to the first, and the width finished in the same manner, finishing it two thicknesses of metal and clearance wider than the punch. All four sides are finished in this manner, and the inside or bottom is finished flat and square with the sides. When the finishing of the die has been done properly, extra care being taken at the corners, the inside of the die will present a smooth appearance, and very little polishing will be required. The two holes H H for the pad springs J J are then let in by drilling, and the pad I is got out. This pad is of mild steel, about 5-16 inch thick, and is finished to fit easily within the die. A hole is drilled and tapped in the center and the pad stud F is screwed tightly into it. This pad stud is also threaded at the other end for the adjusting nuts L. The parts of the die are then assembled within the punch, and we are then ready to make the trial draws, and find the blank, as the exact size and shape of it have to be found before either punch or die can be finished.

One Way of Finding the Blank for a Rectangular Shell.

To make these trial draws, when constructing dies of the type shown here, two things are necessary—first, a blank holder ring, which afterward forms a permanent part of the die, and, second, a trial spring barrel and plate. The blank holder is usually a forging of tool steel, and it is shown at N N in both the plan and the cross-sectional view of the die in Fig. 363. This

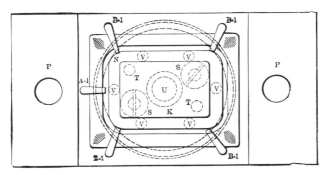

FIG. 363.—PLAN OF DIE.

blank holder should be about $\frac{3}{8}$ inch thick, and, after being planed on both sides, it should be worked out on the inside to templet, to fit nicely at all points around the drawing punch K. The outer edges of the blank holder are left rough until the blanking die has been finished.

We now work out several different sizes of templets, in size and shape somewhere near what we think will be required to form the shell, transferring an outline of each size, and marking the duplicates, upon a flat sheet of stock. The templets are to draw up and the outlines for reference afterward. These templets should be got out of the same stock that is to be used for the shells. The manner of making the trial draws is shown in Fig.

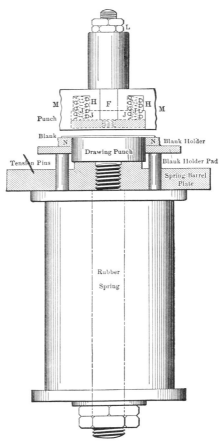

FIG. 364.—ARRANGEMENT FOR FINDING SIZE AND SHAPE OF BLANKS.

364. The spring barrel is of rubber, 4 inches in diameter and 6 inches long, with a clearance hole straight through it to admit the barrel stud, which is screwed tightly into the bottom of the barrel plate. The tension pins for supporting the blank holder

pad are six in number, and they are made extra strong so as to allow of using the spring barrel for trial draws of a number of different sized shells. These pins have to be finished all to exactly the same length, so as to allow of the blank, which is to be drawn up, being held with an equal tension at all points. The parts of this trial spring barrel are assembled as shown with the plate resting on the press bolster, and the barrel projecting down through the hole. The drawing punch is located on the plate, and the blank holder pad and blank holder are placed around it, as shown. The tension adjusting nuts on the end of the barrel stud are then adjusted so that there will be sufficient tension between the blank holder and the face of the punch, so that when the punch descends and the blank is drawn up into it, the metal will not crimp or wrinkle.

One of the templets or blanks which we have got out, is now placed on the blank holder, getting it approximately central with the drawing punch. The punch proper, in which is embodied the drawing die, is fastened within the ram of the press, and the barrel plate shifted and set so that the die is central with it. The punch is then brought down, by revolving the press flywheel by hand, until the templet or blank has been drawn up into it. The punch is then raised and the drawn shell is expelled by the spring pad I. We are now able to determine where we have any excess of metal and where we have a deficiency of it in the blank. We now take another blank and increase or decrease the size at any point that the shape of the drawn shell may require. We then transfer an outline of this templet to a sheet, after which we draw it up. By repeating this operation a few times we are at last able to determine the exact size and shape of the blank. Sometimes the blank may be found in two trials, and often, when the shape is odd or intricate, it is necessary to make quite a number of templets and trial draws before the exact size and shape of the blank can be determined.

Finishing the Blanking Portion of the Die.

Having found the correct blank for the shell, and having made a perfect templet, we can go ahead and finish the die. By reverting to Fig. 360, the method of construction will be clearly understood. The forging for the blanking die is first machined on the bottom and the ends at P P and O. A hole is then drilled at each end, as shown, and the forging is bolted tightly on the table of the milling machine. Then by using the vertical attachment the die is finished to templet, finishing it straight for about ⅜ inch of its depth and then undercutting as shown at Q Q. The outside of the die is then sheared away, leaving about 3-16 margin all around the cutting edge, as shown in the plan of the die. The blank holder ring N is then finished to fit nicely within the die, finishing the outside so that the opening for the drawing punch will be exactly in the center of it—this calls for very accurate work. The blank holder is then hardened, drawn, and ground true and flat on both sides.

Locating the Drawing Punch Within the Die.

To locate the drawing punch K central within the blanking die, the blank holder N is entered within the blanking die and the drawing punch K is located within the blank holder. Four holes are then drilled through the back of the blanking die and transferred into the drawing punch, two holes for the flat-head screws S S and two for the dowels T T. The punch and blank holder are then removed and the holes for the six blank-holder tension pins V drilled through, distributing them evenly or equally around the inside of the die. After the holes for the four stripping pins B1 and the stop-pin A1 are drilled and the hole for the spring barrel stud U let in and tapped, we are ready to harden and temper the die.

Hardening the Cutting Die.

To do this right the die should be carefully heated in either a gas muffle or a charcoal furnace to an even cherry red and then quenched in a tub of water, which should not be too cold. After hardening, the die should be placed on the fire and slightly warmed. The face should then be ground and the outside margin and the inside polished. To temper the die, heat a flat block of cast iron (large enough to hold the heat for some time) and when it is red hot place the die face up on it, wipe and polish top with an oily piece of waste and the various stages of temper can be noted, and when a light straw appears remove the die and allow it to cool off slowly.

Finishing a Square Blanking Punch.

The finishing of the blanking punch is a very simple matter, all that is necessary to attain good results being a little care and the application of a few methods of construction which have become standard. The punch is placed on an arbor and located on the miller centers and the four sides are milled down to almost the finish size. The edges of the punch are then slightly beveled, and it is placed under the press with the drawing punch raised so as to locate itself in the punch by straddling it with two pieces of stock, and the punch sheared a little ways into the blanking die. It is then removed and the surplus stock is worked away and then filed until it is a snug fit within the die. After the face of the punch has been slightly sheared, and the edges of the drawing die slightly rounded and highly polished, the punch may be hardened and then tempered by laying it alternately on each of its four sides on a hot plate, tempering the cutting edges to a dark blue and leaving the inside or drawing portion as hard as possible. When finishing the blanking portion of the punch, care has to be taken to do it so that the drawing portion will be perfectly central.

The drawing punch K is hardened and drawn slightly. It is then fastened and located within the blanking die by means of two flathead screws S S and the two dowels T T. This punch should be highly polished for the inside of the shell to present a smooth appearance. The four stripper pins should be of stiff drill rod and bent and driven into the base of the blanking die in the position shown, projecting out over the blanking die so that the blanking punch will just clear them. The stop-pin A1 is also of drill rod. The two spring barrel washers W and Y are of cast iron, and are faced on both sides, as are also the adjustable nuts Z.

Use and Action of the Die.

When in operation, the punch and die are set up in the press in the relative positions shown in Fig. 360, and the stroke is set so that the pad will bottom. The strip of metal to be punched is then fed under the stripper pins and against the stop-pin A1. The punch descending, the metal is punched and the blank is held between the faces of punch and blank holder, the tension on it increasing as the punch descends and the rubber spring barrel compresses, and the shell is drawn. As the punch reaches the end of its stroke, the drawing punch K forces the shell solidly against the pad I, flattening the bottom and squaring the edges. As the punch rises the drawn and finished shell is expelled from the punch by the spring pad I, and as the press is inclined, it drops off at the back through gravity, while the scrap is stripped from the punch by the four stripping pins.

Combination dies of the design and construction here shown can be used to the best advantage for the blanking and drawing of shells which are not required to exceed ⅞ inch in height, as, in order to draw that amount, the rubber spring barrel is compressed to the maximum, and to compress it more would cause the metal to either stretch excessively or to split. So when it is desired to draw shells over ⅞ inch in height, more than one die is required.

A Set of Dies for Decorated Tin Boxes of Rectangular Shape.

In no branch of modern sheet-metal manufacturing, have dies and press fixtures been adopted and developed with better results, than in the manufacture of decorated tin boxes of rectangular or irregular shapes. As these boxes have almost completely superseded the old pasteboard and small wooden kinds, the number of skilled and well paid mechanics constantly engaged in making improved tools for their cheap and rapid production is enormous. It may not be irrelevant to say that in the manufacture of such articles, results are attained, both as to cheapness and rapidity of production, which are not equaled in any other branch of sheet-metal working.

The following description and accompanying illustrations are of a set of dies for the production of vaseline boxes and covers, the dimensions of which were required to be: 3⅞ inches long by 1 13-16 inches wide by ¾ inch deep. The operations required to finish the box and cover are shown by the half-tones, Figs. 365 to 368. Fig. 365 is the result of the first operation; that of punching out the blank and drawing it as shown. Fig. 366 is the appearance of Fig. 365 after the second operation, which consists of trimming the edges of the blank and drawing it to the height shown. The third operation consists of forming the narrow bead in the four sides of the box, as shown in Fig. 367. Fig. 368 shows the cover of the box, which is blanked and drawn and paneled in one operation.

First Operation for Rectangular Shells.

The first operation, Fig. 365, is accomplished with the punch and die shown in vertical cross section in Figs. 369 and 370 and showing plans of the punch and die respectively. This punch and die is of the single-acting, combination blanking and drawing type, and is of a construction which will allow of the best results being attained at the minimum of cost and labor. It also possesses a number of new and improved features which facilitate production.

As shown in Fig. 369, the cutting or blanking die is finished from a forging of mild steel with a tool steel ring welded on for the die proper. Beneath the blanking die is the punch plate, on

FIG. 365.—FIRST OPERATION.

FIG. 366.—SECOND OPERATION.

FIG. 367.—THIRD OPERATION.

FIG. 368.—THE COVER.

which are located the spring barrel stud, the drawing punch and the blanking die; the latter located by a dowel at each end. The drawing punch is located and fastened on the punch plate by two dowels and two screws, as seen in the plan view, Fig. 370. The blanking die is finished with three degrees of clearance and the blank holder ring is machined to fit it. The cutting die is hardened and drawn to a light straw and the face is sheared so as to have four or five high spots equidistant around the cutting edge. The stripper on the die consists of a piece of sheet stock worked out to a clearance size for the punch, and located at the back of the die on two pieces of tubing B B by two cap screws

A A. This kind of stripper works better than the usual bent pins, and should be used wherever possible. The stop consists of a stud driven into the die base and an adjustable squared piece of stock let into an inclined hole and located by a setscrew. The six tension pins, the buffer or spring barrel and washers, as well as the shape of the blanking die are shown in Figs. 369 and 370.

The punch consists of two parts, the blanking punch, the inside of which acts as the drawing die, and the pad, which also acts as the knockout. The shape of the cutting edge of the

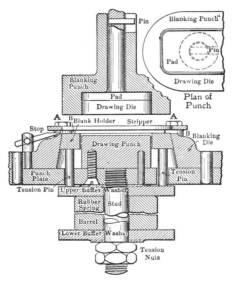

FIG. 369.—CUTTING AND DRAWING DIE FOR FIRST OPERATION.

punch is the exact shape of the blank required to form Fig. 365. The manner in which the blanking and drawing of Fig. 365 is accomplished can be understood from Fig. 369, as can also all other points of construction.

Fundamental Practical Points for Making Irregular Shaped Drawing Dies.

The fundamental practical points to be kept in mind when constructing a die of this kind for working decorated stock are as follows: Make three templets; one for the drawing die, an-

other for the drawing punch and a third for the corners so as
to get the proper radius. Finish the drawing die, the punch
plate, the two sides of the blank holder ring and the inside, and
the drawing die, before starting on the cutting die or punch.
Then make your trial draws until the proper blank is found.
When you have an exact blank, finish the cutting die and the
outside of the blank holder ring, and fit the blanking punch.
Take a cut off the die base after the die has been hardened. For
decorated metal allow .006 inch clearance in the drawing die;
that is, finish the drawing die .006 inch and two thicknesses of
metal larger than the drawing punch, while for plain tin allow
about .0035 inch. By doing this there will be no necessity for
easing up with files or grinding, and the designs on the metal will
not be marred or scratched. Round the edges of the drawing die
smoothly; if the draw is very short, 1-32 inch will be enough,

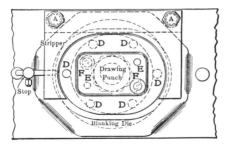

FIG. 370.—PLAN OF COMBINATION DIE.

and if long increase it accordingly. Be careful to get all the
corners of the drawing punch the same radius and those in the
die also (plus two thicknesses of metal and clearance) and lap
very smooth. By keeping the above points in mind no trouble
will be encountered when constructing a die of this type.

Trimming and Drawing Die for Second Operation.

For the second operation, that of trimming the edge of the
portion of the blank which is still flat and finishing the draw,
the double-acting punch and die, Fig. 371, are used. This die
is used in a double-acting press. The plunger or punch consists of the holder, a mild steel forging, the trimming punch and
the drawing punch. The holder is located on the face of the

press ram and fastened by two cap screws through G G. The cutting punch is located in a machined seat sunk into the face of the holder and is fastened by four flat head screws. The plunger proper or drawing punch, fits the inside of the trimming die and is finished with a taper stem for locating and fastening it in the press; the drawing punch portion is finished very smooth and is hardened.

The die consists of the cast iron bolster, the trimming die

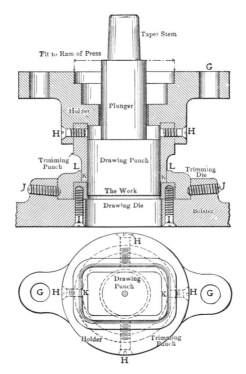

FIG. 371.—DOUBLE-ACTION TRIMMING AND RE-DRAWING DIE FOR SECOND OPERATION.

and the drawing die. The trimming die is located within a machined seat in the top of the bolster and is fastened by four headless screws J. The drawing die is located within a machined seat in the bottom of the trimming die and is fastened to the bolster by four flat head screws from the bottom. The drawing die is left very hard and is lapped to a dead finish and the upper edges rounded, while the lower edges are left sharp and act as a stripper for the work.

The action of this die when in operation can be understood from Fig. 371, in which is shown the work after the cutting punch has descended and trimmed the edges and has stopped (holding the flat portion tightly on the face of the drawing die, by the action of the press) while the plunger or drawing punch continues to descend and draws the metal into and through the drawing die, producing the shell shown in Fig. 365.

The Use of Trimming Dies for Drawn Work.

The reasons why a second drawing die of this type is necessary in order to produce shells of the height shown are: In the first place, it is almost impossible to produce shells of any, except

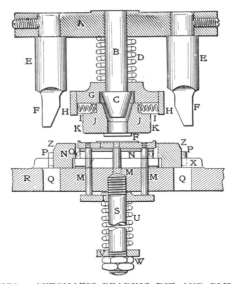

FIG. 372.—AUTOMATIC BEADING DIE AND PLUNGER.

very shallow, depths with true edges without a trimming operation, because the flow of the metal while it is being drawn is such that the slightest defect in the blank will show up in a jagged edge in the drawn shell, and the deeper the draw the greater the effect in the walls of the shells. Secondly, any defect in the construction of the press or in the alignment of the ram with the bolster, or any inaccuracy of parallelism in the parts of the punch and die, will contribute to raggedness in the walls of all drawn work of rectangular or irregular shape. The only way to overcome this is to trim the edges in a second operation in a cutting die of the type shown or with rotary shearing cutters.

The Beading of the Shell.

Fig. 372 shows the die and plunger used to form the bead in the four walls of the shell of box shown in Fig. 367. The bead does not extend entirely around the shell, but, instead, runs to within about ⅜ inch of each corner. Fig. 373 shows a plan of the plunger and Fig. 374 a plan of the die. From the three illustrations the construction and operation of the tools can be

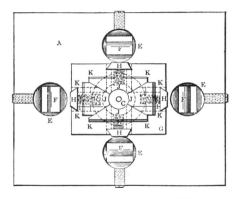

FIG. 373.—PLAN OF PLUNGER OF AUTOMATIC BEADING DIE.

understood. The die and plunger are automatic and are constructed, the one to expand and the other to contract, by the action of the down and up strokes of the press ram.

The die consists of, first the bed plate, Fig. 372, which is a mild steel forging with a raised surface X in the center in which the four sections N of the beading die proper are located to move in and out in dovetailed channels. These four sections are of tool steel and have a bead milled out on their faces, as shown by the dotted lines in profile at O in Fig. 372. They are beveled at Z for the faces of the plunger studs F, and are forced outwardly together by the springs Y. The pins P prevent them from expanding too far. The shell is located on the spring pad L, Fig. 372. This spring pad is worked by the four tension pins

M, the lower ends of which rest on the large washer T, which is located on the spring stud S. The spring U, the washer V and the two nuts are the other parts.

The plunger is shown in section in Fig. 372, and in plan in Fig. 373. The stem (not shown) of the body plate A is fitted to the ram of the press. The four inclined faced studs F are for contracting the die sections N. The expander B is located and fastened in the stem of the body plate by means of a strong taper pin (not shown). The holder is then milled dovetailed to admit the four expanding sections J. Small pieces H are dovetailed into the sides of the holder as backs for the springs. The bead on the sections is shown at K. The sections J are hardened and drawn to a light straw, as are also the sections N in the die.

The manner in which the die is operated can be understood

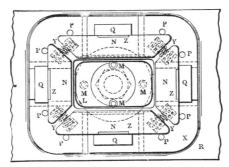

FIG. 374.—PLAN OF AUTOMATIC BEADING DIE.

from Fig. 372. The shell is placed upon the spring pad L and located by the raised ribs at the side and back. As the plunger descends, the four sections enter the shell until they strike the bottom, when the spring pad is forced downward. When the spring pad is halfway down the inclined faces of the studs F encounter the portions Z of the sections N in the die, and commence to contract them. As the spring pad bottoms on the bolster, the sections N touch the walls of the shell and remain stationary, while the inclined faced studs and plunger continue progressing downward and the four sections are expanded by the plunger at C, the sides or sections expanding until the beads are produced in the walls of the shell. As the plunger rises, the four punch sections contract by the action of the springs I, and are withdrawn from the shell, while the die sections expand by the action of the springs Y, and the spring pad L raises the beaded shell to the top of the die, to be thrown off by the operator. The shell as beaded in this die is shown in Fig. 367.

The cover, Fig. 368, is produced in one operation in a die of the same construction as the one shown in Fig. 369. As the draw is rather shallow no trimming die is necessary. Instead, in order to produce the edge shown, the blank must be exact in shape and size at all points.

Rules for Figuring the Approximate Size of Blanks for Drawn Shells.

All die makers that have had much experience in making drawing dies, know that there is no way of figuring out the *exact* size of a blank for a shell of a given depth and diameter. In fact, the only way to secure a perfect blank is by the "cut and try" method described in another part of this chapter. However, although a *perfect* blank cannot be found by figuring, a blank of approximately the correct size can be found by so doing. As it is always well to know how to do this in order that the correct blank shall be found in as few trial draws as possible, we give here a method which has worked well in practice.

The way to figure out the approximate size of a blank for plain cylindrical shells is as follows. Take the outside diameter of the shell to be drawn and add it to the length or depth of same. Then add to this 1-32 inch for every 3-16 inch of depth, and the resulting total will be very near the exact size of the required blank. For deep shells this rule will allow of finding a blank which, when the shell is drawn, will leave enough for trimming, while for shallow shells, which will draw perfectly square across the top, a slight reduction in size will be necessary. The amount to deduct will become apparent after the first trial draw.

As a simple example of how to find the blank, say the height of the shell is to be 2.625, and its diameter (outside) 2.225. Allowing 1-32 inch to every 3-16 inch of height, as 2.625 equals 42-16, we get 14-32 or .4373 to add to the added total of height and depth. Thus we have the following:

Height of shell to be = 2.625 in.
Depth of shell to be = 2.225 in.
Allowance to add on = .4373 in.

As the total of this, 2.625+2.225+.4373, equals 5.2873, the diameter of the blank should be a little over 5 and 9-32 inches.

There are any number of rules for figuring the size of blanks, in which the principle upon which the finding of the diameter is based, is that the area of a drawn shell equals the area of the blank from which it is drawn. But as it *never* does, because of the fact that all sheet metals stretch and run unequally under drawing pressure, the rules work well only on paper. The way to construct a drawing die in the shortest possible time is to figure out the approximate size of the blank in the manner described above, cut out and file up a templet according to the result, make the drawing portions of the die, make the trial draws, discover where there is an excess or a deficiency of metal, make a new templet, which should be almost perfect, draw it up and, if found correct, finish the cutting portions of the die.

In one large shop in Brooklyn, N. Y., where over 100 die makers are employed, they have a man who does nothing but figure out the approximate blanks for the drawing dies and make templets. He makes the templets according to his findings, and they are given to the die-makers, who proceed to make the dies in the manner described above, finding the exact blank as they go along.

The Drawing and Forming of Aluminum.

For the drawing of aluminum shells, tools of the same construction as those used for the production of shells from sheet brass or other sheet metals should be used. The precaution necessary to insure satisfactory results being the use of a proper lubricant, which usually should be a cheap grade of vaseline, not infrequently, however, for deep draws, lard oil will contribute to the attainment of good results. In the majority of cases better results will be derived from the use of vaseline. Never attempt to work aluminum without the use of a lubricant, either in drilling, turning, or press working. For the first two operations use kerosene. Aluminum is properly susceptible to deeper drawing with less occasion to anneal than any of the other commercial metals. When, for instance, an article which is now manufactured in brass, requiring say three or four operations to complete, would usually have to be annealed after each operation, conditions, such as the thickness of metal, depth of draw, etc., determining this; with aluminum, however, if the proper grade is used, it is generally possible to perform these three operations without annealing the metal at all, and at the same time to produce a finished shell which to all intents and purposes is as stiff as an article made from sheet brass.

In order to work aluminum successfully by the use of dies in the power press, particular attention must be paid to the fact that a proper grade of metal is necessary, for either through ignorance or to not observing this fundamental point is the foundation for the majority of complaints that aluminum has been worked and proved a failure. If it should be found necessary to anneal aluminum, it can be readily accomplished by heating it in an ordinary muffle, being careful that the temperature shall not be too high—about 650 or 700 deg. F. The best test as to when the metal has reached the proper temperature, is to take a soft stick and draw it across the metal. If the stick chars and leaves a black mark on the metal, it is sufficiently annealed and is in a proper condition to proceed with further operations.

CHAPTER IX.

The Philadelphia Mint.

Some of the finest and most powerful presses built to-day are used for coining, and nowhere in the world is there a finer lot of such machines than in the new United States mint in Philadelphia. This new mint is the best-equipped and most artistically-modeled coining establishment in the world, and as it now stands has cost over $2,400,000. As a description of this great factory will convey to the reader an understanding of the various processes required in the coining of metal, we will begin with the melting room and proceed onward until we reach the department where the finished coins are turned out.

The bullion used for coin is first received in the deposit room, and from there goes to the melting room. In this room are sixteen melting furnaces. Crude petroleum is used exclusively for heating the furnaces, the temperature of which can be raised to 1,000 degrees.

The keg-shaped crucibles are made of plumbago and are kept piled about the furnaces. These, as needed, are placed in the furnaces and in them are placed the gold and silver bricks, which are brought from all parts of the world and vary greatly in size and shape. Before being turned into coin they must be alloyed with copper until 900 per cent. fine.

The men who do the melting stand before the furnaces wearing huge mittens made of heavy buckskin or crash, padded with pieces of Brussels carpet. When the metal reaches a certain color, which they can detect only after long experience, it is ready to be moulded into ingots. But before this is done a few drops of the molten metal are removed for the assayer.

In moulding, a man whose gloved hands grasp a pair of tongs holding a three-spouted gray bowl in their jaws, dips from each crucible the glowing metal and pours it into a series of clamp moulds. Each set of moulds are then taken by a second man and plunged into cold water. The hardened ingots are next dipped into muriatic acid, which eats away all particles of foreign matter, after which they are placed in a second water bath.

All ingots, whether gold or silver, are moulded to measure a foot in length, but vary up to one and one-half inches in width and thickness, according to the size of the coin to be struck from them.

Each finished ingot comes from the mould with a blunt end, this resulting from the end of the mould where the metal was poured in. A row of machines shear the irregular ends off, after which the bars are passed to bench hands who file off the rough edges.

The filings are caught in oilcloth-lined boxes and carefully saved. Next the ingots are sent to a long table, where they are placed side by side in a row, and a man stamps upon each a number, designating its melt.

The bars now pass to the assayer, who compares the few drops of metal taken from the furnace with the correspondingly numbered lot of the finished bars. If the latter falls below 900 per cent. fine, it must be remelted.

The ingots which have passed the assayer next pass into the rolling department where they are passed between massive rollers fifteen times, reducing them until they are twice the required thickness. Before reducing them further they must be annealed. For this purpose a large annealing and tempering furnace is provided in which the metal bars are heated to a cherry red and quenched in water. They are then put through another series of rolls fifteen times before being reduced to the proper thickness, which, of course, depends upon the denomination of the coin to be made from them. The metal comes from this last rolling operation in strips varying in dimensions up to six feet in length, four inches wide and about one-sixteenth thick.

The flat strips of gold and silver are now fed to presses which are equipped with blanking dies. The strips are fed automatically and the finished blanks drop out at the bottom into a tray. These are the blanks upon which the final designs are to be embossed. The blanks as large as a quarter are cut in a single row from the strip, while the smaller ones are cut in combinations of two and three by gang dies. The scrap strips are returned to the melters.

The blanks are next sent to the cleaning department, after which they are sent to the automatic weighing machines. On each of these machines are ten upright brass tubes into which the blanks are fed. Beneath the tubes is a long sliding bar with a reciprocating motion, each move of which pushes off ten blanks into a small basket on one end of the scale beam. The blanks are weighed instantly and are passed through a series of troughs leading to three boxes. The light blanks fall into the first box, the standard ones into the second, and the heavy ones into the last box. The light blanks are condemned and melted over, while those which are over weight are taken to the adjusting room. Here over 100 women, each with a set of scales and files before her, are employed in filing the edges of the heavy blanks until all are down to the standard size and weight.

The next operation through which the blanks are passed is that of milling. The milling machines put on the flat rim or raised edge which protects the face of the coin from abrasion. The milled blanks are now reheated to a cherry red in an automatic annealing furnace, through which they are fed and at last drop into a copper collender, then lifted by a crane into a bath of muriatic acid, are revolved in this bath and finally dropped into a revolving screen filled with sawdust, which cleans and dries them thoroughly and makes them ready for coining.

Against the wall of the coining room there are twenty-four powerful presses, each with a vertical face of polished steel forged or cast in the shape of a giant letter O. At the front is a box filled with shining blanks which are fed to the machines by women. The blanks are fed beneath the punch through a tube, a pair of automatic fingers taking the lower blank and placing it on the die. The bottom and top of the blank are embossed at the one stroke, and at the same time through the force of expansion, the disk of metal tightens within the fluted collar in the die, thus finishing the coin with the fluted edges. Silver dollars and gold coin are stamped at the rate of 85 per minute, quarters and half-dollars, 90 per minute, nickels, 110 per minute and cents 120 per minute.

From the coining room the finished money goes to the proving department, where its accuracy is again tested. It is then ready for the counting room.

In this department gold coins, silver dollars and half dollars are all counted by weight. They are stacked up inside steel frames and swept off into the pan of a huge pair of scales. The quarters, dimes, nickels and cents are shuffled over large flat boards with parallel strips of brass between which the coins fit loosely. When the boards are filled with money, they are tilted until the coins flowing over them fill all the spaces between the strips. In this way $1,000 in dimes are counted on a single board every eighteen seconds, and thrown into an opening at the front of the counters' table. Leaving the counters, the new money is placed in steel strong boxes to await shipment.

An Embossing Press for Work Requiring Heavy Pressure.

In Fig. 375 is shown the type of press used for embossing sil-

FIG. 375.—AN EMBOSSING PRESS FOR COINING.

ver, britannia, brass, copper, etc., in the manufacture of medals, coin, regalia, jewelry, watches, silverware, etc.

The die is fastened to a slide which is actuated from below by means of powerful toggles. These toggles are made of steel castings, having hardened steel pieces set in at the seats and joints. Adjustment of pressure and die space is effected by means of steel wedges between the punch holder and frame.

This machine embodies several novel features. In order to withstand the tensile strain of 350 tons, which it is designed to exert on the work, the body is made of a solid wrought-iron forging, the center of which is slotted to admit the working parts. The mandrel on which the lower dial rests is made of steel and is operated by toggle joints or links made of tool steel hardened and ground.

In order to obtain the necessary adjustment of the dies to regulate the pressure, a steel shoe is provided above the mandrel, to which the upper die is attached. This shoe is held up in place by four rods passing up to a yoke at the top, and the weight is supported by four large compression springs. The upper side of the shoe is made slightly inclined, and a steel wedge inserted between it and the bearing in the frame. The position of the wedge is adjusted by means of a screw which passes through the side of the housing, and which is operated by the hand wheel shown.

Punching Tools for Heavy Work.

Fig. 376 shows a set of punching tools for punching holes in heavy stock, and Fig. 377 the manner in which they are located and used in a large punch press. The set of tools consist of die block, die holder, die, edge gage, pull off or stripper, punch and punch holder. The die block bolts on the lower jaw to receive the die holder and die, and the die holder is made to fit the die block and bored to fit the various sizes of small dies. When the die is small it is made circular in form to fit the die holder, but if it is large, it should be made to the shape of the die holder to fit directly into the block. The punch holder has a square shank and fits into the ram of the press and is bored to fit the shanks of the small punches. When the punches are large they should be made with the shank to fit directly into the ram of the press. The edge gage bolts to the frame of the press and its edge serves as a gage for the edge of the piece to be punched. The stripper or pull off is a pivoted lever whose forward end straddles the punch and strips the sheet as the punch rises; it is adjustable up and down by means of a pin at the rear end of the lever, so as to accommodate different thicknesses of metal. The Kennedy and Richards patent punches are often used in place of ordinary tools described

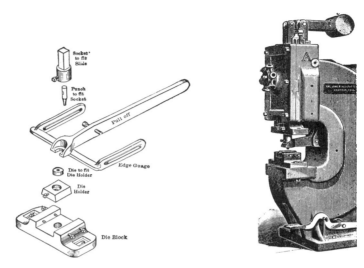

FIG. 376.—SET OF PUNCHING TOOLS.   FIG. 377.—TOOLS IN PRESS.

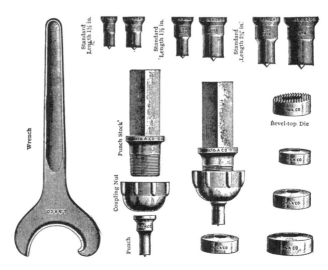

FIG. 378.—PUNCHES, DIES, ETC., FOR HEAVY STOCK.

FIG. 379.—POWERFUL BLANKING PRESS WITH DIES IN POSITION FOR PRODUCING LARGE BLANKS.

above. Fig. 378 shows a collection of punches and dies used for piercing heavy stock. As shown the punches have pointed centers to locate the stock properly by the center punch marks which have been previously laid out on the sheet to be punched. The holders for the punches require no description as the illustrations show all clearly.

Double Crank Presses for Operating Large Cutting and Forming Dies.

For operating large cutting and forming dies, or gangs of punches and dies extending over a large area, double crank presses are decidedly preferable to the ordinary "single crank" type. The two pitmans are so connected that they are always adjusted simultaneously, thus enabling the operator to quickly raise and lower the slide to suit the thickness of dies without any danger of getting the guides out of alignment.

For heavy cutting and forming it is best to use these presses with back gearing, as shown in Fig. 379. In connection with such large presses an automatic friction clutch will be found to give the best results, as it obviates the difficulties experienced with other types of clutches in presses of this class when used for certain kinds of work. The action of such a clutch is practically instantaneous, and it avoids entirely the severe shock which tends to destroy the clutch parts and sometimes causes expensive delays and repairs. In the press shown in Fig. 379 the larger gear wheel instead of revolving continually, is at a standstill until the clutch is brought into action. This constitutes an additional advantage in the saving of considerable wear, and· avoids the necessity of a brake on the crank shaft. The clutch is also operated by means of a hand-lever in such a way that the operator can stop and start the slide instantaneously at any point. This facilitates to a very large extent the setting of the dies.

These double crank presses are used extensively in the manufacture of sheet-iron and steel goods, such as vapor stoves, wrought iron ranges, shingles, paneled ceiling and siding for buildings, cornice work, stove boards, drip pans, armature discs and segments, etc., and for operating gangs of punches for rivet holes in tanks, water pipes, gasometers, kitchen boilers, etc. They are also often arranged and used for forging purposes in the manufacture of hammers and similar articles requiring a series of dies set side by side. When intended for punching holes in long strips of metal, openings are cored in the uprights. The crosshead is guided in long, adjustable bearings, so that cutting and perforating dies, as well as others requiring great accuracy in movement, may be operated.

Heavy Notching Press With Punch and Die in Position.

The press shown in Fig. 380 with punch and die in position is

FIG. 380.—HEAVY NOTCHING PRESS AND DIES.

used for heavy bridge and structural iron work. The press is motor driven and is a very powerful machine. The die is made in sections and the parts are located and fastened within a die block as shown. The punch face is sheared so as to begin to cut

FIG. 381.—HEAVY DISC PUNCHING PRESS AND DIES.

FIG. 382.—STEAM DRIVEN MULTIPLE PUNCH AND DIES.

at the edge of the sheet or beam and progressively punch out the section.

Heavy Disc Punching.

In Fig. 381 are shown a press and set of dies for punching discs 26 inches in diameter from 3-16 high carbon steel. As shown, the die is made in segments, each section having a curved shearing edge so as to make the punching out of the discs progressive and thereby reducing the strain on the press. The sections of the die are located and fastened within a holder. The punch and die holders used in a press of this type should be made so as to receive tools for discs of smaller diameters also. There is an automatic stop on this machine that arrests the slide at any point of the stroke.

Steam-Driven Multiple Punches.

The illustration, Fig. 382, is of a double-geared, steam-driven punch press measuring 10 feet between housings, with throat 6 inches deep. It has a side stand with outboard bearings for cam and countershafts, and is equipped with dies for punching one hundred and twenty $\frac{3}{8}$ inch holes, one inch between centers, in a $\frac{1}{4}$ inch plate. There is a pressure plate over the punches, made in removable sections so that a single punch can be taken out for repair, etc., without disturbing any of the others. This machine has also a slide adjustment which is furnished to overcome the shortening of the punch caused by wear, and an automatic stop which causes the slide to stop at the completion of each stroke. The hold-down is automatic and, after stripping, rises to give plenty of room for the insertion of the plate.

Fig. 383 illustrates another double-geared multiple punch, 104 inches between housings, equipped with dies to punch all of the 64 holes in the tire of a steel harvester wheel 9 feet 6 inches long at a single stroke of the press. This machine has a center bearing for the cam shaft, and side clamping device for centering the strip by hand before punching them. It has slide adjustment which raises and lowers the slide to make up for the wearing down of the punches, and an automatic stop which arrests the slide at the top of the stroke with the punches and dies open to receive the work for the next operation. Machines of this type are made heavier and lighter, belt, steam and electrically driven, and any width between housings with a throat depth to suit requirements.

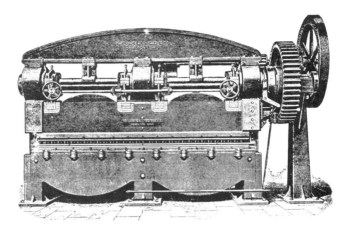

FIG. 383.—MULTIPLE PUNCH PRESS EQUIPPED FOR
PUNCHING 64 HOLES.

FIG. 384.—MULTIPLE PUNCH WITH SPACING TABLE AND DIES.

Multiple Punch With Hand-Feed Spacing Table.

The illustration, Fig. 384, represents a powerful machine capable of punching twenty-six ½ inch holes through ¼ inch plate at each stroke of the slide. Owing to length of the feed required, the table is moved by hand, the distance between centers of end holes being 70 inches. As shown the punches and dies are fitted to holders which allow of their being quickly changed or removed.

Heavy Beam Punching.

In Fig. 385 is shown a heavy steam-driven machine fitted with

FIG. 385.—HEAVY BEAM PUNCHING PRESS, TWO 11-16 HOLES.

tools to punch two 1 1-16 inch holes in the flanges of a 15 inch I beam or do any lighter work. The punches and dies are adjustable so that holes may be punched opposite each other, or staggered, one in each flange or both in line in the same flange. The machine is under perfect control of the treadle, has adjustable rollers to support the beams, and is provided with automatic stop so that the operator can arrest the slide at any point in the stroke.

The machine shown in Fig. 386 is of the same type as the other except it is for heavier work. It is equipped to punch two 1½ inch holes in the flanges of a 30 inch bulb-beam at one stroke, or

FIG. 386.—BEAM PUNCHING PRESS EQUIPPED WITH TOOLS FOR PUNCHING TWO 1½-INCH HOLES IN THE FLANGES OF A 30-INCH BULB-BEAM AT ONE STROKE.

do any lighter work. The adjustable roller frames that support the work swing aside and leave the opening in the lower jaw entirely clear. The punches and dies are adjustable in two directions.

Fig. 387 shows another heavy machine equipped with punches and dies for punching two holes in flanges or six holes in the web of a 24 inch I beam. The punch holders and die holders are adjustable, the minimum distance between centers of the outside holes being $2\frac{1}{2}$ inches and the maximum distance being 38 inches. Each punch is provided with a gag so that it can be made inop-

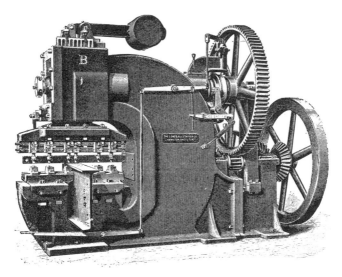

FIG. 387.—BEAM PUNCHING PRESS, DIES FOR SIX HOLES.

erative, if desired, and does not have to be withdrawn in changing from flange punching to web punching.

The machine shown in Fig. 388 is equipped to punch one or more holes in the flanges and the web of I beams, channels, angles, Z-bars or plates, with 15 inch throat. The punches are provided with gags or receding sockets so that they can be made inoperative if desired. The spacing is perfectly controlled by levers and can be instantly changed from zero to full throw by simply moving a lever. One lever adjusts the spacing in multiples of sixteenths and the other in multiples of $\frac{1}{2}$ inch, up to 8 inches, providing for any scheme of spacing or any variation in spacing on the same

FIG. 388.—HEAVY BEAM PRESS WITH AUTOMATIC SPACING TABLE FOR PUNCHING ONE OR MORE HOLES IN WEB OR I-BEAMS, CHANNELS, ANGLES, Z-BARS, OR PLATES.

work. The levers lock in large notches and do not require delicate setting. The table is provided with quick return power movement, independent of the feed, for shifting it back and forth. An automatic hold-down and slide guide, press the work against the gage.

A Beam-Coping Machine Equipped With Coping Dies.

The machine illustrated in Fig. 389 is equipped with double coping dies so that beams can be fed from either side and have both ends coped without turning them around. Punching tools

FIG. 389.—BEAM COPING PRESS EQUIPPED WITH COPING DIES.

to punch the flanges and web of the beams can be substituted for the coping tools, the dies being high and narrow to make room for the lower flange of the beam and get close into the corners. This machine is used to cope the ends of 24 inch beams or punch six ⅞ holes in the web or two 1 inch holes in the flanges, as its heaviest work. As shown, the machine is motor-driven.

Heavy punching tools and machines, such as are shown and described in this chapter, and many other types too numerous to mention, are used principally by boiler makers, bridge builders, ship builders, and structural iron work concerns.

CHAPTER X.

Feeding of Stock a Factor in Production.

In the production of parts and articles from sheet metal by
the use of dies, the proper feeding of the stock is one of the chief
things to be considered, as the efficiency of the finished product
and the cost of its production depends greatly upon the methods
employed for this part of the work.

Although the fact is well known that sheet metal goods manufacturers strive to keep the cost of their tool equipment down to
the lowest figure, and do not hasten to avail themselves of the many
practical devices which are being constantly designed to assist in
the cheap and rapid production of sheet metal parts, they would
find that by installing a thoroughly practical system of feeding
in their establishments, the safety of their operators would be
insured and their profits increased. The improvements which
have been made during the last few years in devices for press
feeding are indeed wonderful, and we feel safe in stating that
there is not a sheet metal part or article in general use to-day for
which some one of the large establishments devoted to the manufacture of sheet-metal working machinery cannot provide an
automatic feeding device to assist in its rapid and cheap production.

Hand-Feeding.

The most common and by far the oldest method of feeding
sheet metal to dies is by hand, and in a number of cases it is the
best. When the metal to be punched comes in short sheets or
strips, or where scrap stock is used, it should be fed by hand,
feeding between a pair of gage plates, or a single one, on the die,
against a stop-pin, as shown and described in the opening chap-
ters of this book. But wherever the nature of the work will allow an automatic feeding device actuated by the stroke of the
press should be used. In the following pages are illustrated and
described a number of the many different kinds of automatic

feeds which are now in general use in all shops where the maximum production from the minimum of labor is desired.

Single Roll Feeding.

When large quantities of pierced blanks, plain blanks, shallow drawn or formed articles which can be produced in one operation, or other work of a like character are required, and the stock from

FIG. 390.—PUNCH PRESS WITH SINGLE ROLL FEED AT SIDE, FOR SMALL BLANKING, PIERCING OR BENDING OPERATIONS.

which they are to be punched can be had in long strips or rolls, a press fitted with a single roll feed as shown in Fig. 390 should be used. The feeds and presses are to be had in a number of different sizes to suit the size and shape of the work, and the feeds and machines are made in different styles, so as to feed from front to back, left to right, or the reverse. The feeds are made with various size rolls with automatic release action for the upper roll, and with hand wheels as desired. The distance which the

FIG. 391.—PERFORATING PRESS WITH AUTOMATIC
DOUBLE ROLL FEED.

stock can be fed at each stroke of the press is governed by the size of the rolls and the adjustment of the feed lever.

Fig. 392 shows a different style of single roll feed and its adaptation and location on a larger press than that shown in Fig. 390. The slide of this press is provided with a wedge adjustment actuated by means of the hand wheel in front. The upper feed roll may be quickly raised by means of an eccentric handle permitting the strip of metal to be accurately placed, released, and readjusted at any time.   The pawl operates on the edge of a tooth-

FIG. 392.— POWER PRESS WITH SINGLE ROLL FEED AT BACK.

less disk, taking its "bite" by means of a wedging action, which permits of easy adjustment and fine spacing.   A machine equipped with a feed of this type is very useful for bicycle chain work, clock and watch parts, Yale key blanks, and many other articles of a like nature.

A Double Roll Feed for Perforated Metal Sheets.

The double roll feed shown in position on the press in Fig. 391 is of the type most generally used for feeding sheets of metal which are to be perforated in regular patterns by means of a single row of dies, or in staggered patterns by means of a double row of dies. As shown, the press is built specially for this feeding device, and as equipped has been adopted extensively on account of its speed of production, the accuracy of its work, and the ease with which the dies and punches may be removed or adjusted. It may be run at from 70 to 100 strokes a minute, according to the class of work done, and feeding the metal through the rolls will punch a double row of holes at each stroke across a 14 inch sheet.

The roll housings are hinged, and each set of rolls has a hand-wheel for quickly adjusting the sheet at the start, or removing at the end. The rolls are actuated by a lever connected at the side of the press, one end to one of the lower feed roll ends, and the other to an adjustable stud in a T slot in the end of the press crank shaft.

Feeding Partly Finished Small Parts and Articles.

Fig. 393 illustrates a method of feeding parts and articles of small size beneath punches. It is used when adapted to a press as shown for letter stamping or reshaping blanks and shells in the manufacture of tin bottle-capsules, burner parts, tin box covers, and many other articles. In this device the die is fastened to a sliding piece, which receives its motion through a cam on the shaft in such a manner as to stand still while the punch is doing its work, after which the slide travels forward toward the operator, who removes the finished piece and locates a new one without endangering his hands by getting them between the punch and die. With a device of this type adapted to the press as shown, a good operator will do from 50 to 100 pieces of work per minute according to the style of the work.

Tube Feeding of Parts Which Have Been Previously Punched.

The stamping, lettering or other die work on small blanks which have been previously punched, such as bicycle chain links, buttons, clock and lock parts, metal novelties, etc., can be best accomplished by means of a tube feed of the type shown on the press in Fig. 394. These devices are built to feed front to back, or left to right, or the other way, as desired. The blanks are put into a tubular holder from which an automatically actuated slide takes them one by one, conveying them into the die at the rate of

FIG. 393.—PRESS WITH CAM-ACTUATED   FIG. 394.—PRESS WITH TUBE
           DIE SLIDE.   FEED.

100 to 150 per minute. In some cases it becomes necessary to add a cam-actuated stop-gage to insure feeding the blank to the accurate position. This stop-gage is constructed similar to the finger-gage shown in Chapter I. The tube feed may be easily removed and a single or double roll feed such as are shown in Figs. 390 and 391 substituted.

Double Roll Feeding for Producing Small Pierced Blanks from Strip.

The double roll feed shown on the press, Fig. 395, is specially adapted for such work as piercing bicycle chain links, washers, watch, clock and lock parts, and many other pieces used in the

FIG. 395.—PUNCH PRESS WITH STAY RODS, DOUBLE ROLL FEED AND DIES FOR PRODUCING SMALL PIERCED BLANKS FROM THE STRIP.

manufacture of hardware, lamps, electric apparatus, etc. The die first pierces the holes and then cuts the blanks, producing from 100 to 150 pieces per minute. On each stroke of the press, at the moment when the pilot pins located in the blanking punch are about to enter the pierced holes, the upper rolls are automatically raised so as to release the strip and permit the pilot pins to shift it into the correct position, correcting any "slip" which may have occurred in feeding, and thereby overcoming the multiplication of error. By means of the hand wheels shown, the strip may be

FIG. 396.—PRESS EQUIPPED WITH DOUBLE ROLL AND LATERAL FEEDS, AND DIES FOR EMBOSSING, BLANKING AND FORMING TIN STAPLES OR TAGS FROM STRIPS OF TIN.

quickly fed to the starting position and the last end quickly re-moved.

Double Roll and Lateral Feeds.

The half-tone Fig. 396 represents a press as equipped with a double roll feed and lateral feed, with dies for embossing, blank-ing and forming tin staples or tags from strips of thin metal.

It illustrates a method of combining feeds for automatically perforating, embossing or lettering, blanking and forming miscellaneous small tin and brass goods; it requires no description as its action is similar to the one shown in Fig. 395.

Double Roll Feed with Automatic Release.

A method of double roll feeding adapted for double-acting

FIG. 397.—DOUBLE ACTION PRESS WITH DOUBLE ROLL FEED
AND AUTOMATIC ROLL RELEASE.

presses for the rapid production of shells which are cut and drawn from the strip in "push-through" dies is shown in Fig. 397. From 60 to 150 shells per minute may be produced by

FIG. 400.

FIG 399.

FIG. 398.

BENCH POWER PRESSES WITH DIAL FEEDS FOR BUTTONS, SMALL BURNER PARTS UMBRELLA TRIMMINGS, ETC.

this method, according to the size and shape of shell.   The roll feed is easily adjusted to different sizes of blanks.   Both of the upper feeding rolls are provided with automatic cam-lifting devices, with hand levers, permitting of opening the rolls at any time or readjusting the strip.   For metal shells (burners, ferrules, umbrella trimmings, thimbles, tin goods, etc.) it can be adapted to the best advantage.

Dial Feeds.

Dial feeds are used for a variety of work, the smaller sizes, such as are shown in Figs. 398 to 400 adapted to small bench presses, being used extensively in the manufacture of buttons, small burner parts, umbrella trimmings, and other light staple articles.   In many cases two or three punches and dies can be made to act simultaneously, performing one after another the necessary operations, either in the finishing of one part or article, or in the assembling of two or more parts of an article, thus doubling or trebling the efficiency of the machine.   Dial feeds of this kind are also used for holding large blanks such as armature disks, rotating the blank successively at each stroke of the press.   The same style of feed fitted with locating sockets to hold and carry the work is shown adapted to a larger press in Fig. 401.   As shown, the press is fitted with tools for performing the two burner operations shown in Figs. 2 and 3.   The shell as fed and located to the sockets in the dial plate is shown in Fig. 1, it being fed around until it has been worked upon by the punches.

Dial feeds of various kinds may be applied to nearly all power presses, as they can be used for automatically carrying blanks, shells, cups, etc., between punch and die to receive a second operation.   They are largely used in the manufacture of brass goods, trimmings, buttons, cartridge and primer shells, tubes for pen holders and pencil cases, and many other specialties.   Two essentially different styles of dial feeds are in general use—the "friction dial feed" and the "ratchet dial feed."

The Friction Dial Feed.

The friction dial feed consists of a smooth circular disk, which revolves continuously, in combination with stationary gages above it, so that the pieces placed on the disk are led accurately under the punch.   In order to insure reliable action in most cases a finger or gripping movement is attached to the feed, which places and holds the piece in the exact position when ready for the descending punch.   The friction dial feed is best for redrawing short shells or pieces which are not liable to topple over.

The Ratchet Dial Feed.

The ratchet dial feed consists of a circular plate which connects with the main shaft through the medium of cams or pawls, so as to receive an intermittent rotary motion.   This disk is pro-

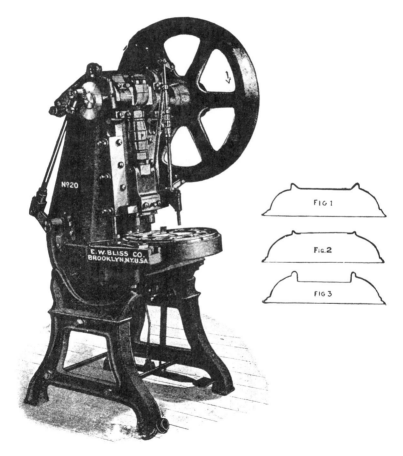

FIG. 401.—PRESS WITH AUTOMATIC DIAL FEED, FITTED WITH DIES
FOR OPERATIONS 2 AND 3 ON BURNER SHELL, FIG. 1.

vided with a number of holes to receive either the work or the dies. By the use of a ratchet dial feed it is often possible, in many cases, to submit the pieces to two or three consecutive operations without rehandling. The feeds shown in Figs. 398 to 401 are ratchet dial feeds.

FIG. 402.—GEARED PUNCH PRESS EQUIPPED WITH FIVE SEPARATELY ADJUSTABLE PUNCH CARRIERS AND AUTOMATIC FEEDING DEVICE.

Burner shell finished on four-punch machine. First operation, **Fig. 1**, made in combination die.

A Press with Adjustable Punch Carriers and an Automatic Friction Dial Feeding Device.

The press illustrated in Fig. 402 is equipped to produce with great speed and economy such articles as lamp burners, stove trimmings, harness oil can tops, small coffee and teapot covers, lantern parts and other similar articles made in large quantities, which require a series of operations after the first cup or shell has been produced in a combination or drawing die.

The first operation shells are placed on the friction dial, whence they are carried automatically by the reciprocating motion or feed from one to another of the several dies, then automatically discharged.

In a press arranged as this one is all dies operate simultaneously, and as the press may be run at a speed of 40 to 60 strokes per minute (according to the size and shape of the shells) its output of 200 to 300 operations per minute is equivalent to the work of 10 to 20 single slide presses fed by hand. As the press may be fed by an inexpensive operator and there is no intermediate handling, the amount of labor and shop room saved, as well as the entire absence of danger to the hands of the operator, are items of very great importance to manufacturers.

Presses of this type are regularly built with four or five punch carriers, but where an additional number of operations are required they are built wider and additional punch carriers provided. Such dies as are used for cutting, forming, perforating, lettering and flanging may be operated in these presses. The number of operations that may be performed is limited to the number that can be done without annealing the shells or parts. Shells requiring a less number of operations than there are punch carriers in the press may be handled just as readily as though the full number of dies permissible were being operated.

The press shown in Fig. 403 is equipped with a different style of dial feed, and is used extensively for redrawing tinfoil bottle caps, caster parts, burner shells and other articles which have been cut and drawn. As equipped it will redraw from 50 to 70 shells per minute, according to the skill and diligence of the operator. The blank-holder slide is actuated on the down stroke by the two cams shown, and is raised by a powerful spring with lever attached to the back of the slide and not shown in the illustration.

The dial feed and bottom knock-out attachment are operated from cams on the outer end of the shaft.

A dial feed as used for work requiring heavy pressure, such as embossed buttons, stem-winder knobs, clock-axle bearings or bushings, etc., and adapted to a press with a cam-actuated knock-

FIG. 403.—DOUBLE ACTING REDUCING PRESS, WITH DIAL FEED AND KNOCK-OUT ATTACHMENT FOR DRAWN WORK.

out for punch and die, and a safety stop attachment, is shown in Fig. 404.

A Double-Action Gang Press with Special Automatic Feed.

The machine shown in Fig. 405 is designed for cutting, drawing and stamping a considerable number of small shells at each stroke. It works with great speed, and effects a considerable saving of stock, as will be seen from the scrap sheet shown on

FIG. 404.—PRESS WITH AUTOMATIC DIAL FEED, CAM-ACTUATED KNOCKOUT FOR PUNCH AND DIE, AND SAFETY STOP ATTACHMENT.

the floor at the left of the press. It is arranged with a special automatic feeding device, as shown, and carries 14 sets of double-action dies, and will produce nearly 1,000 shells per minute. It may also be arranged for more or fewer dies according to what width of sheet, the size of the article, or other special conditions may call for.

FIG. 405.—"BLISS" PATENT TOGGLE-DRAWING PRESS EQUIPPED WITH A GANG OF DOUBLE-ACTING DIES, PRODUCING 14 SHALLOW SHELLS AT EACH STROKE AT THE RATE OF 70 STROKES A MINUTE.

A number of other methods of feeding sheet metal to dies are shown in connection with the dies and presses for various kinds of work in other parts of this book.

Lubricants to Use in the Working of Sheet Metal.

All dies will be found to work better, last longer and produce better results if a proper lubricant is used, and in the following we give a list of the kinds which have proved the best for the work mentioned. When punching iron, steel, copper or German silver, a thin coating of lard oil or sperm oil should be spread over the strips or sheets before punching. A good way to do this evenly is to coat one sheet thickly and feed it through a pair of rolls, thus the oil will spread over the sheet and coat the rolls and a number of other sheets may be run through the rolls and coated evenly. For drawn work this matter of coating the sheets (before blanking and drawing the shells) will be found the best, as the coating of oil on the sheets or strips of metal will be very thin and it will not be found necessary to clean the shells afterward, as the oil will have disappeared during the process of drawing. When the oil is applied with a brush or pad the coating will be so thick that it will be necessary to clean the articles produced. In the drawing of steel shells a thin mixture of grease and white lead will give the best results. For working sheet brass or other soft metals (except in drawing operations) soap water should be used, allowing the strip or sheet to run through a tank filled with the solution as it is fed to the dies. For zinc, soap suds heated to a boiling point and applied as the metal is fed to the dies will allow of the best results being attained. For cutting aluminum use kerosene oil as a lubricant, for drawing it use vaseline.

Although very often dies are used to punch sheet metal without applying a lubricant to the stock, and good results are attained, it will be found that where a lubricant is always used on all classes of sheet metal work the tools will last longer, the results will be better and there will be very little breakage.

CHAPTER XI.

Annealing Defined.

Metals are annealed by being slowly cooled from a high temperature. Annealing generally increases the flexibility, softness and ductility of bodies. When metals have become brittle through excess of strain in rolling, drawing, twisting, hammering, or other mechanical means, their properties may be restored by annealing.

Hardening Defined.

Steel and a number of other metals, if cooled suddenly after having been strongly heated, become harder, more brittle and more elastic than before. If tool steel is heated to a white heat and then plunged into a bath of cold water or mercury, it will become almost as hard as a diamond, very elastic; and so brittle that it can be used only for drilling tempered steel or chilled iron, for coining and engraving dies, and for the hardest kind of files.

Tempering Defined.

Steel may be worked to any shape required in the arts when it is in its softened condition. It is then strongly heated and suddenly cooled, and as this hardening process renders it too brittle for ordinary purposes, something of its elasticity is sacrificed, and a portion of its hardness removed by reheating the steel to a lower temperature and cooling it gradually. This process of annealing is called "drawing" or "tempering." The temper to which the steel is drawn depends on the use to which it is to be put, and is regulated by varying the temperature of the second heating, the higher the degree of heat the softer the steel.

When a steel article has been hardened, then polished or ground and reheated, the film of oxide on its surface becomes, at a temperature of 428 deg. F., of a light straw color, then through intermediate hues to a violet yellow (509 deg. F.), blue (560 deg. F.) ; at 977 deg. F. the steel passes to a red heat. These colors guide the workman in his efforts to temper the tool as required. Light yellow is the temper required for articles or tools requiring a keen cutting edge. A deeper yellow for fine cutlery. Violet is the temper required for table knives, requiring flexibility more than a hard brittle edge, and blue for all tools or articles which are required to be very flexible.

Heating Steel.

Never heat a piece of steel, which it is desired to harden, above the lowest heat at which it will harden, and the larger the piece of steel the more time required to heat it properly, as it will have to be higher than a smaller piece of the same steel, because of the fact that a large piece of steel takes longer to cool than a smaller piece, as when a large piece of steel is plunged into the bath a great volume of steam arises and blows the water away from it, thus necessitating more time in the cooling. Thus when the tool or die is very large a tank should be used to harden it in, into which a stream of cold water should be kept constantly running, as otherwise the red-hot tool would heat the water to such a degree that the steel would remain soft.

Hardening and Tempering Small Tools.

Very small tools such as small piercing punches, etc., should be hardened in an oil bath or in lukewarm water, as if cold water is used they will cool too quickly and come out of the bath cracked or so brittle as to be useless. Never heat a piece of steel for hardening hot enough as to raise scale on it; even when it is a very large piece this can be prevented by heating very slowly in a packing box. When steel has been heated too hot and then quenched the grain is rendered coarse and brittle, and although it may be drawn to the desired temper it will break quicker than a piece which has been hardened at a very low heat and not tempered at all, although the piece which was heated too hot and hardened and drawn will be softer than the other piece.

When hardening long, flat or round objects they should be dipped endwise, holding them perpendicular with the surface of the bath. When this is done the articles will come out perfectly straight, or at least very little sprung. When dipped otherwise such tools will warp. When dipping a half-round tool dip it with the half-round side at an angle of twenty degrees with the surface of the water and it will come out either almost straight or straight.

To draw the temper on small tools use a Bunsen burner, holding the thickest part of the tool which does not require tempering in the blue flame, and as the steel heats wipe it often with a piece of oily waste. By doing this the temper will come up even and will not draw more in one place than in another. Temper slowly so as to avoid having the temper start to run before you are aware of it.

Hardness and Toughness in Steel.

Although few mechanics seem to be aware of it, there is considerable difference between steel which is hard and steel which is both hard and tough, i. e., when a tool has been hardened and tempered to the degree thought best for the work which it is to perform and the edge does not stand up, but instead crumbles away, the steel is hard but is not tough and was heated wrongly in hardening or not quenched right. On the contrary, when a tool has been heated properly and hardened and tempered as it should be, it can be very hard and the edge will hold, because for a given degree of hardness the same degree of toughness has been imparted during the heating and hardening process.

Special Methods of Hardening Tool Steel.

Often when tool steel is bought special instructions will be given as to the method of hardening it. Sometimes those instructions are followed out and often they are not. Now in all cases where such instructions are given don't forget to go by them, otherwise do not buy that brand of steel, but, instead, get a brand which you can harden in the good old-fashioned way. There are now various brands of steel on the market which are used for special purposes and which possess qualities which other brands do not (in regard to cutting at high speeds, removing large amounts of stock, etc.), which require hardening at different temperatures and tempering at special colors. If you need this sort of steel for any purpose, don't try to find out why the special instructions are given, but do as directed, and if the results are what the makers claim for it, it doesn't make any difference if you have to harden it in a cake of soap—the result is the thing.

Hardening Compounds.

In order to harden steel tools or pieces so that uniform hardness and temper will be attained, and so that the steel will come out of the process white and clean, as is often required, the following process may be adopted: First, in the heating of the steel a solution which will protect it from the fire and another to chill it quickly are necessary. This last solution will also give the desired clean white appearance to the steel. The receipt for the first solution is: equal quantities of sal soda and borax in water containing one ounce of cyanide of potassium to the gallon. For the second solution, a strong brine made of salt and water, and about the same amount of cyanide as salt, will do. Have the water hot and add about two ounces of sulphuric acid to each gallon of water used; when mixed put away in a cool place and keep well covered.

To use the solutions proceed as follows: Fill all holes near the edge of the steel with fire clay, then dip into the first solution and place the steeel immediately on the fire while wet. Heat slowly and carefully and be sure not to heat any one portion of the work faster than another, as the slower the heat the more uniform its distribution in the piece. When the proper temperature has been reached, which should be a clear bright red, dip the work straight down into the hardening solution; when it has cooled remove from the bath and work of silvery whiteness and uniform hardness will be the result. When hardening long, slender pieces in this solution, dip them endwise, and do not shake about, but instead revolve, if possible, rapidly.

Tempering in the Sand Bath.

When a number of pieces of the same size or slightly different sizes have been hardened and it is desired to draw them all to the same temper, the sand bath will be found to give the most uniform results. This consists of an iron box filled with sand and heated over a fire to the temperature required. When the sand has been heated to the required degree the tools to be tempered are laid on top and removed when the color denoting the temper required appears. Always remember that the slower the temper is drawn the tougher the steel will be. When steel is heated slowly in tempering and the heat is distributed equally over the entire piece the molecules assume the most stable position with regard to each other, and, when the tool is in use, all

are alike affected by any shock sustained. The effects of heat
on copper and bronze are precisely the reverse of those mani-
fested by steel, as when such metals are cooled slowly they become brittle and hard, but when cooled rapidly, soft and malleable.

Hardening the Walls of a Hole.

Often, in die work, it is desired that the walls of a drawing
die or some other part, such as the inside of a hollow punch,
should be hard and the remaining portions of the piece soft. This
may be accomplished by proceeding as follows: Clamp the die
or punch, as the case may be, between flanges on the ends of
tubes, being sure to have the steel at the proper heat. Then
allow a stream of cold water or brine to circulate through the
tubes and the walls will harden in depth as far as the inside edges
of the flanges, while the remaining portion will remain soft.

Reannealing.

Sometimes a piece of steel, which is to be used for a punch or
die blank, upon starting to machine it, proves hard, although it
has been annealed. When this is the case, never try to finish it
before reannealing it; instead, rough it down, clean out the
centers and anneal it over again. The time required to reanneal
the piece of steel will be more than made up in the machining
of it.

Water Annealing.

Frequently a piece of steel is required for a repair job or
some other job in a hurry, and there is no time to anneal it in the
regular way. At other times a piece which has been hardened
requires to be remachined. When confronted with the above conditions the tool-maker can fall back on the "water anneal," and
after he has tried it a few times he will be delighted with the
results. There are several methods of doing this, and we give
here the best of them all. The mechanic may adopt any of them,
according to the results secured from each. The first method is
to heat the steel slowly to a dull cherry red, then remove it from
the fire and with a piece of soft wood try the heat, as it decreases,
by touching the steel with the end of the stick. When the piece
has cooled so that the wood ceases to char plunge the steel quickly
into an oil bath. On machining the steel it will be found to be
very soft.

The second method for water annealing, is to heat the steel

slowly to a red heat, then allow it to lie in the ashes a few minutes until almost black, then drop it into soap-suds and allow it to cool. Very often the piece of steel annealed in this manner will turn out much softer than if annealed in the regular manner by packing in powdered charcoal and allowed to cool over night. A good way to make sure as to the time to drop the steel into the bath is to allow it to cool until almost black, then touch it with a file; if the steel does not brighten for an instant and then turn blue, wait a few seconds and repeat the experiment. If upon the second trial the blue appears and then a spark right afterward, drop the steel instantly into the bath, and when cool it will be found to be as "soft as butter."

Warping of Tools in Hardening.

Often after carefully hardening a long tool it will be found to have warped during the process, often to such a degree as to make it useless. There is a way to avoid this altogether, or at least, the warp will be so slight as not to affect the efficiency of the tool. To insure against warping, lower the steel, when at the proper heat, squarely into the bath,. lowering it as far as possible into the center of the liquid. When this is done the heat will be absorbed equally from all sides and the tendency to warp excessively will have been eliminated.

The Location of the Hardening Furnace.

Although in a great many shops very little importance is attached to the proper placing and locating of the forge or furnace which is to be used during the hardening processes, it will be found that if the location chosen is in a darkened corner where the sun's rays will not come near it, the best results will be attained. No matter what kind of hardening is to be done, the heating arrangements should never be located where there is too strong a light, or where the sun shines in at any time of the day. If the light is uniform it will not be difficult to attain uniform results, while, on the contrary, if the light it too bright, there is a chance of heating the steel too hot, and, when it becomes darker, not hot enough. When a uniform light is maintained during the day the men become accustomed to it and no trouble is experienced in getting the best results.

Hardening Very Small Parts.

When a large number of very small parts are to be hardened

they should be packed in closed iron boxes, and the box heated. When all the parts have reached the proper heat, they should be dumped into the quenching bath, of either oil or water, as the nature of the work may require. Another way by which small parts may be heated uniform, is by means of a lead bath. Keep the lead at the proper heat and cover the top with powdered charcoal and coke.

Tempering in Oil.

Almost all large shops in which any amount of hardening and tempering are done, have discarded the method of tempering by colors, and have adopted the more reliable method of doing it in oil, gaging the heat by a thermometer. A kettle containing the oil is placed on the fire and heated to the right temperature, the hardened parts are thrown in and left in the liquid until drawn. By this method there is no possibility of over-drawing, as it is impossible for the parts to become hotter than the oil. When tempering in this manner it is not necessary to brighten the work before the operation, and where a lot of such work is done, it will be accomplished much cheaper than if the old methods were used, besides, the most satisfactory results will be attained.

Straightening Hardened Pieces Which Have Warped.

When a piece has been carefully heated and just as carefully quenched, there is little chance of its warping, but when a piece does warp, before it can be used for the purpose required it must be straightened; to do this proceed as follows: Take two V blocks and place them on the bed of an arbor press or a straightening press—either one will do—and place the piece or tool on the V blocks with the concave side down. Then take a Bunsen burner with a hose attached to it for the gas supply, and heat the concave side; do this slowly and do not heat enough to draw the temper. While the steel is hot apply sufficient pressure to spring the punch or tool back in shape. A large number of hardened pieces, which would otherwise be useless, may be saved by straightening them in this manner.

The Use of Clay in Hardening.

Very often in die and tool work it is desired that a piece with a hole in the center should be hard around the outside and soft around the hole, or a punch is required to be hard at both ends and soft in the center. To accomplish these results with ease use clay in the following manner: When the stock around a hole is to be left soft and the outer edges of the piece hardened, fill the hole with clay and pad it at both sides, then heat the piece and plunge it into the water. When cool remove the clay and the stock around the hole will be found to be soft while the outer edges will be as hard as required. To harden both ends of a punch and leave the center soft put a bandage of clay around the center, or desired soft portion, about ¾ inch thick, and bind it with a piece of sheet metal. Heat, and quench, and the desired results will be accomplished.

When hardening dies or other press tools in which there are any holes near the edges of the piece, fill the holes with clay before heating and the tendency to crack will be overcome. When the holes are not filled with clay—when the steel is quenched—steam generates in the holes and cracks start, or excessive warping occurs, due to the fact that the steam does not escape fast enough and the contraction of the metal is unequal.

Hardening Dies.

Of the hardening and tempering of dies and press tools too much cannot be written, as upon the results of this part of their construction depends the efficiency of the tools. For heating dies a gas furnace is preferable, but when this is not at hand a good clean charcoal fire will do.

For hardening large dies it is indispensable to have a large tank, which should be arranged in such a manner as to insure the rapid cooling of the steel. A tank of this kind can be arranged by fixing two or three rods across the inside about 12 inches below the surface of the water, and a pipe let into the tank in such a manner as to insure the circulation of a stream of water from the bottom upward. When the die is to be quenched the water should be turned on and kept running until the steel has cooled. When a good circulation of water is kept up in a tank of this kind there will not be any soft spots in the die.

Hardening Fluids for Dies.

We have heard a good deal about hardening fluids in which it is claimed dies can be hardened better than in water or brine. Such fluids are composed chiefly of acids and we should advise keeping away from them, as where it is not possible to harden die steel in clear water or brine, the steel is useless and should be dispensed with. When quenching the heated steel, dip down straight and don't shake it about, but, after keeping it stationary for a few seconds, move it around slowly, keeping it square all the time. When the die or punch is of an intricate shape, about three inches of oil on the top of the water will toughen it and contribute to helping the steel retain its shape while hardening, and prevent it from warping or cracking during the process. Lastly, immediately after hardening and before grinding, the steel should be placed on the fire and slightly warmed, to take the chill out, and not laid aside for a while, as we have seen dies that were laid aside after hardening (that were intact) after a few hours show cracks.

Steel for Punches.

When small punches are required to punch heavy work or to run at high speeds never use drill rod or Stubs' steel, as such stock is really the poorest stock that could be used for such work, for the simple reason that fine, high carbon steel of this kind, or any other for that matter, crystallizes rapidly under concussion. In place of such stock use the lowest grade of steel which will harden only at a white heat, and the punches will last many times as long as any that could be made from the better grades of stock.

For small punches which are to pierce thin soft stock, or to run at a slow speed, get the best grade of steel on the market, as for such work the finer the grade the better results will be obtained.

Soft or Hard Punches and Dies.

It is often very hard to determine as to whether a punch and die should be hardened or whether one of them should be left soft, and if so, which one. The stock to be worked and the nature of the work have to be considered when deciding this matter. Some classes of work will be accomplished in the best manner by using a soft punch and a hard die; others, when a hard punch and a soft die are used; while in a majority of cases the best results will be obtained by using a punch and die which are both hard. For punching or shearing heavy metals both punch and die should be hard, while for all metals which are soft, and not over 1-16 inch thick, a soft punch and a hard die will be found to work well. By leaving one of the dies soft it will be easy to produce clean blanks, as when the punch and die becomes dull it is only necessary to grind the hard one, upset the soft one and shear it into the die.

Judgment and Carefulness in Hardening.

A great deal depends on the judgment and carefulness of the man who does the hardening in a shop, and in large manufacturing establishments one man should be given the job of doing all the hardening. On this man's efficiency and judgment will depend the increasing or reducing of the cost account, as one piece of steel which has been hardened properly will accomplish many times as much as a piece which has been hardened carelessly. The manner in which the hardener puts the steel into the quenching liquid will be responsible, more than anything else, for having the pieces come out hard and free from cracks. Work with deep recesses will often have to go into the water with the recessed parts first or *vice versa,* according to the shape and location of the recesses. When hardening large pieces which are worked out in the center, a stream of water striking against them is often absolutely necessary. There are some grades of steel which will give the best results if they are removed from the water as soon as the vibration has ceased, and laid aside until cool, while there are a greater number of other brands which will have to be left in the bath until perfectly cool. Experience and good sound judgment are necessary to do good hardening.

The Use of Machine Steel for Press Tools and the Hardening of it.

For a large number of purposes in the line of sheet-metal working, machine steel tools, if properly hardened, will answer as well and sometimes better than tool steel ones, and if the following process is used to harden such tools they will be found to give the best of results and may be used for cutting purposes. In order that the parts or tools may do their work and last long, they must be hardened very deep and come out with a fine compact grain. For dies which are to be used for punching regular shaped blanks from light soft stock machine steel case-hardened tools will give excellent satisfaction, as they are far cheaper to make and will last as long as though made of tool steel.

To do this work properly the following outfit is necessary: A good hardening oven, a number of hardening boxes, a good supply of raw bone, granulated, the same amount of granulated charcoal, some hydro-carbonated bone and the same amount of charred leather. A tank large enough to hold a good supply of water, a small tank so arranged as to allow of heating to any desired temperature, and a bath of raw linseed oil, and the outfit will be complete.

Pack and heat the work as you would for regular case-hardening, and leave in the oven to cool. When perfectly cool heat the pieces in hot lead and quench the same as tool steel. If the pieces are small they should be repacked in the hardening box with granulated charcoal and heated. When packing in charcoal do not mix with any kind of bone or any other carbonizing matter; such substances open the grain, and the object of the second heat is to close the grain. The hardening heat should be as low as possible, and the hardened piece will come out close in grain, with a hard, tough surface all over, while the center remains soft and the piece will be stronger than if made of tool steel.

When machine steel tools are to be used for cutting they should be packed for the first heat in a mixture composed of equal parts of charcoal and charred leather, finely granulated. The use of charred leather gives a much tougher effect to the steel than bone, as the leather is almost free from phosphorus, while bone is not, and as phosphorus makes steel brittle the substance which contains the least amount of it should be used. Tools which are to be used for bending and forming may be packed in bone, which will carbonize them as required. When using either bone or leather an equal amount of granulated charcoal mixed with it will prevent the kernels of bone and leather from adhering and forming a solid mass when hot, and as charcoal is an excellent heat conductor the pieces packed within the hardening box will be heated quicker than if no charcoal were used.

Never use Bessemer steel for such tools as it will not respond to the process; open-hearth steel should always be used to get uniform results.

Hardening Large Steel Ring Dies, so as to Prevent Cracking and Excessive Warping.

To harden large ring dies, which are to be ground after hardening, and which are required to be very hard around the center or hole and the walls, they should be heated in large iron boxes as follows: Put a layer of fine powdered charcoal about 2 inches deep in the bottom of the box and place the die on top of it.

Fill the die and cover it to a depth of about ¾ inch with a mixture of 4 parts powdered charcoal to 1 part of charred leather, then put a loose cover on the box and place in the furnace. After heating about 3 hours or more, according to the size of the die, the die will be at a red heat. It should then be allowed to remain at a low heat for about an hour, which will insure its heating uniformly throughout. The heat should then be increased until the die comes to a full red heat; it is then ready to be quenched.

Remove the box from the furnace, and with two pairs of tongs, and a man at opposite sides if the die is too large for one man to handle, draw the die from the box, clean, and quench squarely into the water, working up and down until the red has entirely disappeared, then let it lie still until cool. When cool remove the die from the water and heat, to remove the strain and chill of hardening, until drops of water sprinkled on it will steam. Then lay it aside in an even temperature where it can cool off slowly.

When large round ring dies are hardened in the manner described above there need be no fear that they will warp, crack or shrink excessively or unevenly.

The Effects of Annealing in Hardening.

Although it is not generally known, the successful hardening of a piece of steel depends on the annealing of it previous to machining it, and in order to harden properly it is necessary that the correct processes of annealing should be understood. Always anneal any odd-shaped piece, or one with an irregular hole in it after having roughed it down. The best way to anneal such pieces is to pack them in granulated charcoal in an iron box, being sure to have as much charcoal at the sides of the box as at the bottom in order that the heat shall not penetrate too quickly. The box should be kept at a red heat for about an hour. The proper heat for such pieces in annealing should always be higher than the heat required to harden the same piece, in fact we have found that a heat almost as high as a forging heat will be the means of overcoming any tension or strain which may manifest itself when the piece is hardened.

Hardening Thin Disks.

The best way to harden thin disks of large diameter is to do it between iron plates with well-oiled surfaces. In heating the disks, it should be done in such a manner as to keep the fire from coming in contact with them.   The best way to do this is to place a flat cast iron plate on the fire and heat it until it is a black heat, then place the disk upon it and heat the plate until the disk has reached the proper hardening heat.   When the proper heat is reached remove the disk and place it upon the lower oiled plate and instantly place the top plate upon it and bear down hard on it until the disk has cooled.

A Welding Kink.

It is often necessary to construct dies from forgings of wrought iron and tool steel, and as the dies when finished are required to be hardened it is necessary that there should be a good weld between the two parts.   To accomplish these results when welding mix mild steel chips—from which all of the oil has been removed—with borax, and there will be no difficulty in producing a clean weld and one which will not buckle or separate in hardening.

Hardening Thick Round Dies.

Often round dies, which are thick in proportion to their diameter, will contract excessively in the center during the hardening process; often to such a degree as to make them unfit for use.   To overcome this, have an arrangement by which a stream of water may be forced through the hole without wetting the outside; allowing the water to only come in contact with the inside of the die.   By doing this the walls of the hole will be hard, while the outside will remain soft, and when the temper is drawn the hole will remain straight and true.   In shops where grinding facilities are not at hand, this method will work excellently.   If possible use strong brine for the hardening fluid.

Hardening Springs.

As very often springs form part of the construction of various kinds of dies, it is well to understand how to harden and temper them successfully.   For small and medium-sized springs, use a solution composed of ½ sperm oil, ½ neat's foot oil with an ounce of resin, and the springs will come out of the bath tempered as desired.   For heavy springs, which have to exert a great deal of pressure, use hot water.   Have the water boiling and plunge the springs, when at the proper heat, into it.   By adopting this method no burning off will be necessary, as the springs will be the proper temper. What is more, they will not break or "crawl up" when in use.

A Substitute for Borax in Welding.

As high carbon steel is frequently used for forgings for dies, and as in order to secure the best results it should be welded at the lowest possible heat, we give here a receipt of a welding compound to use as a substitute for borax.

Pulverize and mix with about 3 pounds of good welding sand, 2 ounces of prussiate of potash, 6 ounces of common salt, 2 ounces of copperas, 1 ounce of black oxide of manganese and 1 ounce of saltpetre.

Hardening Poor Steel.

Very often in making dies we run across a piece of steel which after working up will not respond satisfactorily to the usual hardening processes. When this is the case prepare a solution composed of two handfuls of common salt, one ounce of corrosive sublimate to about six quarts of water, and when the steel has reached a good red heat plunge it into the bath. The corrosive sublimate gives toughness to the steel and the salt hardness. This solution is deadly poison; exercise care when using it.

To Anneal Doubtful Steel.

There are some kinds of steel which will not anneal satisfactorily even when packed in an air-tight box in powdered charcoal. To anneal steel of this kind cover it with fire clay, and heat to a red heat and allow to cool over night in the furnace.

Annealing in Bean Water.

Down in New England where beans are *appreciated* they anneal steel very satisfactorily by heating it to a cherry red and when cooled to a black plunging it into a bath of water in which beans have been boiled.

Bluing Bright Sheet Metal Blanks.

To blue bright sheet metal blanks, or other small parts, heat a ladle full of core sand, put the blanks in and shake the ladle over the fire until the required color appears. Another way to blue such parts is to heat a mixture composed of 10 pounds of saltpetre, 1 pound of black oxide of manganese. Put the work in a wire basket and sink the basket into the center of the mixture. Keep the basket revolving and remove when the proper color appears on the parts.

Machining Mild Steel Forgings.

When machining mild steel forgings, or any other material for which water can be used as a cutting lubricant, use instead of soap water strong sal soda water. It will work better than the other on either lathe or planer.

Laying Out Dies.

When laying out dies, first have a bright smooth surface and use blue vitriol and water for coloring. By using this solution the surface will be coppered nicely, and all templet lines will show up fine. If the surface of the steel is oily add a little oil of vitriol to the mixture and the oil will be eaten away and a nicely coppered surface will result.

Cutting Aluminum.

For cutting, turning, drilling, blanking or drawing aluminum coat the sheets or parts with kerosene oil or coal oil.

Softening Chilled Cast Iron Dies for Drilling.

As drawing and forming dies are very often made of chilled cast iron, and as sometimes holes are required to be drilled in them, it is well to know how to soften it to allow of drilling the holes. To do this heat the die to a cherry red and let it lie on the coals. Then place a piece of brimstone, circular in shape and a little less in diameter than the hole to be drilled, on the spot where the hole is to be. Let the die lie in the fire until it has died out and the metal has cooled, and the brimstone will have softened the iron entirely through within the radius of its diameter when solid.

Hints and Suggestions as to the Proper Method of Using Files.

As nothing contributes more to success in die-making than a well-defined understanding of the proper use of files we have embodied in the following a number of hints and suggestions which will be found valuable and prove practical guides in the art of filing. We are indebted for the data, etc., to the Nicholson File Co., of Providence, R. I., and herein acknowledge our thanks for the same.

Very few mechanical operations are more difficult than that of filing well. Unlike the tool fixed in the iron planer, whose movement is guided by unyielding ways, the file must be guided by the hand, and the accuracy with which this is done, will depend largely upon the patience and perseverance given in prac-

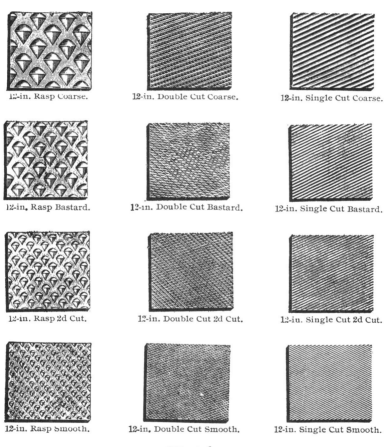

12-in. Rasp Coarse.   12-in. Double Cut Coarse.   12-in. Single Cut Coarse.

12-in. Rasp Bastard.   12-in. Double Cut Bastard.   12-in. Single Cut Bastard.

12-in. Rasp 2d Cut.   12-in. Double Cut 2d Cut.   12-in. Single Cut 2d Cut.

12-in. Rasp Smooth.   12-in. Double Cut Smooth.   12-in. Single Cut Smooth.

FIG. 406.

tice; the "guiding principle," involved in many other tools and operations, being wanting in most applications of the file. While a perfect file is necessary to secure the best results in filing, knowl-edge as to the selection of the proper file for the work in hand, and skillfulness and practice in handling it, are equally essential.

A severe test in filing would consist in producing a true, flat surface upon narrow work, or say that whose width does not exceed one-eighth the length or stroke of the file. To the uninitiated, this would seem to require that the file should have a perfectly true and straight surface, but were it practicable to make the file absolutely straight lines across the work, even were this operation possible, the pressure, if applied to each end of the file, as is the usual custom, would give it sufficient spring to cause a rounding to the surface of the work.

Therefore, to produce a flat surface, under this severe test, or even under more favorable circumstances, the file should have a convexity given to its surface.

Convexity in Files.

Undoubtedly few, even of the old filers, have given the subject of convexity as it bears upon broad surface filing, the thought it is entitled to. It is known to many mechanics that a file which will bite and cling, with the accustomed downward pressure, upon wrought iron, or soft steel, will require a greater pressure to prevent it from glazing or slipping over the work, when applied to broad cast iron surfaces. This is owing to their glassy nature, and their extremely granular formation, requiring that the teeth should enter the surface deeper than in the more fibrous metals, or they will soon glaze over, and become dulled or shiny, thus giving to the file the appearance of being soft, while the contrary may be the fact.

Considerable convexity is, therefore, needed in such cases; for, while it gives greater control of the file from the point to heel, it also presents fewer cutting points to the work, with a given pressure downward, than in the less convex file—the bite being increased in proportion to the increase of the convexity; the ability, therefore, to increase it more or less, at the will of the operator, is of considerable importance.

In finishing many kinds of work, the absence of a suitable convexity limits the usefulness of the file—as in the preparation of the valves of steam engines, tables of printing presses, stereotype plates or other work requiring a true surface and in the finishing of accurate blanking and drawing dies.

While an absolutely true surface is confessedly unattainable, it is evident that, as in the above cases, a degree of perfection is sometimes desirable beyond what the necessities of other work may require; and to be able to touch the exact spot indicated by the straight edge or surface plate with the file, is to utilize it in a manner which could not be done if the convexity did not exist.

Files Properly Handled.

Before using the file, it should first of all be properly handled; not, as is too often the case, by driving the handle half way down upon the tang, and thereby doubling the chances of breaking it, but by forcing it well up to the shoulder. Some of the file handles found on the market will not stand this amount of driving, without splitting; in such cases, the tang of an old or worn-out file, of similar dimensions, should be heated, taking care, of course, not to draw the temper, and the hole in the handle burned out to nearly the desired size and shape, before driving it upon the tang. It not infrequently happens that the tang hole is not drilled central, or is badly out of line; this may also be corrected by using a heated tang.

Of the many file handles of special construction hitherto devised, there are none which have, as yet, combined that simplicity, utility and economy necessary to take the place of the ordinary wooden handle; nor do we think it possible to improve upon a wooden handle that is conveniently formed and properly ferruled for most applications of the file, provided it be firmly affixed, and carefully used.

Devices for Holding Files.

The file, when used in ordinary manner, considerably exceeds the length of the work; but when such is not the case, as in filing large table surfaces, and shaping out recesses of considerable length, or when, from causes, the ordinary handle will not answer, it then becomes necessary to grasp the file by holders of special construction. These special devices (many of which are quite rude) are numerous, and vary to suit the particular shape of the file and the work to be performed.

Short pieces of files, of special construction, are sometimes clamped to the slide rest, to be used upon work revolving in the engine lathe, and are soldered or screwed to bent handles when required to be used in finishing in and around the bottoms of shallow cavities.

The necessity, however, of this last and troublesome method of holding the file may be avoided, by the use of the stub file holder, Fig. 407. Woodworkers not infrequently clamp one or more files to pieces of board, or fasten them by means of staples and wire pins, or by cutting in, in such a manner as will enable them to smooth out grooves, or true up the edges of their work, using the board or holder as a gage.

Bent rifflers are oftentimes required in reaching certain irregular shaped cavities in drop dies and irregular shaped drawing and forming dies.

In filing large surfaces, the tang is frequently bent upward, as in Fig. 409, to admit of the hands clearing the work, when

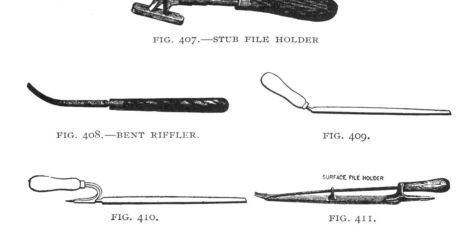

FIG. 407.—STUB FILE HOLDER

FIG. 408.—BENT RIFFLER.   FIG. 409.

FIG. 410.   FIG. 411.

the file passes over the surface; sometimes a crank-shaped holder is employed, having one end fitted to the tang of the file, while the other is fitted to receive the handle, as in Fig. 410. These devices, which facilitate somewhat the handling of the file, do not give that perfect control which enables the operator to manipulate it at will, nor do they aid in governing its convexity.

The improved surface file holder, illustrated in Fig. 411, was designed especially to meet these points, thus enabling the skillful operator to do much of the work with the file which has hitherto been done with the scraper.

To have the file truly and firmly handled or properly affixed to a suitable holder is the first step in point of economy, as well as in the production of good work.

Height of Work.

Various ideas very naturally exist among mechanics, as to the height at which the jaws of the vise should be set from the floor, for use in filing; arising largely, no doubt, from the varied nature of the work upon which the advocates of the different ideas have been accustomed to operate.

For filing general work, the top of the vise jaws should be placed so as to be level with the elbow of the workman, which will be found to range from 40 to 44 inches from the floor—therefore 42 inches may be considered as an average height, best suited for all heights of workmen, when the vise is to be permanently fixed. This position enables the workman to get the full, free swing of his arms from the shoulder; the separate movement of the wrist and elbow should be done away with, as much as possible.

If the work to be filed is small and delicate, requiring simply a movement of the arms, or of one hand and arm alone, the vise should be higher, not only in order that the workman may more closely scrutinize the work, but that he may be able to stand more erect.

If the work to be filed is heavy and massive, such as large cutting dies, requiring great muscular effort, its surface should be below the elbow point, as the operator stands farther from his work, with his feet separated from 10 to 30 inches, one in advance of the other, and his knees somewhat bent, thus lowering his stature; besides, in this class of work, it is desirable to throw the weight of the body upon the file, to make it penetrate, and thus, with a comparative fixedness of the arms, depend largely upon the momentum of the body to shove the file.

It will therefore be seen, that in fixing the height of the vise, the nature of the work and the stature of the operator should be considered, if it is deemed necessary to apply the principle correctly.

Grasping the File.

In using the large files, intended to be operated by both hands, the handle should be grasped in such a manner that its end will fit into, and bring up against, the fleshy part of the palm, below the point of the little finger, with the thumb lying along the top of the handle, in the direction of its length; the ends of the

fingers pointing upward, or nearly in the direction of the operator's face.

The point of the file should be grasped by the thumb and first
two fingers, the hand being so held as will bring the thumb, as its
ball presses upon the top of the file, in a line with the handle,
when heavy strokes are required. When a light stroke is wanted,
and the pressure demanded becomes less, the thumb and fingers
may change their direction, until the thumb lies at a right angle,
or nearly so, with the length of the file, the positions changing
more or less, as may be needed to increase the downward pressure.

In holding the file with one hand, as is often necessary in filing light work, pins, etc., the handle should be grasped as already
described, with the exception that the hand should be turned a
quarter turn, bringing the forefinger on top, and lying along the
handle nearly in the direction of its length. In this position,
the freest action of the hand and wrist may be made upon light
work.

Amateurs will find by following these directions, the movements of the file will be simplified, and made somewhat easier
than if grasped at random and without consideration.

Carrying the File.

The most natural movement of the hands and arms in falling
is to carry the file in circular lines, the several points of the limbs
being the center of motions; this movement with a convex file
would apparently give a concavity to the work, but the real tendency, especially on narrow work, is the reverse, owing to the
work acting as a fulcrum, over which the file moves with more or
less of a rocking motion, giving an actual convexity to its surface, except when in the hands of a skillful operator. The real
aim, therefore, should be to cause the file to depart only so much
from a true right line as will be necessary to feel that each inch
of its stroke is brought into exact contact with the desired portion of the work; and by thus changing the course of the stroke
slightly, thereby preventing "grooving," a more even surface
results and the work is completed sooner.

The movements here referred to have reference to those in
which both hands are used upon flat work, requiring nicety and
trueness of finish, and the difficulties to be overcome in producing

even a comparatively true flat surface with a file require much practice on the part of the operator.

In filing ovals and irregular forms, the movements, while not considered so difficult or trying, nevertheless require considerable experience and a good eye, to so blend the strokes of the file upon the round or curved surfaces as to give the best effect; the varied nature of the work upon this class of surfaces, though much might be said, prevents any detailed definition as to the movements of the file, within the limit of this article.

In point of economy, the pressure on the file should be relieved during the back stroke; this will be apparent to any one who will examine the formation of the points of the teeth (see illustration, Fig. 406), when it will be seen that the file can only cut during the ordinary or advancing stroke, and that equal pressure during the back stroke must be very damaging to the points of the teeth.

Draw-Filing.

Files are sometimes used by grasping at each end, and moving them sidewise across the work, after the manner of using the spoke-shave. This operation is known as draw-filing, and is usually performed in laying the strokes of turned work, lengthwise, instead of circular, as left from the lathe finish, as well as when giving a final fit to the shaft that is to receive a coupling; cases, generally, in which no considerable amount of stock is to be removed, and thus any defection from the principle of construction or arrangement of the teeth of the file are not so readily apparent.

Files, as they are ordinarily made, are intended to cut when used with a forward stroke, and the same file cannot work smoothly, or to the best advantage, when moved sidewise, unless care is taken that the face of the teeth present themselves, during the forward movement of the file, at a sufficient angle to cut, instead of scratching the work. To accomplish this the angle at which the file is held with respect to the line of its movement, must vary, with different files, depending upon the angle at which the last or up cut is made. The pressure should also be relieved during the back stroke, as in ordinary filing.

When properly used, work may be finished somewhat finer and the scratches more closely congregated than in the ordinary use of the same file; as, in draw-filing, the teeth produce a shearing or shaving cut.

First Use of a File.

In economizing the wear of the files intended for general purposes, consideration should be given to the kind of material which they may be subjected to, in the different stages of their use.

In the ordinary use of the machine shop, the first wear of these files should be in finishing the larger surfaces of cast iron, bronze, or brass metals, all of which require a keen cutting tooth; they may then be made to do good execution upon the narrower surfaces of these metals, also upon wrought iron and soft steel; as a file that has been used more or less upon this kind of work will not tear the surface of these metals and will consequently do more effective work. To obtain the best results, the file suited for general purposes is not so well adapted to filing brass or other similar soft metals as those whose teeth are arranged for this purpose.

New files, particularly double cuts, are severely worn down by use upon narrow surfaces, as the strain comes wholly upon a few teeth and frequently breaks them.

Preparing Work.

The corners or thin edges of iron castings are very likely to become chilled, and a thin scale or skin produced over the entire surface of the casting, caused by the hot metal coming in contact with the moist sand of the foundry molds; this outer skin is usually much harder than the metal beneath it, and many times the thin edges or corners are chilled so as to be harder even than the file itself.

The necessity, therefore, of removing this scale and chilled surface becomes readily apparent, and all mechanics who give any consideration to the proper and economical use of the file will be careful to see that the scale and sand are first removed by pickling, and the surfaces which have become chilled by grinding, before applying the file.

If it is impossible or impracticable to remove the scale by pickling, a file that has been used until it is too dull for narrow steel work may be employed; the teeth will then not be broken by the hard scale.

Pickling the Work.

The pickle for gray iron castings is generally made by mixing sulphuric acid and water, in the proportion of two or more parts of water to one of acid, and is usually kept for this purpose in a trough lined with lead.

The articles to be pickled are sometimes immersed in this bath, where they remain for a short time; they are then removed and the acid is allowed to act upon their surfaces until the scale has loosened, when they are washed off with water. More often, however, the pickle is dipped from the trough and poured over the castings, which are placed on a sloping platform (thus allowing the acid to return to the trough), where, after remaining for a sufficient time, they are washed. When dry, the castings are either rattled, or scraped and cleaned with old files and wire scratch-brushes, until the surface is freed from scale and sand.

To pickle brass, or gun-metal castings, a mixture of nitric acid and water may be used, in the proportion of, say, one part acid to five of water; the treatment being the same as that of the iron castings. While not in general use upon the coarser kinds of brass work, the pickle is desirable for smaller castings, or those requiring to be protected with lacquer.

When Oil Should Not be Used.

All files, when they leave the manufactory, are covered with oil to prevent them from rusting. While this is not objectionable for many uses to which the file is put, there are cases where the oil should be thoroughly removed, as when the file is to be used in finishing the large cast iron surfaces which are of a glassy nature; the principal difficulty being to make the file "bite," or keep sufficiently under the surface to prevent glazing; otherwise the action not only hardens or burnishes the surface operated upon, but dulls the extreme points of the teeth, thus working against the desired end in both directions.

When Oil May be Used.

Oil may, however, be used to good advantage on new files, which are put immediately to work upon narrow fibrous metals of a harder nature; in such cases it is not uncommon, with good workmen, to fill the teeth with oil and chalk.

Oil is also useful on fine files, in the finishing of wrought iron or steel, as by its use the teeth will not penetrate to the same degree, and the disposition to "pin" and scratch the work is materially less than when used dry.

Cleaning the File.

The dust and small particles removed from the material operated upon are always more or less liable to clog and fill the teeth. This tendency is especially aggravated when the file is used upon wood, horn and such other materials, as upon being mixed with the oil in the teeth, become baked, when dry, and thus prevent the teeth from penetrating the work, to say nothing of the appearance of being worn, or the tendency to injury from rust.

It therefore becomes necessary that the file should be cleaned not only at intervals during its use but carefully before being laid aside, if the best results are to be attained.

This cleaning is done in several ways; sometimes, in the finer files, by rubbing the hand over them, or by drawing them across the apron of the workman (which is a more common method upon the large files); by the use of a strip of old or worn-out card clothing, tacked to a piece of wood, having a handle-shape at one end—a device which is usually rudely constructed by the operator.

The file card and file brush, illustrated in Figs. 412 and 413,

FILE CARD   FILE BRUSH

FIG. 412.   FIG. 413.

will be found excellent tools, and master mechanics should see that every person in their employ using a file is furnished with one or the other of them, and insist that they be used, if he deems it desirable to economize in the wear of his files.

In removing oil from the teeth of a new file, a ready way is to rub chalk or charcoal across the teeth, and brush thoroughly. By repeating the operation a few times, the oil will be entirely absorbed, and the file will be in the best possible condition for use upon cast iron.

When the teeth of files are clogged with wood, or other soft substance, which has become baked into them, if held in boiling hot water for a few moments, the imbedded substance becomes so loosened, that it may be easily carded out of the teeth. If the operation is quickly performed, any moisture remaining will be readily evaporated by the heat retained in the file.

Care in Putting Away.

One of the most destructive customs among a large number of mechanics of the present day is that of loosely throwing their files, fine and coarse, small and large, into a drawer filled with cold chisels, hammers and other tools.

Now when we consider the small portion of the points of the teeth which is worn off by extreme wear, and that to effectually dull them for some kinds of work requires but slight rubbing upon a hard substance, it will be easily seen that the evils of this habit should be more carefully considered by the master mechanic, and suitable provision made to avoid its destructive tendencies.

CHAPTER XII.

MISCELLANEOUS DIES, FIXTURES, PRESSES, DEVICES AND SPECIAL
ARRANGEMENTS FOR SHEET METAL WORK.

Artistic Die-Making.

As a rule it is popularly supposed that the finer classes of die work can be turned out only in shops equipped with the latest improved tools, and if one were to make the assertion that many of the shops in which the finest of such work is done possess only such tools and machines as are to be found in any little country jobbing shop, he would be laughed at. Now, while an equipment of up-to-date machine tools is always to be desired in any

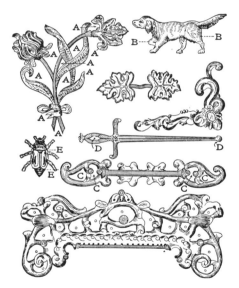

FIG. 414.—SAMPLES OF ARTISTIC DIE WORK.

line of mechanical work, in order that less shall depend on the skill of the workman and more on the machines, it is a fact that a skillful workman can often accomplish the most astonishing results with tools that are far from being what they should be.

In Fig. 414 are shown a number of samples of work which are remarkable principally from an artistic standpoint and for the principles of construction adopted in the tools used to produce them. The dies and fixtures used to produce these pieces were made in a little shop in Brooklyn, New York, the machine tool equipment of which consisted of: One medium sized lathe, a speed lathe, a shaper, two drill presses, large and small; an emery wheel, a forge and an old German screw press. There were six men employed in this shop, one being an engraver and the others die and tool-makers. The class of work turned out in this shop would bear favorable comparison with that turned out in any other shop in the country, and what is more they turned it out at a good profit for the "boss." This little shop has been in exist-

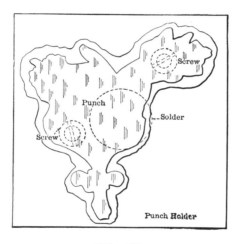

FIG. 415.

ence for a number of years, and we hope that it will continue to do good work for a number of years to come, for we dearly love the "little shop."

The flower design shown in Fig. 414 was produced in three operations; embossing or striking up the design, piercing or punching out the sections marked A, ten in all, and trimming and punching out the finished piece. The embossing die is not shown, as its construction will be understood from the other cuts. Fig. 416 is a plan of the piercing die. The punch for this die consists of the regular cast-iron holder and machine-steel pad in which the ten piercing punches are located, after which solder (hard) is run around them at the face of the pad. These punches are left soft and when dull are upset and sheared into the die so as to punch clean again. Fig. 415 is a plan of the blanking and trimming punch for the finishing operation. It is fastened to the holder by two flat head screws let through from the back, after which solder is run around the face, as shown by the irregular line around the punch. This punch is also left soft. Any die-maker who has made many dies in which gangs of piercing punches had to be located will appreciate the skill required to

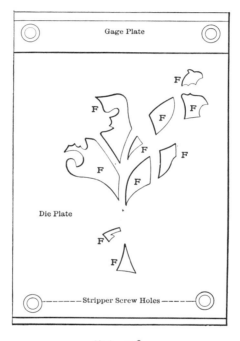

FIG. 416.

locate ten irregular shaped punches, as in Fig. 416, so as to have them in perfect alinement with the dies.

Fig. 417 is a plan of a gang die used to produce the sword shown in Fig. 414 in one operation. The work to be done consists of embossing or striking up the design at K, then moving the metal one space and piercing the two small holes D D, Fig. 414, at the dies M M, and lastly blanking out the finished piece at the blanking die N. The construction of this die is shown plainly in the engravings, and very little description is necessary. The embossing die and the blanking die are two pieces of tool steel with one end of each finished to the angle on which the dies are laid out. The two pieces of steel are fitted to the bolster in a seat between F F, and are located with their

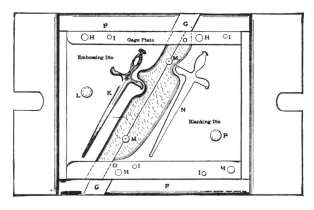

FIG. 417.

inner ends tightly together by strong taper pins at L and P. The piercing dies are two tool steel bushings, hardened, lapped and ground to size, and forced into holes in the inner faces of the blanking and embossing dies.

The punch used with this die is shown in Fig. 418. The

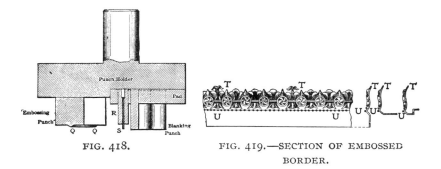

FIG. 418.   FIG. 419.—SECTION OF EMBOSSED BORDER.

blanking and piercing punches are fastened and located in a pad, while the embossing punch is located on, and fastened direct to, the face of the holder by screws and solder, not shown. The piercing punches are, because of their small diameter, No. 60

drill, forced into supplementary holders R, and are allowed to project beyond the face sufficiently to allow of their passing through the stripper and stock and entering the die. The blanking punch is made longer than the others, so as to pass through the stock and enter the die before the other punches touch the stock, thus preventing an unequal drawing of the metal by the action of the embossing punch, and also insuring the proper locating of the "follow" operations on the work, as it is fed along the die-face.

In Fig. 419 we show a section of an embossed border which was produced in strips 36 inches long by the gang die shown in Fig. 420.

The strips of metal are fed from left to right and are first acted upon by the embossing punch and die and are then fed for-

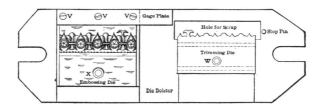

FIG. 420.—PLAN OF DIE.

ward and trimmed. The stripper is located on the trimming punch and is of the usual spring type. The embossing die and the trimming die are located in dovetailed channels in the bolster by taper pins at X and W. The points T T, in Fig. 419, are the gage points for locating the work in the proper position on the trimming die, the stock being fed forward until the point strikes the stop-pin.

To finish these embossed strips so that four of them will form a picture frame when soldered together, two bending operations are necessary. The results, after the operations, are shown at the right end of Fig. 419, while the dies used to accomplish the results are shown in Figs. 421 and 422.

The punch and die for the first bending operation are shown in Fig. 421, giving an end view and a front view of both sections. The punch and die for the second bending operation are shown in Fig. 422. The manner in which the work is accomplished may be understood from the end view of both sets of tools, in which the work is shown by heavy dark lines as located upon the dies in position for bending. These dies were 37 inches long, and when it is considered that they were machined and finished in an

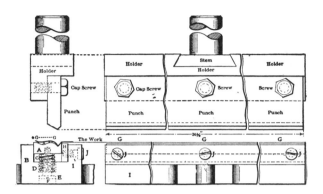

FIG. 421.—PUNCH AND DIE FOR FIRST BENDING OPERATION.

18 inch stroke shaper, it will be conceded that considerable skill was involved in the accomplishing of the desired results. All working parts of these dies, except the spring and fastening portions, and the holders, were of tool-steel and were left soft, as the

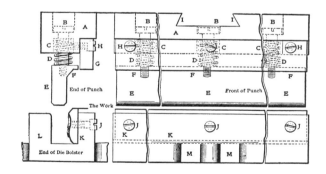

FIG. 422.—SECOND BENDING OPERATION.

shop did not possess the necessary facilities to allow of their being hardened.

The animal design shown in Fig. 414 was produced in one operation by means of a die similar to Fig. 417, the work done comprising embossing, piercing two holes at B B and blanking out the finished piece. The beetle, shown in Fig. 414, was also produced in a die of this construction, there being two holes pierced at E E, the stock used being thin sheet copper, while for the dog, brass was used.

The maple leaf design was produced in one operation by an embossing and trimming die.

The piece shown at the bottom of Fig. 414 is the best of the lot, and required but two operations to produce. In the first operation, the metal was embossed and the piece was blanked out, while in the second the portions marked by the dots were pierced. The making of the piercing dies for this piece was a job worthy the skill of any die-maker, as the piece had to be produced clean and free from burrs, fins and irregular margins. In the piercing twenty punches were used. They were all let into and fastened in a machine steel pad, and solder run about the face of the pad.

When it is considered that the people who go to this little jobbing shop, where the above dies were made, to have tools made, do so because they can get them cheaper and as good as if they went to some of the larger shops, and when the tool equipment of the shop and the classes of work produced in it are also considered, the skill of the men and the mechanical and business ability of the "boss" may be imagined.

Dies for Punching Leather Shoe Tips.

For the production of shoes and various other articles of leather, the parts of which are required to be pierced in fancy designs, the work of the tool-maker plays an important part, as the variety and number of tools used is very large, and, as they are kept in quite constant use, even their renewal gives employment to a large number of mechanics. In the following we will describe the means employed for the production of elaborate designs, which are accomplished by punching.

In Fig. 423 are shown samples of work, full size, produced in this manner, and in Fig. 424 the type of die used. The construction of the dies for their production entails a lot of accurate work, both in the laying out of the shapes and designs and in the finishing of the tools.

The principles of construction involved in these dies differ somewhat from those usually carried out in the making of dies for sheet-metal working, as the conditions under which the tools are worked and the material pierced are different. In Fig. 424

is shown a die complete, and in Fig. 425 are the essential parts of the same—the die plate, the stop and the stripper.   The die is made to pierce eighty-eight holes of comparatively small diameters.   This number is small compared with some designs.   The

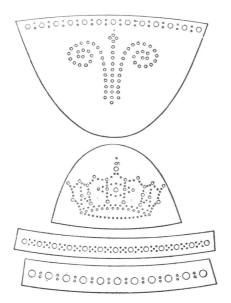

FIG. 423.—SAMPLES OF LEATHER TIPS.

crown shown in Fig. 423 requires 137 holes, and others even more.

For the die plate Fig. 425 a piece of annealed tool steel is finished all over and left about 5-16 inch thick.   The stripper

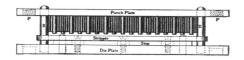

FIG. 424.—PERFORATING DIE FOR LEATHER TIPS.

plate is then got out and finished to a thickness of about 5-32 inch.   This stripper plate is clamped to the face of the die plate and holes are drilled for the two dowel-pins, as shown at D D in the die plate and at K K in the stripper.   Three more holes are

then drilled for the fastening screws, as shown at F F F in the
die and at J J J in the stripper. The two dowel-pin holes are
carefully reamed, and the stripper is removed from the die. The
three screw holes are tapped in the die and enlarged in the
stripper for clearance, and the two dowel-pins are forced into the
holes D D in the die.

We now take a piece of hard sheet brass and, after getting

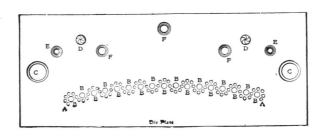

Die Plate

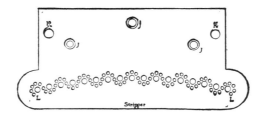

Stripper

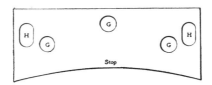

Stop

FIG. 425.—PARTS OF DIE.

it perfectly straight, the design is laid out upon it, the holes are
spaced, prick-punched and drilled to size. In the making of the
templet care must be taken to get it accurate and the holes evenly
spaced for the design to present a symmetrical and artistic appearance. Note the fancy design of the templet shown in Fig.

426. The templet being finished, we fasten the stripper plate and the die together by screws and dowels, and soft solder the templet to the stripper, so that the design will be in the position shown in Fig. 425, transfer the holes through it to the stripper plate, and drill entirely through it and the die, being sure to keep the drill sharp and using lard oil freely. After the holes have been drilled, the templet is removed and the holes in the stripper are slightly countersunk at the top, while those in the die are reamed to a very slight clearance from the back. The two holes C C are now drilled and countersunk for fastening the die plate to the press bolster.

We now take another piece of steel and finish it to the same

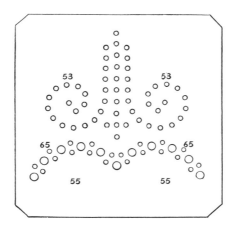

FIG. 426.—A TEMPLET.

size and shape as the die plate for the punch plate, and after locating it true on the die we clamp it there and drill two holes at E E through both, and ream them to 5-16 inch. These holes are for the punch and die alining dowels. The two dowels are made to the length shown and the ends are rounded. The pins are then driven into the holes E E in the die, and the two corresponding holes in the punch plate are reamed so that the plate will slide up and down on them without play. The punch plate is now located on the face of the die by means of the dowels, a pair of thin parallel strips are placed between them, and the holes are transferred through the die to the punch plate and drilled through. The punch plate is then removed from the die and the holes are countersunk at the back, a hole is also drilled and tapped at each end to fasten it to the press plunger.

The punches are made from drill rod of the correct size, are forced into the punch plate, as shown in Fig. 425, and are upset at the back, first entering all the smaller punches and grinding them on the ends, getting them sharp and even with each other, by entering them into the die and allowing them to project through slightly, and grinding them all while thus supported. The larger punches are then fastened into the punch pad and ground in the same manner, leaving them about 3-32 longer than the others, as shown. The stop-plate, Fig. 425, is got out and finished to allow of adjustment, all the parts are assembled as shown in Fig. 424, and the die is complete.

In use the punch plate is fastened to the press plunger by a screw at each end, and the die-locating dowels E E are entered into their holes in the punch plate. The ram of the press is then brought down until all the punches have entered the dies, and the die plate is securely fastened to the press bolster. The construction of the dies in the manner here described insures perfect alinement of all the punches with the dies, and the dowels E E secure the setting of the tools in the press. For this work neither punches nor dies are hardened.

A Cheap Grinder for Round Dies.

As there are a large number of shops where a lathe center grinder is unknown, and where they worry along and try to do good work with soft centers, or at the best, one hard center and the other soft, I think the small tool post grinder shown in Figs. 427-428 will if adopted, prove the means for overcoming these obstacles that prevent the production of first-class work. We have often, when in various shops, had our attention called to the condition of the lathe centers. Really, it was terrible; here one with the point burred up, and there another running out fearfully. Then again, the slipshod manner in which they were repaired, first turned down to gage with a wide-nose tool, and then filed to a finish, after which they were hardened and drawn. And they were then expected to run true! The day is past when this sort of work would do. All centers should be turned, hardened and drawn, and then ground true while in the lathe. This is the only correct way to finish lathe centers.

The grinder shown in Figs. 427 and 428 respectively is about

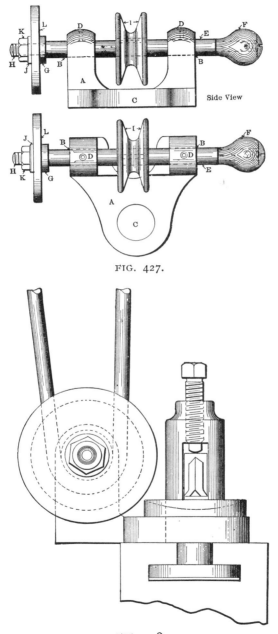

FIG. 427.

FIG. 428.

as cheap and compact a tool as could be devised for the purpose
mentioned, and can be used to advantage for other work as well
as center grinding. In fact one of the best uses to which it can
be put is the grinding and finishing of round dies and punches.
Whenever dies of the combination blanking and drawing type
are constructed, this grinder will answer the purpose as well as,
if not better than, a more expensive one, as it can be easily
handled, requires very little adjustment, and can be laid away on
a shelf or in a drawer when not in use. The engravings show
clearly its construction and no further description is necessary.
A wooden drum, which is fastened opposite the countershaft of
the lathe, drives the grinder by means of the round belt shown
in Fig. 428, the wheel, of course, revolving in an opposite direction from the work. When grinding a blanking die that tapers
slightly (that is larger at the back than at the cutting edge) the
grinder is set off to the proper angle, and the carriage of the lathe
is moved up until the wheel of the grinder is near the face of the
die. Then, while the die is revolving slowly, and the wheel fast,
the handle, F, Fig. 427, is grasped and pulled in and out slowly,
feeding the wheel to the die by the cross slide, until it has been
ground to the size required.

*A Compressed Air Drop Hammer for Making Sheet Metal
Caskets.*

What is certainly one of the largest drop presses ever built
for working sheet metal is here illustrated in Fig. 429, in its
principal features. This hammer was built by the Perkins Machine Co., of Boston, Mass., and was designed for the special
purpose of making sheet metal caskets, the different parts of
which, ready to be assembled, are shown in Fig. 430, after being
struck up from the plain sheet. A casket complete is shown in
Fig. 431.

This drop hammer will handle a blank 30 inches wide by 7½
feet long of No. 22 gage sheet steel. The distance between the
guides is 8 feet, the stroke of the hammer being 5 feet. The
height of the press over all is 17 feet, and it occupies a floor space
of 4 x 12 feet. The largest cover it will make will measure 6
feet 7 inches by 24 inches, the form of the cover being shown
in Fig. 430. The piston and hammer weigh 3 tons, while the
cast iron anvil weighs 12 tons. The dies used for producing the
casket parts are composed of cast iron bodies faced with steel.

FIG. 429.—COMPRESSED AIR DROP HAMMER, WEIGHT 64,000 POUNDS, USED FOR MAKING SHEET STEEL CASKETS.

The piston rod may be said to be attached to the hammer in two ways: First it is keyed into the block, then a short length, just above the block, is reduced in diameter to receive a collar which is bolted to the top of the hammer, as shown in the illus-

FIG. 430.—THIS ILLUSTRATES THE DIFFERENT PARTS READY TO BE ASSEMBLED AFTER BEING STRUCK UP FROM THE PLAIN SHEET BY THE DROP HAMMER.

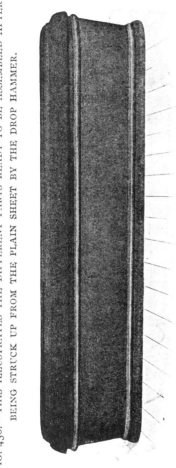

FIG. 431.—SAMPLE OF WORK ACCOMPLISHED WITH THE 64,000-POUND COMPRESSED AIR

tration. This double protection was deemed necessary owing to the fact that should the piston rod break while the air pressure was on the result might be disastrous as far as the cylinder head was concerned.

In using the hammer it was found that a stroke of 3 feet was amply sufficient to upset the metal, although long enough to allow a drop of 48 inches. Some idea of the distortion which takes place may be conceived from the fact that the cup formed has a depth of 4½ inches, the contour being plainly indicated in the half-tones, Figs. 430 and 431.

The machine is made so as to allow of the operator handling it with perfect ease, allowing the hammer to drop every two minutes, thereby producing 30 complete covers for metal caskets every two hours.

A Special Blanking and Piercing Die.

The punch and die shown in Figs. 432 to 436 was designed

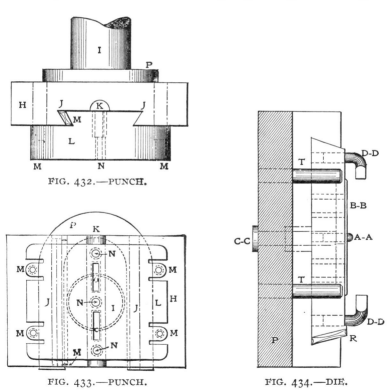

FIG. 432.—PUNCH.

FIG. 433.—PUNCH.

FIG. 434.—DIE.

and used to produce pierced blanks of the shape shown in Fig. 437, which were required to interchange perfectly. As the making of this punch and die involves some new principles and illustrates an improved method for producing work of great accuracy, a description is here presented.

After a templet of sheet steel was made and finished, as shown in Fig. 437, we were ready for the die, which is shown

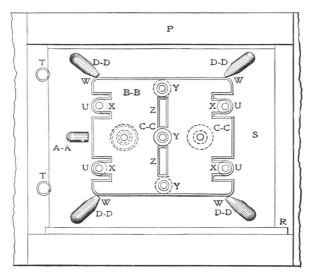

FIG. 435.—PLAN OF DIE.

in different views in Figs. 432-433. The die blank, after being fitted to the bolster, was ground on the face and then drawn to a dark blue. The templet was clamped to the face of the die and

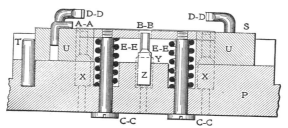

FIG. 436.—CROSS-SECTION OF DIE.

an outline of it transferred to it with a sharp scriber. The corners of the outline were drilled and reamed to the radius required with a straight reamer, as were also the ends of the wings.

The stock between these points was then worked away and the templet carefully worked through the die from the back, finishing all parts of the die perfectly straight (no clearance being allowed) so that the templet would fit perfectly at the cutting edge, and all the way down through the die. The inside of the die was then finished and polished as smooth as possible, after which the holes for the four stripping pins D and the gage pin A were drilled. The die was then hardened, heating it to an even cherry red, and when quenching it dipping perfectly straight, thereby avoiding as far as possible the tendency of the steel to crack or warp excessively. The die was immediately warmed to take the chill out, after which the face was ground and drawn to a straw temper.

The punch is shown at L in Figs. 432 and 433. A piece of well-annealed tool steel, after being roughed out and finished in a dovetail at the back, was tinned on the face and the templet sweated on. The punch was then worked out, first in the shaper and then with the file, down to the edges of the templet, leaving a margin of about .003 of an inch at all points. Then, by using the templet on the face of the punch as a leader, the punch was gradually sheared into and through the die, in the press, removing the punch several times during the process and filing away the surplus stock curled up by the shearing. The punch was then fin-

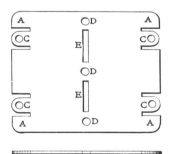

FIG. 437.—THE BLANK.

ished and polished until it fitted nicely within the die. The holes for the piercing dies (M) were transferred through the templet to the face of the punch by using center drills, which fitted exactly the holes in the templet. The holes were then drilled through the punch and reamed from the back to the required diameter, allowing them to taper slightly. The oblong piercing dies O shown in Fig. 433 were drilled and worked out to the edges of the holes in the templet, allowing them to taper the same amount as the round piercing dies. The templet was then removed from the face of the punch, which was then ready to be hardened.

The hardening of the punch was a difficult thing to accomplish successfully, as the tendency to warp and the possibilities of cracking were considerably greater and harder to overcome than with the die, the presence of the piercing dies being a factor greatly to our disadvantage. All the piercing dies in the punch were filled with fire clay to within about 3-16 inch of the punch

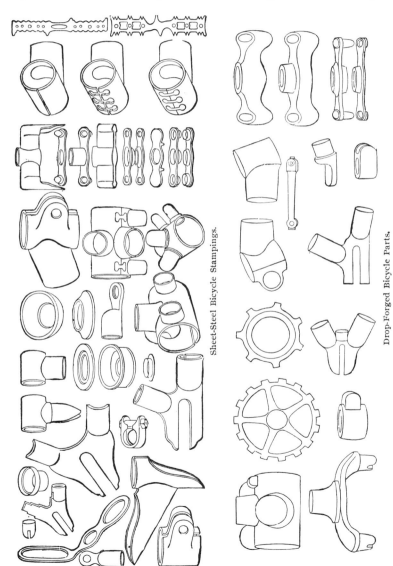

Sheet-Steel Bicycle Stampings.

Drop-Forged Bicycle Parts.

FIG. 438.—SAMPLES OF BENT AND FORMED DIE WORK.

face. The punch was then heated in a gas muffle and quenched in a tank of water which had been first slightly warmed and with about 3 inches of oil on top. The punch came out all right except for a few tight spots which were lapped down. The use of the oil contributed greatly to the successful hardening of the punch—the warming of the water also helped. The face of the punch was ground, after which it was drawn, tempering the edges to a dark blue by standing the punch alternately on each side on a hot plate; the rest of the face, which comprised the piercing dies, being tempered to a straw.

The die S, Fig. 435, was now tightly fastened within the bolster by the key R and against the two Stub steel pins T T. The punch was inserted within the die until its face rested on the bolster. The holes for the seven round piercing punches X and Y were transferred through the punch by means of a center drill, and also the outlines for the oblong piercing punches Z. These outlines were then milled with a "butt" mill, so that two pieces of finished tool steel, about $\frac{1}{8}$ inch larger all around than the finish size, could be driven in, holes being drilled completely through the bolster, so that they could be removed when required, as shown by the dotted lines in the cross-section view of the die. These two punches were then reduced and finished by inserting the blanking punch within the die and shearing the two punches Z up into the dies O. They were then hardened and drawn to a dark blue, and driven into their respective positions. The holes for the round piercing punches in the bolster were drilled and enlarged by counterboring, the seven punches finished, hardened, drawn to a dark blue and driven tightly into the holes. The faces of the piercing punches came within $\frac{1}{8}$ inch of the face of the blanking die.

The spring stripper plate B was worked out to fit freely within the blanking die. Two holes were drilled in the bolster to admit the stripper studs C, and were counterbored to admit the springs E. The springs, studs and stripper plate were then assembled in the die and bolster as shown in the cross section, Fig. 436. The gage pin A and the four scrap stripping pins D were made and fastened within the die as shown in the plan view.

The holder for the punch was of cast iron, finished with a dovetailed channel in the face to allow of locating and fastening the punch, as shown in Fig. 432, by the key M. A hole was drilled straight through the holder at K, breaking through into the dovetailed channel in the face to act as an outlet for the central piercings.   Holes were also drilled through for the punchings from the dies X.   The punch and die were now set up in the press, the body of which was tilted back to an angle of 25 degrees, and the intermediate horseshoe-shaped pad P was

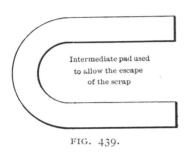

Intermediate pad used to allow the escape of the scrap

FIG. 439.

placed around the stem I of the punch-holder H, in the position shown in Figs. 432 and 433, thus insuring the easy escape of the piercings or scrap. The metal to be punched was 1-16-inch flat cold-rolled stock, and was fed beneath the stripper pins D-D and against the stop-pin A-A, and, the punch de-scending, the blank was punched into the die and held securely between the face of the stripper plate B and the blanking punch L.   All the holes were then pierced, and on the return stroke the stock was stripped from the punch by the four pins D-D, while the finished blank was stripped from the die by the stripping plate B, the blank falling off the face of the die at the back through gravity.

The rapidity with which a punch and die of this improved construction can be worked, and the absolute interchangeability of the product should commend it for all work which is to be produced in large quantities and in exact duplication, thus allow-ing for the increased cost of the die.

The Cutting of Armature Disks.

According to the size and quantity of disks required they are usually cut in one of the following ways:

1.   For very large diameters or relatively small quantities, the shearing of the outside and inside circles is done on circular shearing machines.   These disks are then notched on a notching machine and the key-notches on the inside are usually slotted after the disks have been put together by means of a vertical shaping machine.   For disks 18 inches or less in diameter, with small center holes, as shown in Fig. 440, a circular shear may be used for the outside and the inside punched on a strong power press.

2. For such disks as are made in large quantities and which are of moderate diameter (for street-car motors, for instance), the best factories use power presses with tools so arranged that the inside with its keyseats and the outside with its notches are

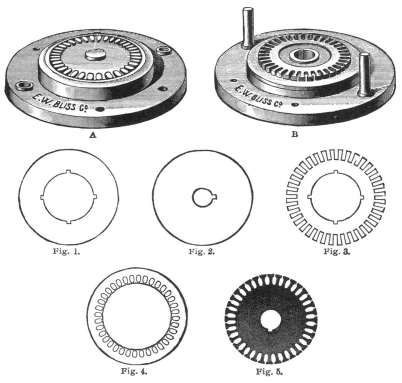

A   B

Fig. 1.   Fig. 2.   Fig. 3.

Fig. 4.   Fig. 5.

FIG. 440.—ARMATURE DISK DIES AND SAMPLES OF DISKS.

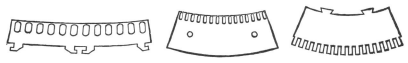

FIG. 441.—ARMATURE SEGMENTS.

cut simultaneously at one stroke, as shown in Fig. 440. This constitutes the quickest, most accurate, and most economical way of manufacturing armature disks in large quantities. The presses used for these dies are provided with knockout attachments which discharge the scrap and the disks so as to lie loosely on top of the dies, whence they may be easily and quickly removed.

The requirements of armature work for electric motors and dynamos have led to the construction of presses which differ in essential points from those used for other styles of sheet-metal work. The usual form of armature is made up of annular disks with notches on the outside or inside circumference. As it is essential to have the outside and inside exactly concentric, it has been found best to adopt dies which, by cutting them simultaneously, eliminate the inaccuracies which are almost unavoidable when the cutting is done in two or more operations. In many cases the notches and keyseats are also punched at the same time, all of which calls for tools having "throw-out pads," in addition to the cutting parts, so as to automatically push the disks and scrap out of the dies and punches.

3. In the many cases where dies mentioned in connection with the second method would be too costly to be economically used, we recommend the cutting out simultaneously of the plain outside and the notched inside as indicated by Fig. 440. This method produces an absolutely concentric blank ready to be notched, and, as the outside notches are cut separately, the power of the presses is equal to much larger diameters than those specified in connection with the second method. The notching is then done on notching presses.

From the inside scrap which results from the punching of the large disks, the projections corresponding to the key notches are usually removed by a die which at the same time cuts the inside with its key slots, thus working the scrap over into smaller disks without any loss of stock.

4. In some works it would not pay to use the dies mentioned for the third method, which dies are still somewhat expensive, on any but the most current sizes of disks. In that case we recommend dies which cut the outside and inside separately by means of a combination die in a single-acting press.

The Cutting of Armature Segments.

For segments used in very large qauntities the outside and the holes or notches are frequently cut simultaneously by means of dies which are so arranged that they discharge the scrap and the segments automatically from the lower and the upper tools. A press equipped in this manner and designed specially for this class of work is shown in Fig. 442. It will cut the inside and outside simultaneously on plain disks, Figs. 440 and 441, up to 35¾ inches in diameter when disks are not less than 3 inches wide, and up to 14 or 15 inches diameter when all the outside notches are also cut at the same stroke, as shown in Figs. 440 and

FIG. 442.—ARMATURE DISK-CUTTING PRESS WITH DIES IN POSITION.

441. It is also used when equipped with a set of dies of the type shown for cutting segments or sections complete at one stroke, with all their teeth or holes, up to 35¾ inches long. Most segments have their plain outsides cut first, and are perforated or notched separately in a second operation.

A Multiple Piercing and Projecting Punch and Die.

The punch and die shown in Figs. 443 to 445 was used to produce the results shown in Fig. 447 in the drawn shell shown in Fig. 446. In this die the usual positions of the punches and dies are reversed, the punches being below and the dies above. At first a bolster F of cast iron was bored and faced as shown, and the holder G, for the punches, of tool steel was turned up and

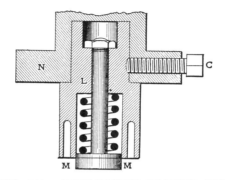

FIG. 443.—CROSS-SECTION OF UPPER DIE.

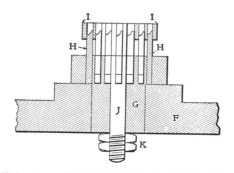

FIG. 444.—CROSS-SECTION OF LOWER DIE.

fitted to it. The holder G was then laid out for the holes for the punches, which were nineteen in number, by indexing in the milling machine. They were then drilled through and reamed to size and the holder hardened. The holes for the dies in L, which had been finished from tool steel as shown to fit the holder N, were then transferred through the holder G to the face of L at M M. They were then drilled and reamed to size.

The die L was hardened and drawn to a light straw temper and the face ground.   Nineteen punches, all of the same length, of Stubs steel, were finished and sheared on the side as shown at H H, each one exactly the same amount.   They were then hardened and drawn to a blue and forced tightly into their relative positions within the holder G, resting on the face of the bolster F.   The stripper for the punches (shown at I I) was finished to fit freely over the punches H H with a stud J fastened in the center and fitting freely within a hole in the holder G, and

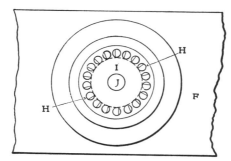

FIG. 445.—PLAN OF LOWER DIE.

FIG. 446.—THE SHELL.   FIG. 447.—THE SHELL FINISHED.

equipped with two jam nuts to regulate the height.   The outside diameter of the stripper I I was the same as the inside diameter of the shell, Fig. 446.   The stripping arrangements on the die L require no description.

When in action the cap was located on the stripper I I, and, the die descending, it was held between the two, while the punches pierced and pushed the projections up into the dies, which were set so that the punches would enter it far enough to just leave a narrow section of each of the projections united to the cap and leave all of them stand off at the same angle.

When the die rose a spring within the circle of punches caused the stripper I I to rise and strip the cap from the punches, while the stripper on the die stripped it from the dies. The shell was then removed from I I by hand. The projections thus made on the cap served as vents for small jets of gas as part of a special gas burner, causing the jets to be directed off at an angle and thereby increasing their range.

Drawing and Punching Continuous Strips of Hemispheres.

In Fig. 448 are shown two views of a strip of thin sheet brass that has been drawn and punched to resemble a number of brass balls joined together. These were made in continuous strips and were used for ornamental purposes on wood fixtures. The strip of stock left after the operation is shown in Fig. 448.

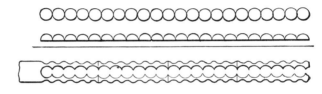

FIG. 448.

The punch and die used for this job are shown in Figs. 449 and 450, respectively.

In this case the punch, Fig. 449, was made first. A cast iron holder F was first machined. A piece of tool steel G was then got out 3 3-16 inches long by ⅞ inch wide, to be used as a holder for the forming punches, and to act also as the trimming punch. This piece of steel was left ¾ inch high half way from the right-hand side while the other half was reduced to ½ inch. It was fastened to the face of the punch holder by four fillister head screws J J J J and the two dowels, L L, placed so as not to interfere with any of the holes for the punches. The holder was then set up in the miller with the front facing the spindle. The stock to be worked on was .010 inch thick and the balls were to be ¼ inch in diameter; we were to draw six and trim six at each stroke after the first.

After the work was set up a center drill was used, and, starting from the left-hand side, the first hole H for the forming punch was centered. A drill was then used .020 inch less than

¼ inch and the holes were drilled almost through. The table was then moved forward exactly ¼ inch and the next hole was centered and drilled, and the other four in the same manner.

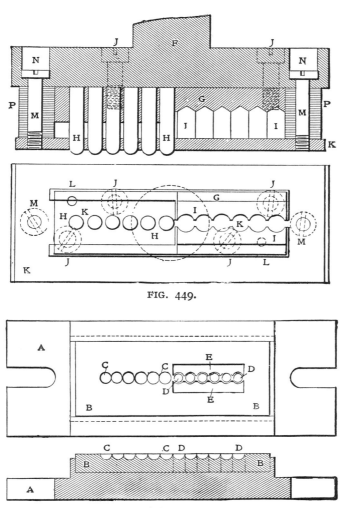

FIG. 449.

FIG. 450.

The table was then moved another ¼ inch, and the next hole was centered and drilled and reamed with a special rose reamer .002 inch larger than ¼ inch to the depth shown at I I. Then, with accurate spacing, the other five were finished likewise. After all this was done the holes just run into each other (the six at the right, we mean) and were touched up and finished to leave open spaces 3-32 inch wide between to hold the metal together after punching. The punch G was then removed from the holder.

Before finishing the punch the die, Fig. 450, was got out. A blank B of tool steel was planed and fitted to the bolster A. A butt mill was then made and finished to a ⅛-inch radius and stoned to dead sharp edges. The die B was strapped to an angle plate on the miller table facing the spindle, and with the butt mill in the chuck the first forming die was finished by letting the mill in just .130 inch, then coming back and moving the table ¼ inch and finishing the next one, and the same with the other four. The six trimming dies D D were placed and milled in the same manner to .005 inch less in depth than the others, leaving six circles just ¼ inch in diameter, the lines of which served as guides for finishing the cutting dies. This was done by drilling and cutting out two sections E E, one on each side, and from the back one degree taper from the cutting edge to just the edges of the circles, leaving a neck between each 3-32 inch wide, as will be seen in the plan view, Fig. 450.

The punch was then carefully hardened and drawn and entered into the die, just fitting and showing the tight spots. These were then eased up and the die hardened and drawn to a blue. The face of the die was then ground down .005 inch, thereby leaving the forming dies ¼ inch deep and the cutting dies .120 inch and leaving a margin around them, this being necessary as the edges would not stand up if left dead sharp. Holes were then let into the bolster A to allow the escape of the scrap.

The stripping was done on the punch in the following manner : A stripper plate K, of 5-16-inch flat cold-rolled stock, was made and worked out to fit around and within the punches as shown; that is, fitting freely around the drawing punches H H and within the trimming punches I I. Two studs or screws M M were then made and let down through the body F, shouldering in the bottoms of counterbored holes N N and screwing into K tightly. This allowed the stripper plate to move up and down freely when in action. A piece of good stiff rubber P, ⅞ inch thick, was then placed between the face of the holder F and the stripper plate K, being cut away in the center to clear the punches. When the screws M M were tightened and adjusted to hold the stripper plate K perfectly level, there was enough tension in the rubber P to allow of the stripper acting as a blank holder while the drawing was being done and to strip the metal afterward. We neglected to state the holes for the drawing punches H H were drilled all the way through the holder to allow them to shoulder against the face of F.

The punches were next made and finished .105 inch in diameter, and the points, with a special forming tool, to a radius of .0525 inch. They were then hardened and drawn to a straw at the forming ends. The ends of H H and the forming dies C C were lapped to a high polish. After all parts were assembled and adjusted the tools were set up in the press and a roll of metal of the width required was placed on a reel on one side and to wind up automatically at the other side.

It will be seen that by placing the stripper and the metal holder on the punch the work is constantly before the operator, and there is no trouble in locating it on the die. The strip was first entered and moved in far enough to cover the six forming dies and project slightly over the trimming edge. The punch descending, the metal was held by the pressure of the stripper K while it was being formed and drawn, and trimmed on the end. At the next stroke the strip was moved along far enough to allow of the six half-balls previously drawn to locate themselves within the seats of the trimming dies D D. The punch then formed six, and trimmed six, at each stroke, cutting the scrap in the die in sections, as shown by the cross-lines in Fig. 448. The strip was moved continually until the entire length was finished, trimming and forming nicely, there not being a burr or a line to show where the successive sections commenced or finished. The one thing most necessary in work of this kind is accuracy in spacing, as the die cannot be used, as is usually the case, as a gage to transfer the locating points for the punches.

Watch and Clock Makers' Power Presses for Sub-Press Work.

Fig. 451 shows a type of power press which is made in a number of different sizes and styles, and they are specially adapted for the manufacture of watch and clock work, jewelry, and other articles of a similar character. They are essentially the same as other solid back presses, but are made with considerably more distance between bed and slide so as to accommodate "sub-presses" such as the illustration shows. A bridge bolster is used to shorten this distance if ordinary cutting or forming tools are also to be operated in the press. Such a bridge bolster

FIG. 451.—WATCH AND CLOCK MAKERS' POWER PRESS EQUIPPED WITH A "SUB-PRESS" FOR DELICATE PUNCHING.

is shown on the floor in the illustration. These watch presses are frequently furnished with an adjustable stroke, permitting to vary the movement of the slide in accordance with the construction of sub-presses of different sizes, and also with a positive stop attachment, which makes it impossible for the operator accidentally to make two strokes in succession if he should forget to take his foot off the treadle.

Sub-presses are now almost entirely used for the delicate dies required in the manufacture of watches and clocks. These dies are generally so arranged as to cut the outside and perforations of the pieces simultaneously, thus insuring the accuracy of the relative finished points. By the use of sub-presses the most accurate work may be accomplished with ease, as the dies may be always kept finely adjusted for the work and the alinement will be perfect.

An Automatic Trimming Machine, a Beading Machine and a Double-Head Crimping Machine.

The half-tone, Fig. 452, represents an automatic trimmer

FIG. 452.

recently designed for trimming seamless tin boxes, brass, copper, zinc and aluminum shells, lamp collars, etc., from 1 to 3 inches in diameter, and from ¼ to 1¾ inches deep. It is provided with a device for cutting the rings of scrap into short pieces so that they may fall freely and avoid clogging. This machine will trim from 35,000 to 40,000 shells a day. The action of the machine is automatic throughout, it being only necessary to keep the feeding chute supplied with shells. The rapidity and perfection of the work produced in machines of this type make them invaluable in the manufacture of articles like those mentioned above. A separate feeding chute, disk and cutters are required for each size of shell.

The strongly-built machine shown in Fig. 453 is used for

FIG. 453.

beading, corrugating and embossing sheet iron stove bodies, stove pipe, powder kegs and similar work; also for tin, zinc and brass. It has steel shafts 2½ inches in diameter and 4 inches center to center; also steel cut gears with a proportion of 4 to 1. The driving pulley runs continuously, and is connected at will to the driving shaft by means of a friction clutch controlled by the treadle. An adjustable apron gage is provided and also an extension arm with adjustable roller support for long cylindrical work. For short work this outer support is not required, and is so attached as to allow of being quickly removed if desired. The rolls are brought together by means of a screw and hand wheel, while strong spiral springs throw them apart when released by the screw. A pair of embossing rolls are shown on the machine.

The machine shown in Fig. 454 is a double-head crimping

FIG. 454.

machine and is used to crimp round cans on the outside, either one or both ends, at one operation. A pair of crimping disks are required with each size of can, and the ends of the cans have to be slightly sunken.

Hand Bending Fixtures.

We sometimes come across a bending job in sheet metal that for one reason or another it would be impracticable to do in the press, sometimes for want of a press, and oftener because the tools themselves would be too expensive. The bending shown in

Figs. 455, 456 and 457 was of this character. Fig. 455 shows the blank, of sheet brass 1-16 thick, with three holes pierced in the position shown, one ¼ inch at B and two 3-32 inch at A.

The first bend was the one shown at A, Fig. 456, which was to bend over the end so that both holes would match and leave space enough to insert the small roller a, Fig. 457, the holes forming for the roller to turn freely in. The bending was done in the jig, Fig. 458. C is an oblong block of cast iron with two ears cast on to allow of its being fastened to the bench; this was the body of the jig. E is a piece of tool steel worked out and finished in the way shown, and fastened by screws and dowels. This acted as the bending form. It was cut away taper at F and also cut away at the bottom, and left with a square shoulder, so as to allow the work to slip under it. This shoulder also acted

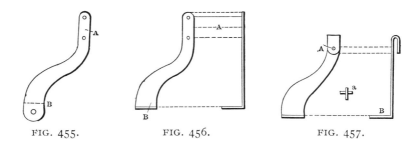

FIG. 455.   FIG. 456.   FIG. 457.

as a gage to push the work against. This piece was hardened and drawn. H was the bender, which consisted of a machine steel forging, turned and finished on centers, leaving a square shoulder and bearing at each end. The handle portion was finished on centers also. It was then cut away to the center, as shown at I, to within one inch from the end. The side pieces, or bearings, G G, were got out and finished and fastened, one at each side of the block C, so that when the bender was down, the center or flat part I would be level with the top of the block C. The pieces G G were held by screws and a dowel, as shown. The gage pin K was let in, and the block cut away to allow of the easy removal of the work. The work was located in position for bending by entering the hole B over the gage pin K, and pushing it under and against the piece E, as shown. This finishing the jig, it was fastened to the bench by two wood screws through the ears D D, and was ready for work. The work being in position, the bender H was brought up quickly by hand, which caused the end of the work J to bend over the thin part of the former E, which finished the operation. The piece was then removed and another inserted.

The second bend, the one at B, Fig. 457, was a simple right angle bend, and was done in the same manner as the first, as will be seen from the two views in Fig. 459, using the same style of block as in the other case, the same kind of side pieces, and in

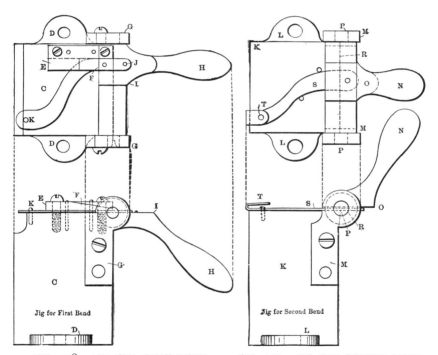

FIG. 458.—JIG FOR FIRST BEND.   FIG. 459.—JIG FOR SECOND BEND.

fact the same mode of construction throughout, except that the bender N was of a different shape. It was cut away to the center, as the other was, and after the ends or journals were inserted within the side pieces M M, they were set above each side of the block enough so that when the bender N was in position shown in the bottom view, there would be just space enough for the work S to pass under freely. Instead of the bending form E used in the first operation, the edge of the block was used as such. After the work S was placed in position on the block, the gage pin T entered into the hole in the work as shown, and the sides of the work held between the two stop pins, the bender N was brought down sharply, which caused the part of the work projecting over the edge at R to be bent over the edge of the block at P, which completed the bend and finished the piece.

A Combination Blanking Die for Heavy Stock.

The punch and die shown in Figs. 461 and 462 were made

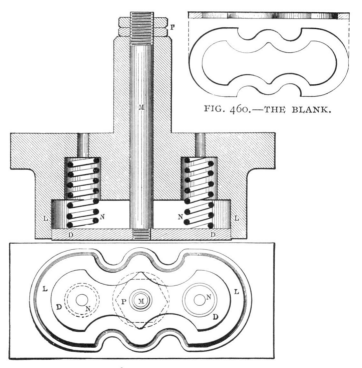

FIG. 460.—THE BLANK.

FIG. 461.—THE PUNCH.

for producing at one operation blanks from 3-16 inch cold-rolled sheet steel of the shape shown in Fig. 460. As the drawings are very clear and as the construction can be understood from descriptions of similar dies in other parts of the book, a very slight description will suffice.

The punch and die portions were forgings, with mild steel

backs and tool steel faces. They were machined and finished in the milling machine. In making the punch, L, it was first turned and machined to finish the stem and then milled around the outside and inside to the shape of the templet, this being accomplished with ease by soldering the templet to the face of

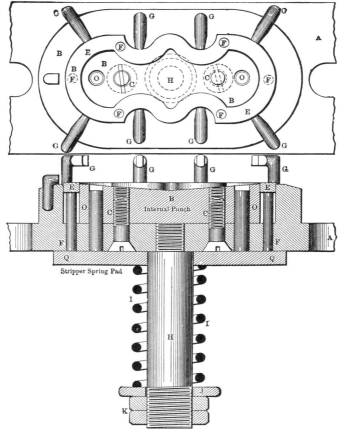

FIG. 462.—THE DIE.

the punch and using the vertical attachment on the universal milling machine, and leaving about .007 inch of surplus stock all around. The edges both inside and outside were then nicely beveled, after which the punch was sheared into the die A by fastening both punch and die in the press in which they were to be used when finished, thus making sure of a perfect match of all the cutting edges.

Tool Holder and Tools—Self-Hardening Steel.

The sketch, Fig. 464, shows a simple, home-made tool-holder for lathe or planer, with set of tools for it in Fig. 465, neither of which will require description. A set of these tools and a holder of the construction shown will be found handy things for a tool or die-maker to have in his drawer.

A great many toolmakers complain about self-hardening steel cutting tools, and say that it is impossible to accomplish fine results in turned or planed work with them, and for that reason

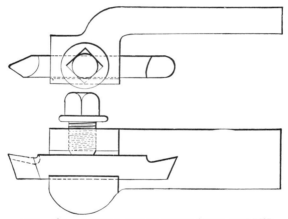

FIG. 464.—SIMPLE HOME-MADE TOOL-HOLDER.

a great many will not use them. Now, when they say that for fine work they are useless, they are right, as it is impossible to get the edges of such tools keen enough to allow of taking smooth finishing cuts. But for the preliminary work or roughing, for medium cuts and feeds and coarse thread cutting, machining cast iron in the shaper, planer or lathe, and for turning brass castings, and also for accomplishing different operations on cast-iron repetition parts in the turret lathe they are unequaled, and should always be used where the production of machine parts at the minimum of cost and labor is imperative. For face milling of large castings where inserted tooth cutters are adaptable, the self-hardening steel tools will be found to give the best

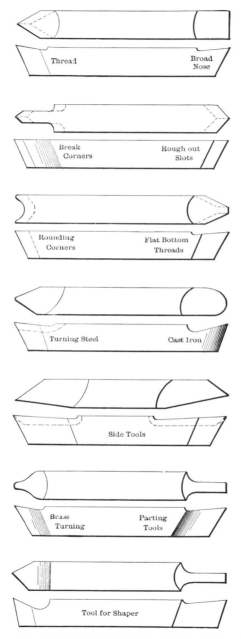

FIG. 465.—SET OF SELF-HARDENING STEEL CUTTING TOOLS.

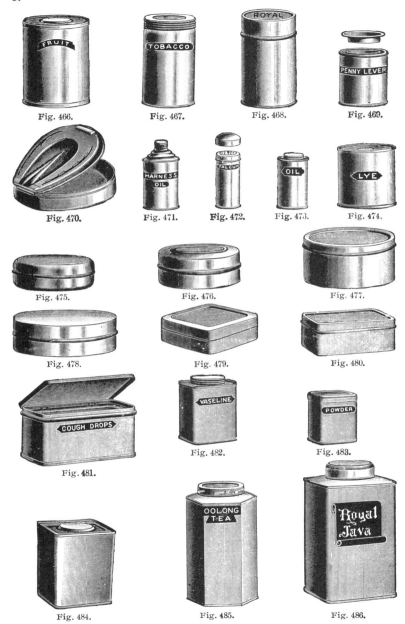

Fig. 466.   Fig. 467.   Fig. 468.   Fig. 469.

Fig. 470.   Fig. 471.   Fig. 472.   Fig. 473.   Fig. 474.

Fig. 475.   Fig. 476.   Fig. 477.

Fig. 478.   Fig. 479.   Fig. 480.

Fig. 482.   Fig. 483.

Fig. 481.

Fig. 484.   Fig. 485.   Fig. 486.

FIGS. 466 TO 486.—SAMPLES OF FINISHED ARTICLES FROM COMBINA-
TION AND DOUBLE-ACTION DIES.

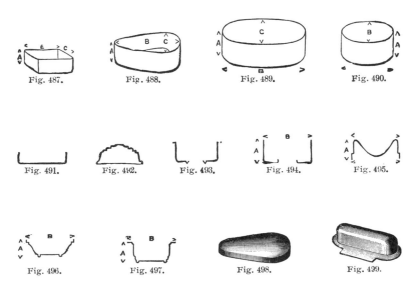

FIGS. 487 TO 499.—PARTS FROM COMBINATION AND DOUBLE-ACTION DIES FOR LAMP FOUNTS AND LAMP LININGS, CLOCK CASES, REFLECTORS, LANTERNS, OILERS, ETC.

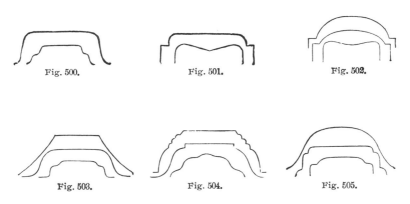

FIGS. 500 TO 505.—DIAGRAMS OF PARTS FROM COMBINATION AND DOUBLE-ACTION DIES FOR TOYS, PEPPER BOX COVERS, BURNERS AND GAS FIXTURE PARTS, CURTAIN-POLE ENDS, DOOR-KNOB HALVES, ETC.

results. There are a number of brands of this steel on the market, in which it will be found possible to hold an edge sufficiently keen to allow of their being used for the purposes above enumerated.

Rules for Calculating the Speed of Power Presses.

To calculate the proper speeds of power presses according to directions given by the manufacturer, use the following rules, according to conditions:

The diameter of driven given to find its number of revolutions. Rule.—Multiply the diameter of the driver by its number of revolutions, and divide the product by the diameter of driven. The quotient will be the number of revolutions of the driven.

The diameter and revolutions of the driver being given to find the diameter of the driven, that shall make the number of revolutions.

Rule.—Multiply the diameter of the driver by its number of revolutions and divide the product by the number of required revolutions of the driven. The quotient will be its diameter.

To ascertain the size of pulleys for given speeds.

Rule.—Multiply all the diameters of the drivers together, and all the diameters of the driven together; divide the drivers by the driven. Multiply the answer by the known number of revolutions of the main shaft.

CHAPTER XIII.

LAYING OUT BLANKING DIES TO SAVE METAL.

The present day cost of sheet metal is so exceptionally high that every effort should be made when it is used in connection with punch press work, to get the greatest possible amount of blanks from the least possible amount of metal. In order to do this the blanking dies must necessarily be properly laid out to obtain the desired results; and this article is therefore written with the idea in view of giving an idea as to how blanking dies are laid out in order to save metal.

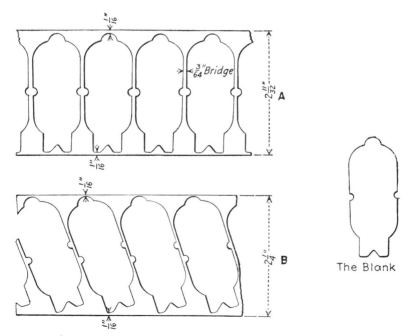

FIG. 506.—SHOWING HOW CONSIDERABLE METAL CAN BE SAVED BY CUTTING THE BLANKS DIAGONALLY FROM THE METAL STRIP.

Before laying out a blanking die there are a few essential things to be taken into consideration some of which are as follows: The amount of blanks wanted; the metal thickness of the blank; the laying out of the dies so that in cases where there are two or more holes in the die that the die when completed will be strong enough to stand up to the work for which it is intended. Also that the dies are properly laid out as regard spacing distance and that they are laid out central with the die blanks from which they are made.

To make the above more explicit, it may be added that, if the required amount of blanks is large, it often pays to make a double or a triple blanking die. If, on the other hand, the desired amount of blanks is small, then a single die should be made.

The metal thickness of the blank is important as it governs the length of "the bridge," i.e., the narrow strip of metal that separates one blank from another while they are being cut from the strip of stock. (See *A*, Fig. 506.) The length of the bridge should be the same as the thickness of the metal to be cut to insure good results, and to prevent the bridge from breaking while the stock is being run through the dies.

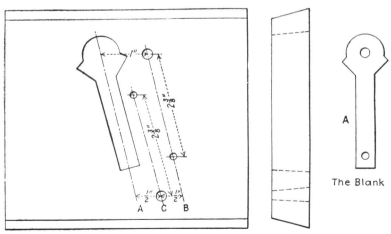

FIG. 507.—SHOWING PLAN AND LAYOUT OF DIE FOR CUTTING THE BLANK A FROM STOCK SHOWN IN FIGS. 508 AND 509.

When there are two or more holes in a die, care should be taken to see to it that the die is laid out so that the holes are not too close together, in order to prevent a "weak die" that is apt to break or crack before the first hundred blanks are cut.

A blanking die must be properly and accurately laid out. If not, when the metal is run through the die, the cut out holes in the stock will run into each other, which means imperfect or half blanks will be the result.

All blanking dies should be laid out "central," i.e., central with the length and width of the die blank. This helps to save time for the Toolsetter in setting up the tools in the press. It sometimes happens that the Toolsetter finds, after he has the tools partly set up in the press, that he must take them out and shift the position of the die in the die bed one way or another, simply because the working part of the die was not laid out central with the die blank. The dies as laid out and shown in the cuts herewith, are laid out central with both the length and width of the dovetail steel die blanks, and give a good idea as to how blanking dies are laid out "central."

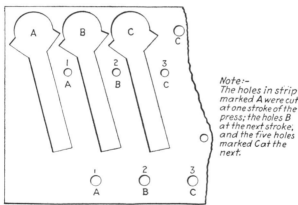

FIG. 508.—SHOWING STOCK AFTER IT HAS BEEN RUN THROUGH THE FIRST TIME.

Fig. 506 gives a good illustration of a most commonly used method for laying out blanking dies in order to save metal. This is done by laying out the blanking dies so that the blanks will be cut diagonally from the metal strip. By comparing the strip A (from which the blanks have been cut at right angles, with the strip B) it will be seen that the strip A must be $2\frac{11}{32}$ inches wide, while the strip B is only $2\frac{1}{4}$ inches wide.

The layout for this die is so simple that it really does not have to be shown, for the reason that the die is laid and the outline of the blank is scribed on the face of the die blank diagonally with the sides of the same, similar to any one of the punched-out holes shown in the strip B.

There are times when the required amount of blanks is so small, they do not warrant the expense of making a double blanking die; but, nevertheless, in order to save metal, the punched-out holes in the metal strips must match in very closely together and still not run into each other. Fig. 509 is a good illustration of a strip of stock of closely matched-in holes cut by a single blanking die, and yet the holes do not run into each other. The manner in which this is done is very clearly shown by the strip of metal shown in Fig. 508. By referring to the blank A, Fig. 507, it can be seen that there are two round holes punched

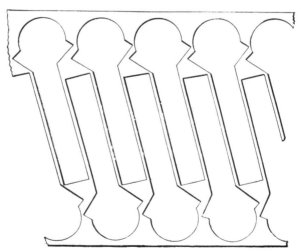

FIG. 509.—SHOWING STOCK AFTER RUNNING THROUGH THE SECOND
TIME.

in the center of, and at both ends of the blank. Now, in laying out the die, Fig. 507, these holes are laid out so that when the strip of stock is run through the die the first time, as shown in Fig. 508, the four holes for two blanks are cut the same time the finished blank is being cut from the stock. This is done in order that the holes numbered 1, 2, and 3 can be pierced out in an exact central position between the holes from which the blanks are cut. When one-half of the order has been filled the piercing punches are removed, and the stock run through the die the second time. Pilot pins in the blanking punch act as leaders for the metal by first entering the pierced-out holes and thereby correctly guiding the metal before it is cut from the strip by the blanking punch.

In laying out the blanking die as shown in Fig. 507, it can be seen that the center line A is the center line for the blanking part of the die. B is the center line for the two pierced holes for the blanks that are cut from the stock the first time it is run through. The center line C is the center line for the pierced holes 1, 2, and 3, Fig. 508, and is exactly half way between the center lines A and B, as shown in the cut.

Fig. 510 shows the layout of a double blanking die for cutting two brass T-shaped blanks at every stroke of the press. Fig. 512 shows that after the stock has been run through the die the

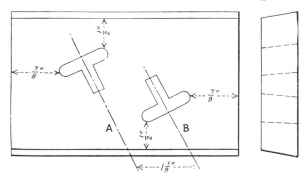

FIG. 510.—SHOWING PLAN AND LAYOUT OF DOUBLE BLANKING DIE FOR CUTTING TWO T BLANKS AT ONE TIME FROM STRIPS OF STOCK SHOWN IN FIGS. 511 AND 512.

second time, the metal is pretty well used up. The reason this strip is run through the die the second time is, that every strip of metal has two sides, and therefore there are two narrow strips of metal about $\frac{1}{16}$ of an inch wide that must be considered as waste after the strip has been run through the dies. By making use of a wider strip it can be seen that there is only a waste of two $\frac{1}{16}$ inch strips for the sides and one of $\frac{3}{64}$ inch for the center, which amounts to $\frac{11}{64}$ inch. As the amount of waste for two narrow strips is $\frac{1}{4}$ inch, there is a saving of the difference between $\frac{1}{4}$ inch and $\frac{11}{64}$ inch, or $\frac{5}{64}$ inch. Another point in favor of this method is, that wide brass costs less per pound than narrow brass.

In connection with the above it may be added that in some cases where a double blanking die is used and the blanks to be cut are small, that a wide strip of stock is sometimes run through a half a dozen times or more in order to effect a saving of metal.

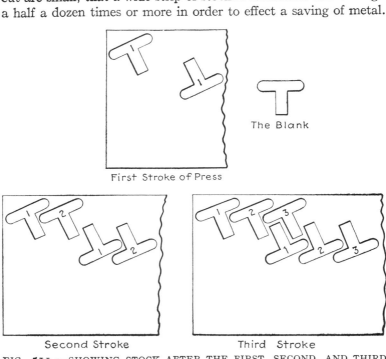

First Stroke of Press

The Blank

Second Stroke   Third Stroke

FIG. 511.—SHOWING STOCK AFTER THE FIRST, SECOND, AND THIRD STROKE OF THE PRESS.

Fig. 511 shows how the blanks are cut from the stock after each stroke of the press and the manner in which the holes closely match in with each other in order to use up all the metal possible.

Fig. 510 shows the layout for this die and hardly needs any explanation. The distance between the center lines A and B is $1\frac{1}{8}$ inch (one inch and one-eighth) and represents the exact distance which allows for the bridge of metal between holes and the matching up of the holes in the strip after the second

stroke of the press.   The reason that the holes are so far apart
is to make the die strong enough to stand up to the work for
which it is intended.   By way of further explanation and again

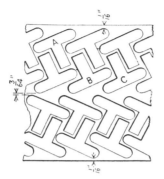

FIG. 512.—SHOWING STOCK THAT HAS BEEN RUN THROUGH THE
DIE THE SECOND TIME.

referring to Fig. 512, it can be seen that if the die was laid out so
that A and B were the holes for the die, the die would be alto-

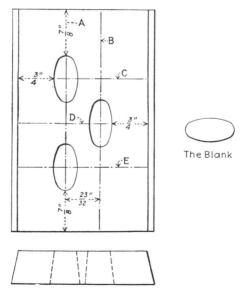

The Blank

FIG. 513.—SHOWING PLAN AND LAYOUT OF TRIPLE OVAL
BLANKING DIE.

gether too weak, as the holes would come too close to each other; but, by skipping the hole B we have A and C, which gives the correct layout for a strong, substantial die.

Fig. 513 shows the layout for a triple blanking die for blanking three oval blanks at one time, while Fig. 514 shows a strip of stock

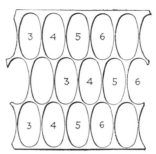

FIG. 514.—SHOWING STRIP OF STOCK AFTER IT HAS BEEN RUN THROUGH THE OVAL BLANKING DIE SHOWN IN FIG. 513.

after it has been run through this die, and very clearly shows that the die is laid out so that the oval holes in the center of the strip match in very closely with the holes on the sides of the strip. For instance, the center hole in the strip numbered

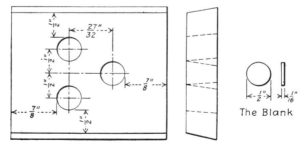

The Blank

FIG. 515.—SHOWING PLAN AND LAYOUT TRIPLE BLANKING DIE FOR CUTTING THREE ROUND BLANKS FROM STRIPS SHOWN IN FIG. 516.

3 matches in exactly half-way between the outside holes numbered 4 4 and 5 5, while the center hole number 4 matches in between 5 5 and 6 6 and so on.

In laying out this die as shown in Fig. 513, the lines A, C, and E are the center lines for the outside holes, while the lines B and D are the center lines for the center oval hole in the die. The rest of the lines and figures speak for themselves. It may be well to say by way of further explanation that in order to make this die strong enough, one hole is also skipped in laying it out. When the stock is run through the die the three oval holes marked 3, Fig. 514, are cut at one stroke of the press, after which the holes marked 4 are cut and so on until the strip is run through.

Fig. 515 shows that the layout for a blanking die for cutting three round blanks at one time is a most simple one to lay out. In laying out this die, one hole is also skipped to make it substantially strong. The diameter of the blank, which is $\frac{1}{2}$ inch plus the bridge of metal, $\frac{1}{16}$ inch, equals $\frac{9}{16}$ inch, the distance from the center of one punched-out hole in the strip of stock, Fig. 516, to the center of the other which is taken into consideration and the holes in the die blank laid out at an angle of 30 degrees with each other as shown in the cuts. In running the stock through the die the three holes marked 2, Fig. 516, are cut at one stroke, of the press; on the next stroke the holes marked 3 are cut and so on.

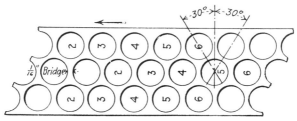

FIG. 516.—SHOWING STRIP OF STOCK AFTER IT HAS BEEN RUN THROUGH THE DIE SHOWN IN FIG. 515.

In connection with the above it should be added that all round dies, whether the diameter of the blank is large or small. no matter if the amount of blanks to be cut at one time are two or twenty-two in number, must be laid out at an angle of thirty degrees, in order to obtain the greatest amount of blanks from the least amount of metal.

Fig. 517 shows how considerable metal ean be saved by running the metal through the second time and by having the holes from which the blanks have been cut match in with each other as shown at B. The strip of stock marked A shows that in running the metal through only once that there is a considerable amount of metal wasted between the blank holes as shown at X; and also that the distance from the center of one hole to the center

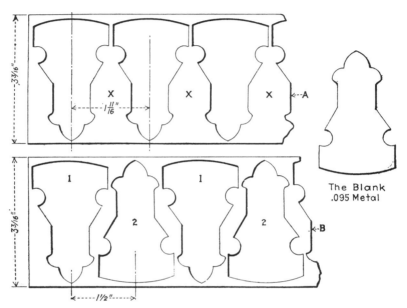

FIG. 517.—SHOWING HOW CONSIDERABLE METAL SCALE FULL SIZE CAN BE SAVED BY RUNNING THE STRIP THROUGH THE SECOND TIME.

of the other is $1\frac{11}{16}$ inches (one inch and eleven sixteenths). The strip B, shows that very little of the stock is wasted and that the center distance from one blank hole to the other is only $1\frac{1}{2}$ inches (one inch and one half).

Running through the strip as shown at B, is not a question of laying out the blanking die, but rather one as to the manner in which the stock is run through the die. In running the strip of stock through the first time, the finger stop on the press is adjusted so that the blank holes marked 1 are cut, while the holes marked 2 are cut when running through the second time.

A shearing and piercing die for cutting the diamond-shaped blank shown in Fig. 519 is shown in Fig. 518. The advantage

gained by using a die of this type is that after the first stroke
of the press, the round punchings cut from the two pierced holes
in the blank is the only metal wasted until the end of the strip
is reached.   This is due to the fact that the width of the blank
is such that no blanking is necessary, as the sides of the strip
form two sides of the finished blank.

Fig. 519 gives a good idea as to how this is done.   The strip of
stock as shown is fed under a stripper and two gauge plates not
shown which are fastened to the die bed.   On the first stroke of
the press the cross-sectioned piece and the cross-sectioned punchings marked 1 are cut from the strip, after which the stock is

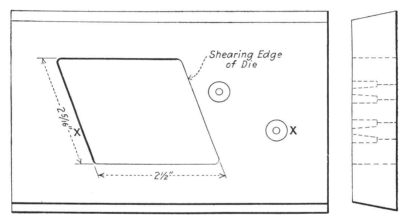

FIG. 518.—SHOWING PLAN OF DIE FOR SHEARING AND PIERCING
THE DIAMOND-SHAPED BLANK SHOWN IN FIG. 519.

fed forward so that the diagonally-sheared end is brought to bear
against the stop A of the punch as shown in Fig. 520.   On the
next stroke of the press a finished blank and the punchings numbered 2 are cut from the strip, and so on as clearly shown by the
dotted lines.   The press runs continuously until the entire strip
is run through.

The construction of this die, Fig. 518, shows that the shearing
edge of the die is wider than the strip.   This not only gives
ample room for feeding the strip through the die, but also allows
for the rounding corners as shown, which give the die added
strength, and acts as a preventive to cracking while the die

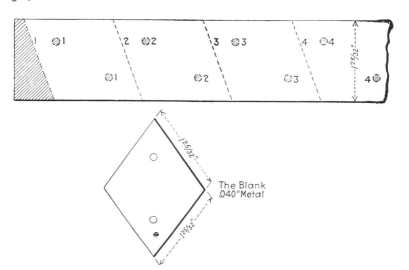

FIG. 519.—SHOWING HOW THE FINISHED BLANK IS SHEARED FROM
THE STRIP OF STOCK.

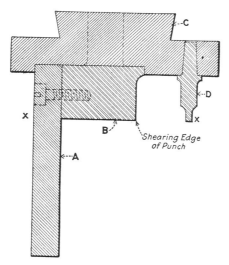

FIG. 520.—PLAN OF PUNCH, SHOWING CROSS-SECTION VIEW OF
THAT PART OF THE PUNCH WHICH ENTERS THE DIE AT XX,
FIG. 518.

is being hardened. The length of the large hole in the die is $2\frac{1}{2}$ inches (two and one-half inches) which is $\frac{23}{32}$ inch longer than the width of the blank, which is to allow for the stop A of the punch. Inserting bushings in the die as shown for piercing the two holes in the blank is up-to-date die practice and is most always done when there is ample room for doing so without weakening the die. Other reasons for using bushings is that in case blanks are required with larger or smaller holes, that

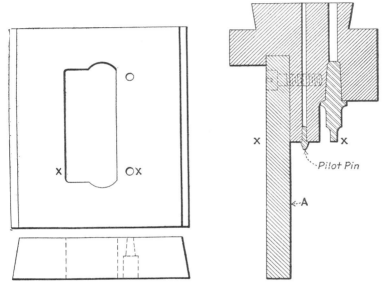

FIG. 521 —PLAN OF DIE.   FIG. 522.—PLAN OF PUNCH SHOW-
ING CROSS-SECTION VIEW OF THAT
PART OF THE PUNCH WHICH EN-
TERS THE DIE AT XX, FIG. 521.

the bushings can be readily driven out and new ones inserted; or if the edges of any one of the holes should flake or chip off, it will not be necessary to regrind the entire face of the die, which would have to be done if the die was a solid or one piece die. The bushing would be simply driven out and a thin sheet steel washer placed between the bottom of the bushing and the die, and the raised-up bushings could be then ground flush with the face of the die in less time than it takes to tell.

In making the punch as shown in Fig. 520, it can be seen that the shearing punch B has a round shank which is driven into the dovetail punch holder C. Across the face of the holder C a channel is milled which allows for the sides of the shearing punch and the stop A, which is made a tight fit between the shearing punch and the punch holder C. The stop A is further secured to the shearing punch by two philister head screws. The stop A, as already explained, acts as a stop or gauge for the end of the metal strip, and also helps to support the shearing punch while it is shearing the blank from the strip of metal, as the shearing punch and the stop A are made a good sliding fit to the hole in the die. When set up in the press, the stop A

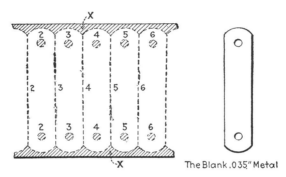

The Blank .035″ Metal

FIG. 523.—SHOWING HOW THE BLANK IS SHEARED AND PIERCED FROM THE STRIP OF STOCK.

is always in the die, the end of same never coming up above the face of the die. Two piercing punches one of which is shown at D, are held by taper shanks and driven into the punch-holder as shown, and are used for piercing the two holes in the diamond-shaped blank.

Figs. 521 and 522 show another set of tools for piercing and partly blanking the narrow blank shown in Fig. 523, together with the strip from which it is cut. These tools are similar to the ones shown in Figs. 518 and 520, with the exception that the circular ends of the blanks are cut at the same time the blank is cut from the strip. It will also be seen that there are no piercing bushings used in this die, for the reason that the holes for retaining the bushings would come so close to the cutting edge of the die as to weaken it.   By referring again to Fig. 521, it can be seen that the part of the die into which the stop A is fitted, is made shorter in length than the length of the blank, in order that the cut off sections of the strip marked X, Fig. 523, will readily clear the stop A while the strip is being run through.

The strip of metal as shown in Fig. 523, shows that the only amount of metal wasted is that part which is cross-sectioned, and that the rest of the strip is converted into blanks.   The figures placed on the strip explain just how the blanks are cut from the strip after each successive stroke of the press; and from what has already been said with reference to the tools as described in the preceding pages no further explanation seems necessary.

INDEX.

A

398   INDEX.

INDEX. 399